AFRICAN CHRISTIAN LEADERSHIP

The American Society of Missiology Series, published in collaboration with Orbis Books, seeks to publish scholarly works of high merit and wide interest on numerous aspects of missiology—the study of Christian mission in its historical, social, and theological dimensions. Able presentations on new and creative approaches to the practice and understanding of mission will receive close attention from the ASM Series Committee.

American Society of Missiology Series, No. 54

AFRICAN CHRISTIAN LEADERSHIP

Realities, Opportunities, and Impact

Edited by

Robert J. Priest and Kirimi Barine

ORBIS BOOKS
Maryknoll, New York 10545

ORBIS BOOKS
Maryknoll, New York 10545

Fathers and Brothers
MARYKNOLL™

Founded in 1970, Orbis Books endeavors to publish works that enlighten the mind, nourish the spirit, and challenge the conscience. The publishing arm of the Maryknoll Fathers and Brothers, Orbis seeks to explore the global dimensions of the Christian faith and mission, to invite dialogue with diverse cultures and religious traditions, and to serve the cause of reconciliation and peace. The books published reflect the views of their authors and do not represent the official position of the Maryknoll Society. To learn more about Maryknoll and Orbis Books, please visit our website at www.maryknollsociety.org.

Copyright © 2017 by Tyndale House Foundation.

Published by Orbis Books, Maryknoll, New York 10545-0302.

Manufactured in the United States of America.

Manuscript editing and typesetting by Joan Weber Laflamme.

Library of Congress Cataloging-in-Publication Data

Names: Priest, Robert J., editor. | Barine, A. Kirimi, editor.
Title: African Christian leadership : realities, opportunities, and impact / edited by Robert J. Priest and Kirimi Barine.
Description: Maryknoll, NY : Orbis Books, [2017] | Series: American society of missiology series ; No. 54 | Includes bibliographical references and index.
Identifiers: LCCN 2017013356 (print) | LCCN 2017023135 (ebook) | ISBN 9781608337071 (e-book) | ISBN 9781626982420 (pbk.)
Subjects: LCSH: Christian leadership—Africa. | Leadership—Religious aspects—Christianity. | Christianity—Africa.
Classification: LCC BV652.1 (ebook) | LCC BV652.1 .A37 2017 (print) | DDC 262/.1096—dc23
LC record available at https://lccn.loc.gov/2017013356

To past, present and future African Christian leaders
who have demonstrated exemplary servant leadership,
with thanksgiving for their unsparing efforts
to make the African continent
a better place for its people.

L et us, your servants, see you work again;
let our children see your glory.
And may the Lord our God show us his approval
and make our efforts successful.
Yes, make our efforts successful!
—PSALM 90: 16, 17 (NLT)

Contents

Tables

List of Figures

Preface to the American Society of Missiology Series

The purpose of the American Society of Missiology Series is to publish—without regard for disciplinary, national, or denominational boundaries—scholarly works of high quality and wide interest on missiological themes from the entire spectrum of scholarly pursuits relevant to Christian mission, which is always the focus of books in the Series.

By mission is meant the effort to effect passage over the boundary between faith in Jesus Christ and its absence. In this understanding of mission, the basic functions of Christian proclamation, dialogue, witness, service, worship, liberation, and nurture are of special concern. And in that context questions arise, including, how does the transition from one cultural context to another influence the shape and interaction between these dynamic functions, especially in regard to the cultural and religious plurality that comprises the global context of Christian life and mission.

The promotion of scholarly dialogue among missiologists, and among missiologists and scholars in other fields of inquiry, may involve the publication of views that some missiologists cannot accept, and with which members of the Editorial Committee themselves do not agree. Manuscripts published in the Series, accordingly, reflect the opinions of their authors and are not understood to represent the position of the American Society of Missiology or of the Editorial Committee. Selection is guided by such criteria as intrinsic worth, readability, coherence, and accessibility to a range of interested persons and not merely to experts or specialists.

The ASM Series, in collaboration with Orbis Books, seeks to publish scholarly works of high merit and wide interest on numerous aspects of missiology—the scholarly study of mission. Able presentations on new and creative approaches to the practice and understanding of mission will receive close attention.

THE ASM SERIES COMMITTEE
Jonathan J. Bonk
Angelyn Dries, O.S.F.
Scott W. Sunquist

Acknowledgments

The editors would like to acknowledge the help of everyone involved, particularly the chapter authors and others who helped supervise and analyze the research, including José Paulo Bunga, Adelaide Thomas Manuel, and Kalemba Mwambazambi. Over eight thousand people completed our survey; dozens granted us in-depth interviews, and scores of graduate and undergraduate students helped carry out the research. Without their assistance this book would not have become a reality.

Numerous individuals advised on the research, its findings, and/or provided feedback on chapters of the book—including Miriam Adeney, J. Kwabena Asamoah-Gyadu, Dwight Baker, Johan Boekhout, Daniel Bourdanné, Edward Elliott, Matthew Elliott, Casely Essamuah, Zachs-Toro Gaiya, Evan Hunter, Joanna Ilboudo, Wambura Kimunyu, Samuel Kunhiyop, Gerald Macharia, John Maust, Paul Mouw, Esther Mombo, Peter Ngure, Beverly Nuthu, Timothy Nyasulu, Gregg Okesson, Uma Onwunta, Kersten Priest, Jack Robinson, Theo Robinson, Ian Shaw, Michelle Sigg, Tite Tiénou, Enyidiya Uma-Onwunta, Timothy Wachira, David Waweru, and Darrell Whiteman. Their valuable contributions are acknowledged.

Educational institutions from Angola, Central Africa Republic, Kenya, South Africa, and the USA lent support. These are specifically acknowledged in Chapter 1. Without funding from the Tyndale House Foundation and the vision, support, and commitment of its leaders (Mark Taylor, C. Douglas McConnell, Mary Kleine Yehling, Edward Elliott, and Bob Reekie), this ambitious project would not have been possible. The administrative team worked tirelessly on all the details and logistics to support and enable the work of the group.

We are grateful to Jim Keane and the editorial team at Orbis Books; Jon Hirst and Scott Todd of Global Mapping International, who designed the supporting maps; and Rob Huff of Image Studios for the Africa Leadership Study website design where we also acknowledge the contributions of many others. To all who helped with this project, we are most grateful.

Acronyms

ACATBA	Association Centrafricaine pour la Traduction de la Bible et l'Alphabétisation
AEA	Association of Evangelicals in Africa `
ALS	Africa Leadership Study
ATS	Association of Theological Schools (US)
BWA	Bomaregwa Welfare Association (Kenya)
CAR	Central African Republic
CBO	community-based organizations
CICA	Conselho de Igrejas Cristãs em Angola
CITAM	Christ Is the Answer Ministries
CPDA	Christian Partners Development Agency
DASEP	Departamento de Assistência Social Estudos e Projectos
FATEB	Faculté de Théologie Évangélique de Bangui
FBO	faith-based organization
IBK-MU	Instituto Bíblico de Kaluquembe–Missão Urgente
ICT	information communications technology
IERA	Igreja Evangélica Reformada de Angola
IFES	International Fellowship of Evangelical Students
IMF	International Monetary Fund
ISTEL	Instituto Superior de Teologia Evangélica no Lubango
ITIERA	Instituto Teológico da Igreja Evangélica Reformada de Angola
KSCF	Kenya Students Christian Fellowship
MIERA	Mulher da Igreja Evangélica Reformada de Angola
NCCK	National Council of Churches of Kenya
NEGST	Nariobi Evangelical Graduate School of Theology
NetACT	Network for African Congregational Theology
NGO	non-governmental organization
OIF	Organisation Internationale de la Francophonie

PACLA	Pan-African Christian Leadership Assembly
PIP	Pastoral Instruction Program
SED	Seminario Emanuel do Dôndi
STB	Seminario Teológico Baptista
TCHD	Tenwek Community Health and Development
THF	Tyndale House Foundation
UFEB	Union Fraternelle des Eglises Baptistes
WCC	World Council of Churches
WCD	World Christian Database
WHO	World Health Organization

Foreword

Tite Tiénou

Africans have recognized the importance of leadership for their well-being and for the social, economic, political, and spiritual vitality of the continent. They have convened conferences on leadership, have produced books and various publications on the subject, and have established organizations such as the Africa Leadership Forum (www.africaleadership. org) and the Africa Biblical Leadership Initiative (www.abliforum.org) for the purpose of promoting leadership in the continent. Christians have considered various aspects of leadership in continental venues such as the Pan-African Christian Leadership Assembly (PACLA I, Nairobi, Kenya, December 1976; and PACLA II, Nairobi, Kenya, November 1994). Some of the proceedings of these assemblies have provided material for the academic investigation of Christian leadership in Africa, such as, for example, Hans-Martin Wilhelm's *African Christian Leadership: Cultures and Theologies in Dialogue,* a 1998 master of theology thesis for the University of South Africa.

As readers of this book keep the preceding in mind, they may ask themselves: How does this study of Christian leadership in Africa differ from others? Unlike other documents on the topic, this book is the result of many years of solid qualitative and quantitative research conducted in three countries across a wide range of denominations and ethnicities. This feature alone sets the book apart from others, and it is the basis for important new contributions to understanding the realities of Christian leadership in contemporary African societies.

The focus on contemporary Africa, either in reading patterns or issues of leadership, that is evident throughout the volume rewards the reader with startling discoveries such as "while African Christians read books at lower rates than Americans do, the difference is less than one might expect. African pastors read books at higher rates than the adult US population as a whole" (Chapter 10).

The study was conducted in three countries: Angola, the Central African Republic, and Kenya. By taking into account the current linguistic reality on the continent, this study helpfully focused on one Lusophone country, one Francophone country, and one Anglophone country. This provides nuance and a needed corrective to studies of Christianity in Africa that do not usually consider possible differences among these three linguistic areas. One may nonetheless wonder whether the three countries where the study was carried out are representative of the entire continent in other respects. For example, the religious composition of the population of each of the three countries is majority Christian. What would the results of the study be for a country like Nigeria, for example, with a different and complex religious landscape? This remark is not intended to diminish the importance of this study or its value, but rather to draw attention to the need for studies of the same quality to be carried out in yet other countries.

In my preface to Gottfried Osei-Mensah's book *Wanted: Servant-Leaders* (1990), I wrote, "While many emphasize the need for more and better-prepared leaders for African churches, few have reflected on the nature of Christian leadership itself. Fewer still are those who have written on the qualities needed in African Christian leaders." Over the years Osei-Mensah's book has been significant for leaders. What has been lacking up to now is a study of the opportunities, challenges, and impact of Christian leadership in Africa. This book fills the void.

I commend the authors of the study and the agency that funded it for research designed, conducted, and reported in a coherent and collaborative manner. It is my earnest hope that the overall approach taken in the research and in writing the book will stimulate similar undertakings in the years to come. You will find here many treasures as you read about and further explore African Christian leadership.

Contributors

Kirimi Barine is an author, trainer, publisher, and consultant. He has served and continues to serve in various leadership capacities for organizations in Africa and around the world. He is the founding director of Publishing Institute of Africa, a Nairobi-based publishing, training, and author-development organization. He has authored or co-authored several books, among them *Transformational Corporate Leadership* (2010). Barine delights in training and facilitation of learning experiences as well as consulting on leadership, publishing, and writing. He holds the PhD and doctorate in business administration (with emphasis on leadership and governance) offered jointly and as a dual-degree program by SMC University, Switzerland, and Universidad Central de Nicaragua.

Michael Bowen is associate professor of environmental economics and deputy director of quality assurance at Daystar University. He holds the PhD in environmental economics. In addition to presenting papers at international conferences, he has published a variety of journal articles and book chapters. Among other themes, his writings have focused on Christian marriage and family in Kenya and on the significance of vision and mission in a Christian university. He has served as guest editor for international journal theme issues and has supervised both master's and PhD theses. Professor Bowen has taught at the undergraduate, master's, and PhD levels.

Jurgens Hendriks served as a pastor for ten years before his call in 1985 to teach practical theology at Stellenbosch University, where he has served as professor of congregational studies. Leading congregations through the apartheid transition period was the initial focus of his work and research. In response to the post-1994 increase of postgraduate students from other African countries, he redirected his attention to congregational realities across Africa. His *Studying Congregations in Africa* (2004) was the first publication of the Network for African Congregational Theology (NetACT). Founded in 2000, he became the network's first executive director. He still serves the forty-school network in fifteen African countries as program coordinator.

John Jusu, PhD, serves as Africa regional director of the Overseas Council International and is currently on leave from his position as lecturer in educational studies and dean of the School of Professional Studies at Africa

International University. An ordained minister of the Church of the United Brethren in Christ of Sierra Leone and a missionary of the Association of Evangelicals in Africa, John's focus is on transformational curriculum development. He serves as a curriculum consultant for More than a Mile Deep–Global, as the supervising editor for the Africa Study Bible, and as a member of the Global Associates for Transformational Education. John is also involved in faculty development for many educational initiatives in Africa.

Truphosa Kwaka-Sumba is the principal of Nairobi Campus of St. Paul's University in Kenya. She holds an MA in economics from the University of Manchester (UK). She is a guest editor and columnist with *Leadership Today in Africa* and with the blog her-leadership.com. She is a non-executive board member of the International Leadership Foundation–Kenya and Longhorn Publishers Ltd. She is also a facilitator, trainer, and speaker on leadership, with a special focus on women in leadership, as well as on leadership in Africa.

David K. Ngaruiya is an associate professor and deputy vice chancellor for research, extension, and development at the International Leadership University in Nairobi, Kenya. He holds the PhD in intercultural studies from Trinity Evangelical Divinity School. He served as chair of the Africa Society of Evangelical Theology (2015-16). He has published journal and book articles and served as co-editor and contributor to the book *Communities of Faith in Africa and African Diaspora* (Pickwick Publications, 2013). His research interests include leadership, contextualization, the church in Africa, and the use of digital resources in education. He has supervised graduate research at various levels.

Robert J. Priest is G. W. Aldeen Professor of International Studies and professor of mission and anthropology at Trinity Evangelical Divinity School and holds the PhD in anthropology from the University of California, Berkeley. He is former president of both the American Society of Missiology (2013-14) and the Evangelical Missiological Society (2015-17). His research and writing have included a focus on race and ethnicity, sexuality, short-term missions, religious conversion, and witchcraft accusations. Among his publications is *This Side of Heaven: Race, Ethnicity, and Christian Faith*, edited with Alvaro L. Nieves (Oxford, 2007).

Steven D. H. Rasmussen is a senior lecturer in intercultural studies at Africa International University in Nairobi, Kenya. He received the PhD from Trinity International University in intercultural studies. He has taught for twenty years in East Africa. Previous to his current position he served as principal of Lake Victoria Christian College in Mwanza, Tanzania. He has published a variety of journal articles and book chapters on ethnicity, witchcraft accusations, understandings of sickness in Tanzania, and short-term missions.

Elisabet le Roux is a researcher at the Unit for Religion and Development Research (URDR) at the theological faculty of Stellenbosch University in South Africa. She holds the PhD in sociology from Stellenbosch University; her dissertation is entitled *The Role of African Christian Churches in Dealing with Sexual Violence against Women: The Case of the DRC, Rwanda, and Liberia* (2014). As a faith-and-development expert, she does research in various African countries, focusing particularly on gender and gender-based violence.

Alberto Lucamba Salombongo is a pastor and lecturer in the undergraduate program of the Instituto Superior de Teologia Evangélica no Lubango (ISTEL) in Lubango, Angola. He is also the modular theological program coordinator at ISTEL. He holds a postgraduate diploma in Old Testament from the University of Stellenbosch and is an MTh candidate at the University of Stellenbosch. He is married and has three children.

Yolande A. Sandoua is assistant to the president of Faculté de Théologie Évangélique de Bangui (FATEB) and is FATEB's communication officer. She is currently a PhD student in theology at FATEB. She holds three master's degrees, including an MA in English (American civilization), an MA in theology and mission, and an MTh in African Christianity from the Akrofi-Christaller Institute in Ghana.

Wanjiru M. Gitau is a scholar of Christian history, world Christianity, and missiology. She was a visiting scholar at Asbury Theological Seminary (2015-16). She has the PhD in intercultural studies and world Christianity from Africa International University and an MA in missiology from Nairobi Evangelical Graduate School of Theology. She also has fifteen years of combined pastoral service in dynamic urban congregations and a variety of cross-cultural missional engagements. As a researcher with the Center for the Study of World Christian Revitalization Movements, she is currently writing a book entitled "Reframing the Megachurch Conversation" (working title).

Nupanga Weanzana wa Weanzana is the president of Faculté de Théologie Évangélique de Bangui (FATEB) in Central African Republic and teaches biblical Hebrew and Old Testament (exegesis and theology). He received the PhD in Old Testament studies from the University of Pretoria in South Africa. His area of interest is the Book of Chronicles and the Second Temple Period. Among his publications are several commentaries on Old Testament books in *Africa Bible Commentary* (Zondervan, 2006).

Mary Kleine Yehling is vice president and executive director of the Tyndale House Foundation (THF), where she has served since 1975. Her leadership role at THF, which for fifty-three years has prioritized "Investing in the kingdom," gives her the opportunity and joy of learning about and working closely with Christian leaders, organizations, missions, and churches around the world. She also serves in a variety of ways in her local community as a volunteer and leader in area organizations, choirs, schools, and in her church.

Chapter 1

The Genesis and Growth of the Africa Christian Leadership Study

Robert J. Priest

The recent history of Christianity in Africa involves an extraordinary story. In 1900, there were nine million Christians in Africa. By 2015, there were 541 million (Johnson et. al. 2015, 28). And while Christianity was exploding in Africa, it was declining in countries that had originally sent missionaries to Africa (Jenkins 2002; Sanneh 2003; Walls 1996; Kalu 2005). Today, African Christians make up nearly a quarter of the world's Christian population. While foreign missionaries played important roles in the story of Christianity in Africa, it was African Christians themselves that did the lion's share of the evangelism, with most of the Christian expansion occurring in recent decades, and after colonialism.

This recent growth of Christianity occurred on a continent affected by a history of colonialism, global Cold War politics, ethnolinguistic diversity, International Monetary Fund (IMF) and World Bank structural-adjustment policies, endemic health problems including malaria and HIV/AIDS, failure of development goals, and corruption. In short, the recent growth of Christianity occurred on a continent facing massive challenges related to literacy, education, healthcare, economic development, globalization, peace and security, and the development of healthy governments.

The remarkable expansion of Christianity in Africa in the context of massive social challenges has created unprecedented opportunities for leadership by Christians. Hundreds of thousands of young congregations now provide local platforms for the development and exercise of spiritual and social leadership. And because many of Africa's countries are majority Christian, African Christians also find themselves exercising leadership in a wide variety of business, educational, media, social-service, and governmental venues.

However, in many respects the speed of Christian numerical growth has outstripped available support structures for Christian leadership training and development, particularly leadership training that is contextually relevant. Demand exceeds supply. And while contemporary Christian

1

communities of Europe or North America may have longer histories than many younger African churches, and stronger institutional supports related to the provision of education and leadership training, their theological conversations, leadership curricula, and publications fail the test of contextual relevance in Africa (Tiénou 2006). It takes time, intentionality, sustained work, and material resources to develop and produce the institutional supports and curricular resources needed for African-led contextual leadership development (Phiri and Werner 2013; Carpenter and Kooistra 2014).

Many things that enhance leadership development (for example, books, journals, Internet access, educational facilities, libraries, conferences, access to travel, research grants, writing sabbaticals) require material underpinnings. Religious institutions, especially when compared to governmental institutions, face particular challenges related to such material support. Although seldom considered by scholars of Christianity, the economic stewardship of prosperous congregations, wealthy individual donors, and Christian foundations has always played a strategic role in strengthening religious institutions and ministry initiatives. Consider theological education, with its need for buildings, libraries, faculty salaries, and other supports. Even in wealthy nations, seminaries do not exist solely based on student tuition. Rather, they seek help from significant donors wherever they may be. Trinity Evangelical Divinity School, for example, seeks and receives support from affluent Christians in Chicago and Los Angeles, but also in Hong Kong, Singapore, and South Korea.

Vast disparities in wealth between different regions of the globe have an impact on leadership in different ways. While Africa contains a higher proportion of the world's Christians than does North America, with wide-open opportunities for African Christian leaders to have a positive impact, it contains a much smaller portion of the world's Christian material wealth than does North America (Wuthnow 2009). Many factors critical to leadership development (such as research, publication, education) depend directly on access to material resources. Consider formal education. Despite the strong desire in Africa for education, "fewer than five percent of college-age young people are enrolled" in higher education (Carpenter and Kooistra 2014, 9). Global wealth disparities also are reflected in theological education. The 210 Association of Theological Schools (ATS)-accredited theological schools in the United States, with an average endowment of US$38.7 million, operate within very different economic constraints than do most theological institutions across Africa. The one billion dollar endowment of Princeton Theological Seminary almost certainly surpasses many times over the combined total endowments of all 1,429 theological institutions across Africa listed in the *Global Directory of Theological Education Institutions*.

And yet, Christians are increasingly conscious of themselves as part of a networked worldwide "body of Christ" (Eph 4:15–16), where emerging patterns of global stewardship bridge socioeconomic divides in service of leadership formation and support. This book and the research on which it reports is directly indebted to such a networked body.

BACKGROUND TO THE AFRICA LEADERSHIP STUDY

The original vision for an Africa Leadership Study (ALS) (out of which this book emerged) rather improbably was stimulated by discussions within the board of the Tyndale House Foundation (THF). As board members allocated grants to local ministry initiatives around the world, several were particularly fascinated by the opportunities open to African Christian leaders, by the wide variety of initiatives they were launching and leading, and by the challenges they faced. But board members also noticed that THF giving was often based on subjective information without systematic, context-specific research that would inform the process. They discussed the value to their own work of an India Leadership Study that had been carried out by David Bennett (2002) and contemplated the value of similar research in Africa. While they recognized that many scholars had written about Christianity in Africa, it was felt that such writings seldom focused on the realities that foundations needed help in understanding. For example, they wished for support in understanding dynamics in Africa related to material resources and global stewardship, especially as they relate to leadership training and the exercise of leadership. They wondered which African Christian leaders, and which African-led Christian organizations, were widely respected by local African Christians as having the most positive impact, and in what arenas. And what factors were involved in their positive impact?

Finally, in 2008, board member Edward Elliott, a Chicago-area businessman and founder of the Africa-focused book publisher Oasis International, with encouragement from THF board chair Dr. Douglas McConnell, offered to take the initiative in exploring the possibilities for such a study. Over the next couple of years he consulted program officers of several Christian foundations with interests in Africa. He consulted Robert Priest, a seminary professor and scholar about the research side of the project. David Ngaruiya, a seminary professor in Nairobi, joined Robert Priest to carry out exploratory interviews related to leadership and foundation giving. They consulted with and interviewed over thirty African Christian leaders of churches, theological institutions, and parachurch organizations.[1]

---

[1] Interviews were carried out, and subsequently transcribed, with each of the following: Bulus Galadima, the provost of ECWA Theological Seminary (Nigeria), Desta Heliso, director of the Ethiopian Graduate School of Theology, Joe Simfukwe, principal of the Theological College of Central Africa (Zambia), Katho Bungishabaku, president/rector of Shalom University of Bunia (formerly Bunia Theological College and Seminary), Tite Tiénou, academic dean of Trinity Evangelical Divinity School. Administrators and faculty of Nairobi Evangelical

Next, Robert Priest, Shelly Isaacs, and Mary Kleine Yehling, of the THF, analyzed ten years of THF giving within Africa—and also carried out an initial online survey of two hundred African Christian leaders.

In the summer of 2010, monthly meetings were begun in the Chicago area by an initial planning group made up of Robert Priest, Edward Elliott, Mary Kleine Yehling, and Bob Reekie (a former THF board member). Bob Reekie, the South African co-founder and first president of Media Associates International, brought extensive experience and a strong interest in Africa. Mary Kleine Yehling, the executive director of the THF, brought administrative abilities and sustained commitment to Africa and the ALS project that would, over the next few years, make her central to every aspect of project success. Among other things, this group talked about the implications of what was learned through these interviews and the online survey of African Christian leaders. They spelled out, from the THF perspective, the hoped-for outcomes of the study (see Appendix A).

In November 2011 an expanded international working group convened in Nairobi, Kenya for several days: (1) to consider the feasibility of an Africa Leadership Study, (2) to articulate from an African standpoint the purposes and design of such a study, and (3) to plan the research process. Edward Elliott and Mary Kleine Yehling communicated the Tyndale House Foundation's interest in research on Christian leadership and leadership development in Africa, research that would inform foundation-giving in Africa. They stressed the need for African wisdom to inform donor understanding of leadership needs in Africa. And they also proposed that African Christian scholars help design and carry out a study that would centrally

---

Graduate School of Theology (now Africa International University) included Yusufu Taraki, Douglas Carew, John Ochola, James Nkansah, Peter Nyende, Christine Mutua, Ephraim Mudave (librarian), Robert Carlson, and George Renner. Administrators and faculty at the Nairobi International School of Theology included Emmanuel Bellon, David Ngaruiya, Marta Bennett, and Lois Semenye. Administrators and faculty from Scott Theological College included Jacob Kibor, Esther Kibor, Paul Mbandi, and Joyce Muasa. From Daystar University, Godfrey Nguru, James Ogolla, James Kombo, and Michael Bowen were interviewed. Pastors of churches involved in leadership training who were interviewed included Oscar Muriu, the pastor of Nairobi Chapel; and Muriithi Wanjau, an author and the pastor of Mavuno Church (a megachurch with young, educated, and wealthy members). Others who were interviewed included missionaries (Larry Niemeyer, Jim Harries, and Marvin Smith), Mary Munyi (founding director of Tumaini Ladies Integration Program), Gerald Macharia (enterprise development consultant with the Clinton Foundation), John Padwick (administrator at the Organization of African Instituted Churches), Vincent Wanjau (Evangelism Explosion), Reuben Maina (Christian Mission AID), Wanjau Nduba (Navigators), Steve Maina (chief executive for Chaplains for National Youth Service), Samson Wesaka Mabonga (church planter in the slums), and Mutava Musyimi—a member of parliament, former secretary general of the National Council of Churches, and chairman of the National Anticorruption Steering Committee.

address issues and priorities of concern to African Christian leaders and institutions. Africans on the ALS team were invited to articulate Africa-oriented goals and hoped-for outcomes in this kind of study and to design each step of research in a way that would be responsive to such goals, as well as to the hoped-for goals of the THF. (For the purpose statements finalized at that time, see Appendix A.) That is, while the THF clearly hoped to benefit from the study, it also wished to support a process that would be planned, organized, and implemented with African Christian scholars and leaders at the center.

THE ALS TEAM

This ALS working group was primarily composed of scholars who would supervise and carry out the research. From the beginning, however, it also included advisers representing key constituencies and with pertinent areas of expertise. Over three-and-a-half years the entire group convened a total of four times, with smaller, country-specific working groups regularly convening to plan and carry out research and analysis. Online GoToMeeting sessions often took place. Writing workshops and retreats were also held to evaluate and critique working documents and to draw from one another's expertise and knowledge.

While a majority of the ALS team members had experience with research, several individuals had unusual strengths in guiding the team in research design, implementation, supervision, and analysis. Robert Priest had strengths in both quantitative and qualitative research design and provided leadership throughout the research process. Elisabet le Roux was a research sociologist in the Unit for Religion and Development Research at the theological faculty of Stellenbosch University in South Africa and had extensive experience carrying out research across the continent. Four scholars in the group taught graduate courses in research methods at Kenyan academic institutions: Michael Bowen at Daystar University, David Ngaruiya at International Leadership University, and John Jusu and Steve Rasmussen at Africa International University. All four had significant experience carrying out and supervising research in Africa and on Christianity. Building on this in-country expertise, every phase of research was first field tested and administered in Kenya under the supervision of the above four Kenya-based scholars before being carried out elsewhere.

While most of the team members had a background in theological studies, the core research and writing team was interdisciplinary. Participants held doctorates in intercultural studies (David Ngaruiya, Steve Rasmussen), missiology (Kalemba Mwambazambi), world Christianity (Wanjiru Gitau), education (John Jusu), business administration (Kirimi Barine), economics (Michael Bowen), anthropology (Robert Priest), sociology (Elisabet le Roux), and Old Testament (Nupanga Weanzana). While Jurgens

Hendriks's doctorate was in Old Testament, his faculty appointment was in practical theology and missiology. Others had one or more master's degrees in fields such as economics (Truphosa Kwaka-Sumba), African Christianity (Yolande Sandoua), practical theology (Adelaide Thomas Manuel), Old Testament (Alberto Lucamba Salombongo), and divinity (José Paulo Bunga).

Some individuals with broad Christian leadership connections and experience in and across Africa served at our workshops in a purely advisory capacity. Joanna Ilboudo of Burkina Faso, with diverse leadership experiences, most recently as executive secretary of the Pan Africa Christian Women Alliance (an initiative of the Association of Evangelicals in Africa), helped us keep women's perspectives in view. Originally from Chad, Daniel Bourdanné, the general secretary of the International Fellowship of Evangelical Students (IFES), representing half a million university students in 160 countries, helped us maintain a focus on non-clergy leadership. Both Joanna Ilboudo and Daniel Bourdanné brought insights and expertise on Francophone Africa. Ian Shaw of Langham Partnership and Evan Hunter of Scholar Leaders International attended as advisers with special interest and experience in theological education and with strong theological networks across the African continent. Kirimi Barine, director of publishing and training at Publishing Institute of Africa, drew from extensive experience holding training workshops on writing, publishing, and leadership across the continent. As the project moved into the analysis and writing phase, Barine took on a central editorial role.

Nearly all who were involved in carrying out the research had broad Christian leadership connections and experience in and across Africa. For example, Nupanga Weanzana, president of Faculté de Théologie Évangélique de Bangui (FATEB), in the Central African Republic (CAR), had long, wide, and deep connections to theological leaders across Francophone Africa. Jurgens Hendriks of Stellenbosch University served for years as executive director of the forty-school network in fifteen African countries of NetACT (Network for African Congregational Theology). John Jusu, regional director of the Overseas Council International, curriculum consultant for More than a Mile Deep, and supervising editor for the Africa Study Bible, has served for years as an educational consultant in a wide variety of venues across the continent. For a full list of the ALS team, see the ALS website (www.AfricaLeadershipStudy.org).

SCOPE OF THE ALS RESEARCH

As the ALS team began brainstorming the research process, it was immediately apparent that we could not possibly carry out research across the entire continent. Africa is enormous, larger than China, Europe, and the USA combined. It comprises fifty-five[2] countries, with over two thousand languages spoken.[3]

And yet, as a result of the European colonial impact, people in most African countries use either English, French, or Portuguese as a language of communication and education. These three groups of countries have quite different histories of colonialism and Christian mission and are differently situated linguistically in the contemporary world system. Thus, we wondered if the differences among these three groups of countries might not give us one way to organize our exploration of the variability found within African Christianity.

African countries under the earlier rule of Great Britain would have shared a great deal in common, as would those under France, and others under Portugal. Under British colonialism, for example, traditional African political institutions were accommodated through indirect rule. The British emphasized social and cultural differences among ethnic groups and were less likely to approve European intermarriage with Africans than were the Portuguese—whose mixed offspring were known as *mestiços*. The French and Portuguese employed direct rule and stressed their civilizing mission, binding colonies to the metropole under a policy of assimilation. In French colonies, African educated elite were sometimes granted French citizenship, and a shared currency was used. Forced labor was common in French and Portuguese colonies, but not in British colonies. The British gave greater recognition to common law systems giving rights to property owners and were generally more supportive of freedom of religion.[4] French and Portuguese colonies often limited or prohibited Protestant missionaries (who were mostly English speaking) out of fear that such missionaries would serve British colonial interests. So Protestant missionaries were relative latecomers to French and Portuguese colonies as compared with Roman Catholic missionaries. Education under the French fit assimilationist goals, valuing all things French, and more consistently tried to limit the role of all missionaries. The Portuguese similarly stressed assimilation and the use of the Portuguese language but granted the Catholic Church a quasi-monopoly on education. By contrast, the British allowed both Protestant and Catholic mission schools to administer education. In short, individual

---

[2] Whether Africa comprises fifty-four or fifty-five countries hinges on whether to include Western Sahara as a separate country, a territory which Morocco claims and which the United Nations identifies as "a non-self-governing territory." Since most maps show it as a separate entity, and since the African Union treats Western Sahara as a separate country, we have chosen to follow their lead in this book. Thus our reference to fifty-five countries.

[3] https://www.ethnologue.com/region/Africa.

[4] An exception to the pattern was in Muslim regions under British control, such as Northern Nigeria, where the British themselves prohibited Christian missionaries (Walls 2002, 150–51).

African countries often share significant historical influences with other countries that were subject to the same colonial empire that they were.[5]

Quite apart from this history, African countries with Portuguese or French as the national language are differently situated globally than those with English. Since Protestant missionaries most frequently come from English-speaking countries, their linguistic alignments in Anglophone countries were different than in Lusophone or Francophone ones. In Francophone countries Protestant missionaries often stressed theological education in indigenous languages, not French. But in Anglophone countries, they often supported theological education in English. Literature and educational systems diverge. Protestant Christians in Angola or Mozambique, for example, have weaker ties to the USA than Christians in Ghana or Kenya, and stronger ties to Brazil. The television shows of T. D. Jakes, Joyce Meyer, and Joel Osteen are more likely to be seen in English-speaking countries than in Portuguese or French ones.

Christian foundations or churches in America, because of historical networks, and because of linguistic bridges and barriers, are currently more likely to partner with ministries in Anglophone Africa than with ministries in Francophone or Lusophone Africa. Their knowledge of Francophone or Lusophone Africa is likely to be less than their knowledge of Anglophone Africa.

Indeed, even the world of academia is skewed in similar directions. In a comprehensive study of English-language PhD dissertations focused on world Christianity between 2002 and 2011 (Priest and DeGeorge 2013, 197), it was discovered that Anglophone Africa received disproportionate attention. Eighty percent of Africa's fifty-five countries had only one or two or no dissertations focused on Christianity in that country. By contrast, five English-speaking countries were the focus of half of the Africa-focused dissertations on world Christianity: Nigeria (40), Kenya (36), South Africa (35), Ghana (27), and Uganda (25). More dissertations focused on Christianity in any one of these five countries than in all of Francophone Africa combined (23), with only four dissertations examining Christianity in any Lusophone African country. In short, a majority of research-based knowledge about Christianity in Africa is one-sidedly grounded in research on Anglophone Africa.

In light of the above, the ALS team decided to focus its research on three countries tied to particular streams of colonial history broadly present throughout the continent: one Anglophone, one Francophone, and one Lusophone (Fig. 1–1). It also selected these countries based on the strengths and research connections of the ALS team.

---

[5] The Democratic Republic of the Congo, formerly known as Belgian Congo, while linguistically Francophone, was historically under Belgium, not France, and thus diverges from some of the above patterns.

The Africa Leadership Study focused on one
Anglophone (A), one Francophone (F) and one
Lusophone (L) country in Africa. These countries
are indicated with a white lettered circle and
outlined with a thick border.

Map source: www.gmi.org

Figure 1–1. Africa by colonial language and featuring the three countries
researched

We had several outstanding scholars (Michael Bowen, John Jusu, David Ngaruiya, and Steve Rasmussen) located in key academic Kenyan institutions (Daystar University, Africa International University, Africa Leadership University), scholars who themselves supervised large numbers of graduate theological students with strong connections to Kenyan Christians across denominations. Thus, we selected Kenya as our core Anglophone country. This East African country gained independence from the United Kingdom in 1963. At 582,650 square kilometers, Kenya is over twice the size of the United Kingdom.[6] Its current population of forty-six million has an average life expectancy of sixty-three years, an adult literacy rate of 72 percent, and is 25 percent urban. While Kenyan peoples speak roughly sixty languages,[7] English and Swahili are the *lingua franca* for most. Eight percent of Kenyans identify as Muslim, and 81 percent identify as Christian. Twenty percent of Kenyans identify as Roman Catholic.[8]

Similarly, our ALS team included several scholars (Nupanga Weanzana, Kelemba Mwambazambi, and Yolande Sandoua) from FATEB in the Central African Republic (CAR). FATEB had a significant pool of graduate students that could be drawn on for help with research. Since our ALS team was ideally positioned to carry out research in the CAR, we chose to focus on this Francophone country. This country gained its independence from France in 1960. At 622,984 square kilometers, the CAR is slightly smaller than France. Its current population of 4.9 million has a life expectancy of fifty-three years, an adult literacy rate of 57 percent, and is 40 percent urban.[9] While citizens speak more than sixty languages,[10] French and Sango are the *lingua franca* for most. In the CAR, 14 percent identify as Muslim and 73 percent as Christian. Thirty-one percent are Roman Catholic.[11]

While our initial ALS team had no scholars from Lusophone countries, Jurgens Hendriks and Elisabet le Roux of Stellenbosch University had strong connections with theological institutions and scholars within Angola. Thus, we chose to focus our research on this Lusophone country, with our ALS leadership team subsequently augmented by three Angolan theological faculty (Adelaide Thomas Manuel, Alberto Lucamba Salombongo, and José Paulo Bunga). This country in southern Africa gained its independence from Portugal in 1975. At 1,246,620 square kilometers, Angola is more than thirteen times the size of Portugal and twice the size of France. Its current population of twenty-five million has a life expectancy of fifty-four years, an adult literacy rate of 70 percent, and is 44 percent

---

[6] World Christian Database (April 18, 2016),

[7] http://www.ethnologue.com/country/KE.

[8] Statistics on religion are from the World Christian Database (April 18, 2016)

[9] Ibid.

[10] http://www.ethnologue.com/country/CF.

[11] World Christian Database (April 18, 2016).

urban.[12] While over 30 languages are spoken[13], Portuguese is the *lingua franca* for most. Ninety-three percent of Angolans identify as Christian (50 percent of Angolans are Roman Catholic), and one percent as Muslim.[14]

THE RESEARCH PROCESS

The ALS team designed a two-step research process. The first phase involved administering a survey to 8,041 respondents. The survey results were intended, among other things, to help us identify African Christian leaders and African-led Christian organizations that were perceived by African Christians as having an unusually positive impact in their communities. The second phase of research consisted of in-depth interviews with many of these individuals and organization leaders.

Phase 1 Research

In the first phase, a ninety-three-item survey questionnaire was developed to gather information from a broad cross-section of active Christians in Angola, Kenya, and the Central African Republic. Respondents were asked about themselves and the churches they attended. They were asked to identify key pastoral leaders that they believed were having an unusually positive impact in their communities. They were also asked to identify African Christians with unusually positive impact who were exercising leadership in other social arenas (such as business, medical care, poverty alleviation, education, media, or government). In addition, respondents were asked to identify African-led Christian organizations that they felt were having a high level of positive impact in their communities. Questions then focused on these leaders and organizations—their characteristics, relationships, and leadership development efforts. There were also questions related to the availability and accessibility of books, digital resources, and various leadership training options. (The full questionnaire with responses is available in Appendix B.)

The questionnaire was completed and field tested in Kenya in the first half of 2012; subsequently it was revised and translated into Swahili, French, and Portuguese. In July 2012, Bowen, Ngaruiya, and Priest joined CAR senior directors Kalemba Mwambazambi and Nupanga Weanzana in Bangui, for final field testing and revisions of the instrument in French and for training graduate assistants in administering the survey.

---

[12] World Christian Database (April 18, 2016).
[13] http://www.ethnologue.com/country/AO.
[14] World Christian Database (April 18, 2016).

Kenya

In August, an ethnically and denominationally diverse team of Kenyan research assistants,[15] most of whom were graduate students, received formal training on administering the final survey. Under the supervision of Ngaruiya, Bowen, Jusu, and Rasmussen they spent the last few months of 2012 administering the survey in both English and Swahili to 3,964 Christians across Kenya. They traveled to regions of the country where the population was most concentrated, and where larger denominations and ethnic groups were present. Research assistants were often selected to administer surveys in places where they had strong personal and church networks as well as ethnic ties. While the Kenyan map (Fig. 1–2) does not identify all locations where surveys were filled out, the cities and towns on the map represent places where significant concentrations of respondents filled out the surveys. Surveys were not administered in regions of the country with low population concentrations, low concentrations of Christians, where travel access was limited, and where it might have been dangerous to carry out the research (such as in the heavily Muslim Northeast).

Research assistants looked for active and informed Christians to fill out the surveys. The purpose of the survey was clearly explained, anonymity was assured, and those who filled out the survey were given the gift of a pen with the name of one of the Kenyan sponsoring academic institutions (Africa International University, Africa Leadership University, or Daystar University). Each pen also included the inscription, "'So encourage each other and build each other up' I Thess 5:11." Sometimes research assistants approached individuals one by one. Nearly 30 percent of surveys were filled out by individuals approached in this way. A majority of respondents in Kenya (over 70 percent), however, were part of gatherings where every person in the entire group was asked to fill out a survey. About a quarter of the time, this was in the context of congregationally based groups, such as choirs, worship teams, prayer meetings, women's groups, or meetings of congregational leaders. The rest were in groups composed of participants from more than a single congregation. This included prayer breakfasts, midday prayer groups, pastoral gatherings, university fellowships, youth leader gatherings, men's and women's conferences, school staff meetings, workshops, and in one case, a wedding.

Clearly, this was not a random survey. We specifically intended to survey knowledgeable, active Christians. Among other things, this meant that our Kenyan respondents were well educated, with roughly 90 percent having completed high school, and with less than 5 percent of respondents needing to have the research assistants read the survey to them and record their answers for them. While 8 percent acknowledged not attending church

---

[15] Zephaniah Ananda, Maggie Gitau, Godfrey Isolio, Moses Karanja, Margaret Kariuki, Ruth Kiragu, Rachel Kisyula, Ednah C. Maina, Duncan Malemba, Job Momanyi, Alex Mutuku, Cyrus Mutuku, Sebastian Mwanza, David Njuguna, Hesbon Owilla, Ruth Owino, Philip Tinega, and Angela Weyama.

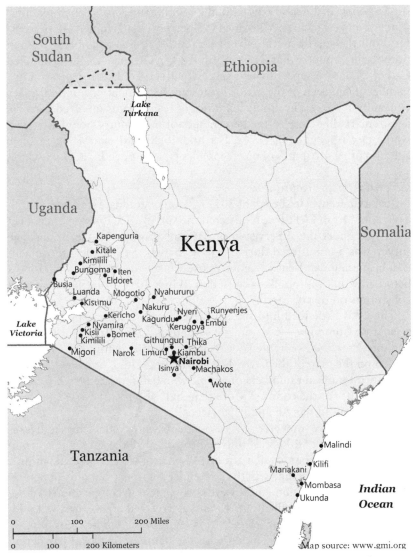

Figure 1–2. Kenya, with towns and cities where research was carried out

regularly, 31 percent of respondents served their church in lay or clergy leadership roles, and an additional 60 percent reported being church members and/or regular attendees.

While we never intended to carry out a random survey, we did intend to survey people in different regions of the country and across denominations, genders, and ethnicities. More men (58 percent) than women (42 percent) filled out the survey. With only 11 percent of respondents being Roman Catholic in a country that is 20 percent Roman Catholic, we undersampled Catholics. But we appear to have successfully surveyed fairly representative numbers from each of the major Protestant denominations in Kenya (see Appendix B, Q.7). The ethnic identities of respondents involved percentages remarkably close to the percentages of the country population as a whole (see Appendix B, Q.76). For additional information on income, age, and other attributes of our respondents, see Appendix B, Q.69–Q.92.

Central African Republic

Just as in Kenya, in the fall of 2012, a team of graduate student research assistants[16] from FATEB administered the survey to 2,294 respondents in the CAR, under the supervision of Mwambazambi and Weanzana. The survey was administered during a time that the Séléka rebel movement was beginning its offensive against government forces, and only months before it would capture Bangui itself in March 2013. This placed marked constraints on our research.

The CAR is divided into sixteen Préfectures with the capital, Bangui, a separate Commune—essentially a seventeenth Préfecture. For logistical and safety reasons, we limited our focus to five cities in four Préfectures, as shown on the map of the CAR (Fig. 1–3). These cities, of course, already contained significant numbers of people who had retreated from violence in other parts of the country. More than half of our surveys (62 percent) were filled out in Bangui and its environs.

In the CAR over 60 percent of respondents were contacted as individuals, with just under 40 percent invited to complete the survey in a group context. Of those contacted in groups, 45 percent were contacted within a congregational grouping, with the remainder in groups that did not pertain to a specific congregation. These were fairly similar in composition to those in Kenya. Those who filled out the survey received a pen engraved with the scripture *"Encouragez-vous les uns les autres et édifiez-vous mutuellement . . .' 1 Thess 5:11"* along with the name of our local partnering institution, *"Faculté de Théologie Évangélique de Bangui."*

---

[16] Belin Boydet, Dzifa Codjia, Didacien Dongobada, Mymy Kalemba, Fatchou Kongolona, Max Koyadibert, Viana Mathy Mataya, Yves Mulume, Jean-Claude Mushimiyimana, Mayambe Elie Muteba, Mavutukidi Lopez Nsamu, Franck Nyongona, Christopher Rabariolina, Frederic Razafimaharo, Paul Sakalaima, Yolande Sandoua, Emmanuel Swebolo, and Elysee Tao.

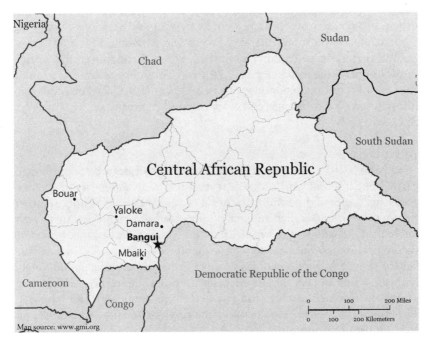

Figure 1–3. Central African Republic, with cities where research was carried out

Again, we intentionally and selectively oversampled those who were well educated and religiously observant. Eighty-nine percent reported being high-school graduates. And while 13 percent acknowledged not attending church regularly, 33 percent of respondents served their church in a lay or clergy leadership role, with an additional 54 percent reporting being church members and/or regular attenders.

Our CAR respondents were disproportionately male (66 percent) and urban. In a country that is 42 percent Protestant and 31 percent Catholic, 92 percent of our respondents were Protestant, with only 8 percent Catholic. But they seem to be fairly representative of the major ethnic groups in the country (see Appendix B, Q.76), and also a broad cross-section of the major Protestant denominations (see Appendix B, Q.7). For additional information on income, age, and other respondent attributes, see Appendix B, Q.69–Q.92.

Angola

In March 2013, Elisabet le Roux and Alberto Lucamba Salombongo carried out training workshops at several different seminaries in Angola. At the insistence of the administrators at our partnering institutions, rather than work with a smaller number of advanced research assistants as we did in the CAR and Kenya, we utilized over a hundred assistants who were theological undergraduates from five theological seminaries.[17] Under the supervision of Adelaide Thomas Manuel, Alberto Lucamba Salombongo, and José Paulo Bunga, these students surveyed 1,783 respondents in half of Angola's provinces, where roughly two-thirds of the population resides. The Angola map (Fig. 1–4) features the towns and cities where we collected most of our data.

Two-thirds of the Angola respondents were approached as individuals, while another one-third were approached in the context of a group, which largely (82 percent) involved congregationally based groupings. Those who filled out the survey received a pen with the scripture *"Exortai-vos e edificai-vos uns aos outros . . .' 1 Tes 5:11."*

The research assistants in Angola were younger and less professionally advanced and connected than those in Kenya and thus found it more difficult to arrange access to larger groups. While the assistants in Kenya were all Kenyan, those in the CAR were mostly from other Francophone countries. With fewer in-country social ties, the CAR assistants were understandably constrained in their access to church groupings by comparison with the Kenya team. Because the Angolan assistants were younger, they seemed to gravitate to younger respondents, with 40 percent of Angolan

---

[17] From Luanda in the north was the Seminario Teológico Baptista (STB) and the Instituto Teológico da Igreja Evangélica Reformada de Angola (ITIERA). In the center of the country in Huambo was Seminario Emanuel do Dôndi (SED), and to the south were the Instituto Superior de Teologia Evangélica no Lubango (ISTEL) and the Instituto Bíblico de Kaluquembe—Missão Urgente (IBK-MU).

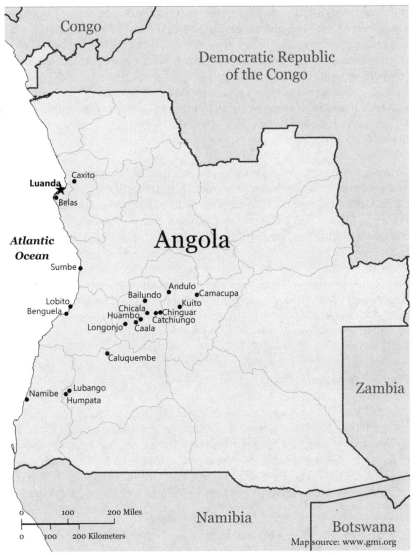

Figure 1–4. Angola, with towns and cities where research was carried out

respondents being under twenty-five years old, compared to roughly half that percentage under the age of twenty-five in the CAR and Kenya. They also surveyed clergy at lower rates than in the CAR and Kenya.

Again, the educated and religiously observant were by intention over-represented in our sample. Eighty-five percent reported being high-school graduates. Twenty-five percent of respondents served in (mostly lay) church leadership positions; an additional 67 percent were church members and/or regular attenders. Our Angola respondents were disproportionately male (66 percent) and Protestant (96 percent). In a country that is 50 percent Catholic, less than 4 percent of our respondents were Catholic. While we surveyed a good cross-section of the Protestant community (Appendix B, Q.7), our sample in Angola was in some respects less representative of the actual population denominationally and ethnically than in the CAR and Kenya.[18]

In total, we surveyed 8,041 respondents in four languages. Our largest and most representative samples were collected in Kenya, where (1) we had a strong team of faculty-scholars with expertise in supervising such research, (2) we had an impressive team of research assistants, many of whom were PhD students with church leadership networks, and (3) we faced fewer security and transportation challenges. Our senior ALS scholars with the most expertise related to survey research spoke English, not French or Portuguese. Thus, the challenges in carrying out our research in Angola and the CAR were compounded. Nonetheless, the data collected in the CAR and Angola provide extremely helpful comparative information on Christian realities in understudied regions of Africa.

Phase 2 Research

Our Phase 1 survey research was intended, in part, to lay foundations for the Phase 2 follow-up interview study. In the survey we had asked respondents to "name a Christian man or woman, outside your immediate family, who has influenced you the most." More than half of the respondents in the CAR and Kenya, and over one-third in Angola, provided the name of a pastor. Clearly, pastors are extremely influential in the lives of

---

[18] For example, 35.5 percent of our Angolan respondents were members of the Igreja Evangélica Congregacional de Angola, although the World Christian Database (WCD) lists this denomination as comprising only 3.5 percent of the Angolan population. According to the WCD, 21 percent of Angolans attend the Igreja Universal do Reino de Deus, yet we apparently surveyed no one from this church. In terms of ethnicity we oversampled those who were Ovimbundu (52 percent of our sample, but only 37 percent of the country population) and Bakongo (28 percent of our sample, but only 13 percent of the country), and undersampled Kimbundu (5.4 percent of our sample, but 25 percent of the country) and Ganbuela (1.3 percent of our sample, and 9.2 percent of the country).

African Christians. Later in our survey, we asked each respondent to name a local pastor who they believed was having the most significant impact in their local community (see Appendix B, Q.20–Q.23). Follow-up questions (Q.24–Q.30) asked about this pastor's gender, age, marital status, ethnic group, breadth of influence, and the extent and manner in which he or she was developing leaders. An initial list of influential pastors for each country was developed based on the frequency with which they were identified as having the most impact, the frequency with which individuals reported being influenced by them, and the extent to which they were deemed to be developing and training others as leaders. Subsequently, each country's ALS senior research directors, in consultation with Robert Priest, developed a priority list from which to select pastors for follow-up interviews. This prioritized list took into account ethnicity, denomination, and region of the country, working to ensure that we would not overly focus on pastors from a single denomination, ethnicity, or locale. While a high proportion of named pastors were older, we gave special consideration to younger pastors with high ratings as well as consideration to women. At this point practical considerations, such as travel dangers in the CAR, or pastors being out of the country at the time, precluded interviews with certain pastors. Where two pastors had roughly equal reasons for being chosen, we sometimes chose the pastor who would require less travel for our senior researchers. Using a protocol developed by the full ALS team, nine pastors were contacted and interviewed (three in Angola, two in the CAR, and four in Kenya). The interviews were subsequently transcribed and reports were prepared on each and made available on the ALS website. Most interviews were conducted by our senior ALS team, but in a few cases research assistants who were doctoral students also conducted interviews. A specific list and more complete description of the pastors we interviewed and reported on are provided in Table 2–1.

In our survey we also asked respondents about local Christian leaders who were exercising important leadership in arenas such as education, business, government, medical health care, or communication and media. Respondents named a wide variety of people, including an architect, judge, medical doctor, general, environmentalist, sex-education teacher, business woman, agricultural specialist, elementary-school administrator, and professor. The leaders were rated individually on a Likert scale in terms of their (1) skill at their work, (2) wisdom and knowledge of their local context, (3) ethical integrity, (4) love and service for others, (5) positive reputation in the community, (6) the extent to which they inspire teamwork and community mobilization, (7) efficiency in use of resources, and (8) the extent to which they were training and developing other leaders. (For full information on data collected on these leaders, see Appendix B, Q.31–Q.50.) Based both on the frequency with which specific leaders were named and how highly they were rated by the above criteria, initial nonclergy leader lists were prepared for each country. Again, the senior ALS team in each country in consultation with Robert Priest reviewed these assessments and refined a prioritized list of leaders from which we would select individuals to interview and report on. Again care was taken to be attentive to gender, age, ethnicity, locale, and specific arena of influence in order to consider as wide a variety of leaders as possible. ALS senior researchers carried out interviews with fifteen chosen leaders (three in Angola, four in the CAR, and eight in Kenya) in accordance with protocols consistent across the three countries, arranged for the interviews to be transcribed, and prepared reports on each that could be made publicly available on the ALS website. A list and fuller description of these leaders is provided in Table 2–2.

Finally, since organizations not only support and foster the training and development of leaders but also provide the institutional frameworks within which leadership is exercised, our survey asked respondents to identify and evaluate Christian organizations having the greatest strategic impact in their local area or region (Appendix B, Q.53–53–Q.68). Each respondent was asked to evaluate the organization using a four-point Likert scale in terms of the extent to which the organization (1) trains leaders, (2) works wisely in the local context, (3) has a good reputation locally, (4) receives strong support from local churches, and (5) allows women to participate in leadership. Taking into account frequency of mention, ratings on the above criteria, and whether or not a named organization (such as USAID) had identifiable Christian links, we developed top lists for each country. The senior leadership team for each country, in consultation with Robert Priest, then selected specific organizations for follow-up interviews. Factors such as locale, the extent to which the organizations were Africa led, and the nature of the organization's activity foci were taken into account in selecting the final organizations for follow up.

Organizations that were international in scope and leadership and that had already been studied in local African settings (such as World Vision, see Bornstein 2005), were sometimes dropped from follow-up consideration, despite otherwise excellent evaluations, while African-initiated and African-led organizations received special consideration. Practical considerations, such as the cost of travel and whether leaders were available to be interviewed, also affected the final selection. For each of the thirty-two organizations we studied (six in Angola, seven in the CAR, and nineteen in Kenya), one to six taped interviews were conducted with organization leaders using protocols prepared by the full ALS team and consistent across countries. These interviews were subsequently transcribed. Supplementary online and print information about the organization was examined where available. A full list of the organizations we studied is provided in Table 6–1, with fuller information on these organizations provided in Chapter 6 and Chapter 7. A final report on each organization was prepared and is available on the ALS website.

Throughout 2013 and into 2014, these interviews, transcripts, and reports were prepared, with reports subsequently made available in all three languages (English, French, and Portuguese) through translation. The chapters in this book build on the above combination of questionnaire-and-interview research.

Phase 3 Research

An additional phase of research that was not part of the original plan was added when a unique challenge—opportunity—arose. As we carried out research in the CAR, the Séléka—a coalition of rebel groups—led a violent coup that culminated in the takeover of Bangui in March 2013. Fighting continued with the Anti-balaka coalition opposing the Séléka. These events not only affected our research, but they influenced many of the organizations and leaders that we studied. Many of these leaders and Christian organizations played pivotal roles in working for peace. Since Christian leaders across Africa have often faced similar contexts of violence and conflict, it made sense for us to avail ourselves of the opportunity to conduct follow-up interviews in 2015 with Christian leaders we had first interviewed in 2012 and early 2013—interviews that focused explicitly on African Christian leadership in the context of violence. Thus, using a specific interview protocol, follow-up interviews were carried out and transcribed, with Chapter 5 in this book focusing specifically on Christian leadership responses during armed conflict.

FOUNDATIONS ON WHICH THIS BOOK RESTS

The quality of any book is directly dependent on its foundations. This book builds on several unusually strong foundations worth recognizing, including the following.

Funding

All quality research involves sustained work over long periods of time. Even when scholars have faculty salaries, their ability to cover research-related expenses and to devote major amounts of time to this (rather than to some other remunerated activity) is greatly enhanced when supplemental funding is available. When the research requires travel and collaboration among multiple countries, such funding is not optional. The most cutting-edge investigations around the world rest on generous funding—something that is often scarce in Africa. This project would not have been possible without the sustained multi-year financial support from the Tyndale House Foundation.

Research

This book is unique in both the amount and nature of the original research on which it rests. It is based on a combination of quantitative and qualitative data collected in four languages across three countries from more than eight thousand people—representing over three dozen major ethnic groups and more than one hundred denominations.

Collaboration

Most academic books present either the work of a single scholar or a collection of essays reporting on the disparate research of diverse authors. By contrast, this book reports on a single coherent research project that was collaboratively designed, carried out, and reported on by a team of scholars. The authors of this book were key participants in every stage of the research and writing process and engaged one another continuously through each stage. The result is a multi-authored book characterized by balance, unity, and coherence.

African Authorship

With a couple of exceptions (Priest and Rasmussen), the scholars who collaboratively designed, carried out, and wrote up the results of this research are themselves African. And while Steve Rasmussen is from the USA, he has spent most of his adult life in Africa. Thus this book largely rests on African scholarship.

Contemporary Focus

History is the academic discipline that commendably has excelled in studying Christianity in Africa. But its success in featuring the past must be matched by a similar prioritization of the present. Consider the online *Dictionary of African Christian Biography,* with its marvelous historical collection of African Christian biographies. One criterion for inclusion in the collection is that the person being written about must be deceased. But if the world's knowledge of Christianity in Africa comes from the historical past and is not matched by equally rich treatments of contemporary African Christianity, our knowledge of Africa may easily be out of date. The ALS research focused not on deceased former leaders, but on active and often youthful contemporary leaders, many of whom make rich use of social media, work in urban contexts, and engage a rapidly changing world. This research focuses on contemporary African Christian reading patterns and on contemporary efforts by African Christian leaders to address ethnic and religious violence, sex education, gender dynamics, environmental issues, and the opportunities and challenges of running faith-based-organizations. Its focus is on the contemporary.

Global Relevance

Early writings about the growth of Christianity in Africa often focused on foreign missionaries, ignoring or subordinating the central role of African Christians. More recently, most writings on African Christianity focus on African Christians as the central actors in contemporary Africa. Readers from outside Africa are encouraged to cultivate a deep appreciation and respect for the dynamism and agency of African Christians but are otherwise seldom given any practical vision for how those outside Africa are, or should be, interfacing with African leaders and partnering on strategic initiatives. By contrast, this book, while also placing the central focus on African Christian agency, nonetheless emphasizes connections within a global community of faith and considers the relevance of our research for a wide variety of interested stakeholders. That is, this book is intended to be of practical help, not only to African Christian leaders but to many from outside the continent who are interested in partnering with, and lending support to, strategic African-led ministries and initiatives.

Augmented by Supportive Online Resources

The authors of this book repeatedly discuss by name and in some detail notable contemporary pastors, leaders in other social arenas (ranging from business to engineering, medicine, law, agricultural development, sex education, drug addiction, youth work, or theology), and highly effective African-led Christian organizations that are focused on a wide range of social and spiritual outcomes. Nevertheless, this book cannot possibly tell the full story of the twenty-four contemporary leaders we examined in depth, or fully report on the thirty organizations we examined, and so we provide a ten-page, single-spaced report on each of these leaders and organizations online, following a specified protocol. Again, this book often refers to results from our ninety-three–item survey of 8,041 respondents and provides a basic descriptive summary of results in Appendix B. But the book does not come close to exhausting what the data reveals. And so the raw data is available online for researchers who wish to use it to carry out further analysis, exploring, for example, how different factors (such as denomination, gender, marital status, ethnicity, educational level, or income) are related.

This book, then, is matched by a parallel website (www.AfricaLeadershipStudy.org) that provides supplementary resources available in English, French, and Portuguese. This site is intended to serve as a pedagogical and research help for professors and students, for scholars, and for all who are interested in networking, planning, and carrying out initiatives related to African Christian leadership. It is envisioned as a resource for African Christians themselves who seek to shape the future.

Our website includes an "About" page with maps, links to participating organizations, and further information about the ALS and its team members. Videos of team members talking about their hopes for the ALS are included. A "Data" page provides links to the questionnaire data (available either in SPSS or CSV) and to the fifty-four ten-page reports about the leaders and organizations that we studied. All of the data is available in English, French, and Portuguese. Copies of the original surveys, of interview protocols, and of guidelines used in conducting the research are also available. A "Findings" page not only features this book but provides a variety of infographics to highlight selected findings from our research. A "Resources" page features a variety of supplementary resources for those interested in the themes of this book. This website is oriented toward the future, not merely the past or present. Of special interest, in this respect, should be the information provided here on funding possibilities through the ALS for small projects that build strategically on the prior ALS results. That is, this seedbed is intended to help additional projects sprout and in time will post reports on these follow-up projects as they bear fruit.

BRIEF OVERVIEW OF THE BOOK

In Chapter 2, David Ngaruiya reminds us that in Africa great interest exists for effective leadership, but that most of the research and writing on the topic features leaders in other parts of the world. He highlights the importance of research and writing that features highly successful African Christian leaders. His chapter introduces us to the leaders we researched and considers the ways in which they exemplify church involvement, vocational commitment, community connectedness, cultural flexibility, endurance under hardship, lifelong learning, empowering mentorship, embrace of technology, and passion for civic engagement. He introduces us to some of the diverse arenas in which they exercise leadership; briefly considers formative influences in their lives represented by family, education, and global travel; and concludes with practical lessons for African Christians today.

In Chapter 3, Wanjiru M. Gitau suggests that the significant leaders we looked at were not merely "born" leaders but went through strategic formational experiences that contributed to their leadership abilities and success. She describes and analyzes the nurturing support that most had experienced in childhood and youth in home settings, schools, and churches. She examines a variety of Christian life-skills instructional programs that most leaders report exposure to in their youth and systematically reviews the role of internships, volunteer service, mentorship, higher education, and being given opportunities to lead, in the leadership formation of the highly regarded leaders we studied. She suggests that this consideration of how leaders were formed should underpin the strategies and priorities of all who are involved in leadership formation in the next generation.

In Chapter 4, Steve Rasmussen builds on the work of social theorists who stress the importance of social capital—of strong social ties characterized by trust and reciprocity. He demonstrates that African Christian leaders achieve leadership success because they have strong social capital—numerous social relationships characterized by trust, commitment, understanding, and shared values. He points out that religious institutions and their leaders often have strong in-group relationships ("bonding social capital"). He finds this true in our data as well. But societies often find that relationships break down around cultural, ethnic, or religious cleavages, and are characterized by distrust, prejudice, grievances and grudges, enmity, and even violence. Thus strong positive social ties across these cleavages ("bridging social capital") become extremely important to good society. Rasmussen demonstrates that effective African Christian leaders are often unusually successful precisely because of their unique ability to forge positive and strong trust relationships that bridge these social divides. That is, they achieve important goals because they are rich in "bridging social capital," and because they make wise use of such capital. Finally, Rasmussen points out that in addition to horizontal differences of culture and identity, people in the modern world, at the local level as well as the global level, encounter incredible hierarchies of wealth, status, and power. These hierarchies often lack vertical relational ties. Rasmussen shows that in such a world successful leadership requires "linking social capital," strong trust relationships that vertically construct positive links across hierarchical divides. He demonstrates the ways in which successful African Christian leaders today exercise linking social capital in the service of shared larger commitments. He suggests that leadership formation must cultivate all three forms of social capital, and the wisdom to exercise them rightly on behalf of kingdom purposes.

In Chapter 5, Elisabet le Roux and Yolande Sandoua illustrate many of the points made in Rasmussen's chapter about how religious leaders draw from their bonding, bridging, and linking social capital to contribute positively to the social good. As mentioned earlier, during the ALS research, the CAR became embroiled in violent conflict. Based on focused follow-up research, this chapter explores the ways in which key Christian organizations—with a particular focus on the role of FATEB—and key Christian leaders worked to contribute to peace and reconciliation within the larger society. The authors examine how bridging relationships were forged and strengthened across denominations and religions (and enhanced with the visit of Pope Francis), and how relationships were facilitated that linked global partners with grassroots needs.

Building on Chapter 5's illustration of the fact that leadership is often exercised within the platform of strategic Christian organizations, Nupanga Weanzana introduces us in Chapter 6 to effective African-led Christian organizations that our research uncovered and studied. He explores their earlier history and the ways these organizations have changed over time. While earlier ministries, especially by evangelicals, were often justified primarily in terms of spiritual outcomes and goals, he suggests that nearly all of the contemporary organizations we examined combine a focus on both "word and deed." Leadership within the framework of these organizations must attend to the complementary ends that are being pursued.

In Chapter 7, Michael Bowen focuses in depth on how faith-based organizations (FBOs) foster socioeconomic development, something which nearly all of the Christian organizations we examined do. He shows that these FBOs are fostering human flourishing in a wide variety of ways. Because these FBOs and their leaders draw on strong local social capital (relationships of trust, reliability, and shared values), they are unusually successful at mobilizing positive grassroots action and accomplishing desired outcomes that align with the Millennium Development Goals. Thus, these FBOs and their leaders gain trust with government officials and win support from both religious and secular global partners. That is, they accomplish strategic ends through what Rasmussen identified as "linking social capital." However, strategic partnerships with disparate religious and nonreligious parties not only empower but also constrain, creating differing levels of tension for FBOs in their ability to retain a prioritized focus on both word and deed. Bowen explores the variable ways in which the leaders of these organizations seek to manage their relationships and resolve these tensions while pursuing desired outcomes through both word and deed.

Several of the FBOs identified by survey respondents as having a high positive impact were led by women. In some cases these were women's organizations. A significant minority of top Christian leaders named by respondents were women. In Chapter 8, Truphosa Kwaka-Sumba and Elisabet le Roux introduce us to seven of these highly effective female leaders and three women's organizations. They describe and analyze the leadership opportunities women have, as well as the challenging and discriminatory realities they face. They describe women's leadership experience as requiring the negotiation of a complex labyrinth. Women need the structural and labyrinthian realities to be analyzed and described for them, with strategic mentorship, support for education, and encouragement to write and publish. We must become self-conscious and deliberate about understanding and counteracting gender-based hindrances to women's leadership if women are to flourish in leadership with their God-given gifts.

In Chapter 9, Jurgens Hendriks points out that Christian leadership in Africa has sometimes been affected by earlier, unhealthy patterns related to chiefdoms, patriarchy, and colonial master-servant relations. But he reports being fascinated to discover through this research that the majority of contemporary Christian leaders who were identified by fellow Africans as having a highly positive impact were, in fact, exemplifying servant leadership to a marked degree, characterized by sustained efforts to empower others. His chapter reports on what he learned about these leaders and their various ways of empowering others. He celebrates what he sees as "a new dawn in African Christian leadership" and suggests a variety of lessons to be learned from the leaders he examined.

In Chapter 10, Robert Priest, Kirimi Barine, and Alberto Lucamba Salombongo describe the reading (and writing) patterns of African Christians and their leaders and analyze the content of African Christian reading. They examine data on the favorite authors of thousands of respondents and show that African Christians are reading African authors and Christian authors at very high rates, but they are reading authors who are *both* African and Christian at very low rates. The authors attempt to analyze the reasons for this and consider its negative implications. They point to evidence that African Christians need and desire more and better (more contextually relevant) publications by African authors and present a variety of suggestions for how various stakeholders might contribute to a stronger presence and influence of African Christian publications.

In Chapter 11, John Jusu helps us reflect on the implications of each earlier chapter for leadership-training curricula in theological schools, universities, and other formal and nonformal educational institutions and programs. That is, this chapter is intended to help all those individuals and institutions involved in leadership training in Africa to consider the implications of the ALS for their own formational programs.

While Christian foundations play strategic roles in contributing to Christian institutions and initiatives worldwide, this is often an invisible or at least publicly unrecognized role. And yet this project would not have been possible apart from the partnership of one such foundation, the Tyndale House Foundation, and the personal commitment of its executive director, Mary Kleine Yehling. In Chapter 12, she describes the context of the work of the THF in Africa and the factors that informed and motivated the decision to engage in the ALS. She reflects on the meaning, purpose, process, and hoped-for outcomes of the ALS from a foundation officer's perspective. In the context of the overall mission and history of the THF she considers the positive benefits of such a study and research partnership, not only for the rest of us, but for Christian foundations themselves. And she demonstrates how a passion for God and God's purposes in the world plays out in global Christian stewardship.

The concluding chapter is a joint chapter, to which our entire ALS team contributed. As we read and reread interviews, pored over survey responses, and discussed our various chapters together, we attempted to synthesize important take-away findings of our research. Chapter 13 thus identifies and briefly articulates seventeen key findings that emerged from our research.

REFERENCES CITED

Bennett, David. 2002. *India Leadership Study: A Summary for Indian Christian Leaders.*

Bornstein, Erica. 2005. *The Spirit of Development: Protestant NGOs, Morality, and Economics in Zimbabwe.* Stanford, CA: Stanford University Press.

Carpenter, Joel, and Nellie Kooistra. 2014. *Engaging Africa: Prospects for Project Funding in Selected Fields.* Grand Rapids, MI: Nagel Institute of Calvin College.

Jenkins, Philip. 2002. *The Next Christendom: The Coming of Global Christianity.* New York: Oxford University Press.

Johnson, Todd, Gina A. Zurlo, Albert W. Hickman, and Peter F. Crossing. 2015. "Christianity 2015: Religious Diversity and Personal Contact." *International Bulletin of Missionary Research* 39/1: 28–30.

Kalu, Ogbu, ed. 2007. *African Christianity: An African Story.* Trenton, NJ: African World Press.

Phiri, Isabel Apawo, and Dietrich Werner, eds. 2013. *Handbook for Theological Education in Africa.* Oxford, UK: Regnum Books International.

Priest, Robert J., and Robert DeGeorge. 2013. "Doctoral Dissertations on Mission: Ten-year Update, 2002–2011." *International Bulletin of Missionary Research* 37/4: 195–202.

Sanneh, Lamin. 2003. *Whose Religion Is Christianity?: The Gospel beyond the West.* Grand Rapids, MI: Eerdmans.

Tiénou, Tite. 2006. "Christian Theology in an Era of World Christianity." In *Globalizing Theology: Belief and Practice in an Era of World Christianity,* ed. Craig Ott and Harold Netland, 37–51. Grand Rapids, MI: Baker Academic.

Walls, Andrew. 1996. *The Missionary Movement in Christian History.* Maryknoll, NY: Orbis Books.

———. 2002. *The Cross-cultural Process in Christian History.* Maryknoll, NY: Orbis Books.

Wuthnow, Robert. 2009. *Boundless Faith: The Global Outreach of American Churches.* Berkeley and Los Angeles: University of California Press.

Chapter 2

Characteristics of Influential African Christian Leaders

David K. Ngaruiya

There is a deep interest across African Christian higher education in preparing Christian leaders for positive impact. Yet most research and writing on leaders, and especially Christian leaders, has focused on leaders in the Global North. For example, there is nothing comparable in Africa to D. Michael Lindsay's (2007, 2014) impressive research on top Christian leaders in America. The result is that when leadership programs and courses are offered in Africa, they are often based on literature and understandings acquired by studying leadership outside Africa. In an attempt to bridge that gap, this book, beginning with this chapter, highlights research that examines successful African Christian leaders who are exercising their leadership in African contexts.

In our survey of eight thousand Christians in three African countries we began by asking respondents to "name a Christian man or woman, outside your family, who has influenced you the most." More than one-third of respondents in Angola, and over one-half in Kenya and the Central African Republic (CAR), provided the name of a person subsequently identified as a pastor. This suggests that pastors are one type of leader in African societies that exercise strategic influence. There are also other types of Christian leaders on the continent.

In order to identify key Christian leaders in Africa—both clergy and non-clergy—we asked eight thousand African Christians to name the Christian pastor who they thought was having the most significant positive impact in their community. Thus, 49 respondents named Dinis Eurico as the Angolan pastor with the most impact, 111 respondents in the CAR named Dr. David Koudougueret, and 46 listed Bishop John Bosco of Kenya. Each respondent was also asked to provide additional information on the pastor, including an assessment of the extent to which this pastor was known for training leaders. Through this process we identified thirty-one

Angolan pastors, twenty-eight pastors from the CAR, and twenty-seven Kenyan pastors who were identified by knowledgeable Christians in their communities as exercising important leadership (see Appendix B, Q.23). We considered both the frequency with which each was listed as an influential leader and the extent to which each was deemed to be successfully training other leaders; we selected nine pastors for in-depth follow-up interviews and reports (Table 2–1).

In our survey we also reminded respondents that

> while pastors of churches are important leaders, there are many other arenas where Christians provide important leadership, such as in education, business, government, medical health care, or communication and media. Some people provide leadership in addressing problems of poverty, HIV/AIDS, ethnic conflict, religious conflict, or unemployment. Some focus on youth, others on women, and others on parents or the aged.

Respondents were then asked to identify the single Christian individual making the most significant difference in their local community in some arena other than pastoral ministry. A variety of follow-up questions were asked about this individual, including gender, ethnicity, arena of influence, and approximate age. Based on the information provided, we identified for further attention twenty non-clergy Christian leaders from Angola, fifteen from the CAR, and twenty from Kenya. One-third of these were female. Respondents were also asked to rate each leader on a Likert scale in terms of (1) skill at their work, (2) wisdom and knowledge of their local context, (3) ethical integrity, (4) love for and service to others, (5) positive reputation in the community, (6) the extent to which they inspire teamwork and community mobilization, (7) efficiency in use of resources, and (8) the extent to which they were training and developing other leaders (for full information see Appendix B, Q.24–Q.30). Taking into account these assessments, while also seeking broad representation in terms of geographical regions, arenas of influence, gender, and ethnicity, a number of key leaders were selected for follow-up interviews and reports (see Table 2–2).

This chapter summarizes some of what we learned through the interviews with these leaders. It begins by examining the qualities identified in the influential African Christian leaders named in the study and also identifies their arenas of influence and how the formation of these African Christian leaders contributed to their leadership development.

	Pastor	M/F	Age	Ethnicity	Region	Denomination
Angola	Pastor Adelaide Catanha	F	62	Ovim-bundo	Huambo	Igreja Evan-gélica Congregacional de Angola
	Pastor Dinis Eirico	M	55–64	Ganguela	Huila Lubango	Igreja Evan-gélica Sinodal de Angola
	Pastor Luisa Mateus	F	45	Bakongo	Luanda	Igreja Evan-gélica Reforma-da de Angola
CAR	Dr. David Koudou-gueret	M	55–64	Banda	Bangui	Eglise Baptistes
	Pastor René Malépou	M	51–55	Mandja	Bangui	Communauté des Eglises Baptistes In-dépendantes
Kenya	Bishop John Bosco	M	56	Kikuyu	Coast	Redeemed Gospel Church
	Bishop Joseph Maisha	M	55–64	Luhya	Coast	Ushindi Baptist Church
	Pastor Edward Munene	M	45–50	Kikuyu	Coast	Kenya Assem-blies of God
	Pastor Oscar Muriu	M	51–55	Kikuyu	Nairobi	Nairobi Chapel

Table 2–1. Pastoral Leaders

	Name	M/F	Age	Ethnicity	Region	Profession
Angola	Eunice Nalamele Alberto Chiquete	F	35	Ovim-bundo	Huila	theology lecturer
	Diamantino Laurendo Doba	M	46	Bakongo	Lu-anda	youth work
	Manuel Missa	M	60	Ovim-bundo	Kuito	school-teacher
CAR	Nestor Mamadou Nali	M	69	Mandja	Bangui	medical doctor
	Mme Marie Louise Yakemba	F	55–64	Ngbandi	Bangui	government official / wom-en's ministry
	Evariste Dignito	M	45–54	Ngbandi	Bangui	civil engineer
	Mme Marie Paule Balezou	F	50–55	From-Camer-oon	Bangui	business / pastor's wife
Kenya	Joseph Kimeli	M	45–54	Kalenjin	Rift Valley	agricultural development
	Cosmas Maina	M	40–45	Kikuyu	Coast	drug addiction professional
	Esther Mombo	F	60–65	Kisii	Central	theology professor
	Isaac Mutua	M	43	Kamba	East-ern	sex-educa-tion teacher
	Patrick Nyachogo	M	26	Kisii	Nyan-za	environmen-talist
	Alice Ki-rambi	F	45–54	Luhya	West-ern	administrator – CPDA
	Onesmus Makau	M	45–54	Kamba	East-ern	judge
	General Kianga	M	65	Kamba	East-ern	military general

Table 2–2. Non-Clergy Leaders

QUALITIES OF EFFECTIVE AFRICAN CHRISTIAN LEADERS

Church Commitment

The church plays a central role in addressing societal problems in distinctively Christian ways. In much of Africa the church is still the first place that people turn in times of need. As one church leader has said, "The Christian community must be rooted in the society within which it has grown up, and its members must be part of that society" (Gitari 2005, 169). The leaders we surveyed realize that if they are to make a difference in their communities, the church is a fitting place to start because many people go there in search of help. Although Africans have been and continue to be active in world evangelization (Tiénou 2008, 173), often under the leadership of clergy, this section briefly examines the important role of non-clergy in the church.

When respondents were asked to identify a non-clergy person as an influential Christian leader, many of the respondents still identified individuals noted for their work within church settings, such as Manuel Missa from Angola. It was in Missa's role as choirmaster and deacon, rather than in his role as educator and administrator of a government school, that he was most recognized for having a significant impact. Thus, even non-clergy members perceived to have the most impact were often found to be serving in some lay position in the church. Most non-clergy members found a way to intertwine their vocation with church ministry and even to serve in positions of responsibility within churches. An example of this is civil engineer and businessman Evariste Dignito from the CAR, who serves as a coordinator for cell groups in his church and is often invited to speak to young people in church contexts. Likewise, Edouard Nvouni is known and appreciated for contributing his skills and resources as an architect toward the construction of church buildings. Many of the women named as non-clergy leaders exercise their leadership with women through church-related ministry structures.

Vocational Excellence

Leaders identified as having the most impact are those who have excelled in their vocations and who often have turned their vocation into a ministry to guide people in value-based leadership. This is especially true for those issues not usually considered to be part of the church's mission. For example, leaders in the CAR and Kenya have taken matters such as ethnic and religious differences that lead to political conflict and have used their vocational strengths to help the church address these challenges.

Such non-clergy leaders include, to name but a few, a medical doctor (Nestor Mamadou Nali), an environmentalist (Patrick Nyachogo), a retired military general (General Kianga), a professor (Esther Mombo), the founder of a large and successful NGO (Alice Kirambi), an agricultural trainer (Joseph Kimeli), a teacher of sex education in schools (Isaac Mutua), and a founding director of two organizations that work with drug addicts (Cosmas Maina).

These leaders are specialists in their fields, with specific and strategic goals that go beyond ministry in the church. When Dr. Nestor Mamadou Nali encountered Jesus, he embraced his vocation and reports, "Now I understand everything that I am doing as a ministry from God. I take every profession as a special calling from God." Some of these leaders have chosen to handle pressing concerns that are taboo to discuss openly in a church context. Due to discomfort with openly discussing drug use or sexually transmitted diseases in church settings, public recognition of the work of these influential non-clergy leaders is sometimes limited. Even with churches that are growing, as they often are in Africa, there is always the temptation for clergy or other church leaders to sweep such issues under the rug.

Community Connectedness

Putnam describes social capital as "social networks and associated norms of reciprocity" (Putnam 2000, 21). Social capital, in other words, is human connectedness in both informal and formal settings. Human connectedness is critical in communities because it is a means by which people encounter and transmit ideas and engage in actions that transform their communities. It is through such connectedness that leaders exert influence. In this study all leaders who were identified as most effective were those who worked within their community. If they extended their ministry to other communities, they still worked through personal connections at the grassroots level. Respondents mentioned those leaders who worked with them and walked with them on a regular basis.

All seven leaders from the CAR, five out of the six leaders from Angola, and eight out of the ten leaders from Kenya had left their country to gain more training and education, but their local commitments brought them back. It is these leaders that the community appears to appreciate because they remain connected to their communities, having returned to share their acquired knowledge with others who could not afford the training. For a full treatment of how these leaders utilized social capital, see Chapter 4 in this book.

Cultural Flexibility

Leadership is always exercised in the context of cultural norms and constraints, and leaders are sometimes successful to the extent that they skillfully adjust to the norms. Consider patriarchal norms. When asked whether their church provides opportunities for women in leadership, nearly a quarter of respondents from Kenya, over one-third from Angola, and nearly half from the CAR answered either "not at all," or "a little." And yet we uncovered significant evidence that many women were exercising leadership, often in ways that did not openly or directly resist patriarchal patterns. Sometimes leadership was exercised within gender-specific venues, that is, by creating separate women's societies through which to exercise influence and impact. Sometimes female leadership was exercised by women married to influential pastors or other leaders. For example, while men exercised formal leadership over Word of Life and Redeemed Academy, their spouses, in practice, were able functionally to exercise significant leadership in these organizations. Sometimes women achieved leadership in political, entrepreneurial, or educational settings—and drew from their status in these settings to exercise leadership in religious venues as well. Others worked strategically to resist and overturn the constraints of patriarchal patterns. A fuller and more critical treatment of African Christian women's leadership is available in Chapter 8.

Endurance under Hardship

Many of the leaders we studied had backgrounds that involved significant hardships. As with many famous leaders throughout history (Blackaby and Blackaby 2011, 41), such challenges and hardships seem to have been the very conditions out of which significant leadership emerged. Consider Bishop John Bosco from Kenya, who grew up in two slums in Nairobi. He was raised by a single mother who sold illicit brews to make a living, and he never knew his father. When his mother became another man's second wife, Bosco was not accepted by his stepfather and had a "difficult" life.

Other leaders, such as Mrs. Balezou from the CAR, who suffered at the hands of an alcoholic parent, grew up in homes where there was neglect either because of harsh circumstances or poor parenting. Nevertheless, their stories are stories of endurance. In a context where the majority of the population lives below the poverty line and under great hardship, leaders who have experienced and overcome similar challenges are deeply appreciated. These leaders' stories are not the "rags to riches" narratives sometimes propagated to marginalized people, but simply the accounts of leaders facing the vicissitudes of life with determination and faith.

Lifelong Learning

Lifelong learning has been described in many ways, and one of those ways is its triadic nature. The key elements of "triadic nature" serve to advance "economic progress and development, personal development and fulfillment, social inclusiveness and democratic understanding and activity" (Aspin and Chapman 2001, 29). In a rapidly changing world, lifelong learning is an imperative for human beings. And in our study, this lifelong learning was characteristic of African Christian leaders.

Of the twenty-three leaders with whom we carried out follow-up interviews, twenty-two had formal education beyond a high-school diploma. This is not surprising, because education in the African context is often revered and desired. For a majority of the leaders, formal education gave them credibility and authority with their community. These leaders not only encouraged others to go on for further education, but they took time for further courses to continue developing themselves professionally, and they frequently were avid readers of both Christian and non-Christian literature (see Chapter 10). The leaders reported reading motivational books either for their own encouragement, or to help them encourage others.

It is not only formal education that has benefited these leaders, but informal learning programs also have helped them improve leadership skills. Such skills help them to address contextual issues that may not have been covered in textbooks. The combination of both formal and informal learning has proved to be most effective because the leaders can combine both classroom and field knowledge to help their communities. While the fundamental principles taught in class are essential, the average person in the community seeks a practical solution, which these leaders are able to provide. As they have disseminated their knowledge to the community, generally in informal ways, African Christian leaders have been able not only to uplift their peers but also to inspire others to pursue an educational degree in a particular field. Some, such as Bishop John Bosco, have even gone as far as to sponsor people's schooling so that they can return and continue to influence the community.

Empowering Mentorship

In a context where leadership succession is often considered a threat, it is interesting that many of these leaders were once led by someone who capably served others. The leaders had the experience of being mentored. "Mentoring is a relational experience in which one person empowers another by sharing God-given resources" (Clinton and Stanley 1992, 33).

Most of the leaders we interviewed emphasized the importance of mentorship, indicating that they were a product of personal mentorship and now mentor others. Mentoring appears strategic in developing new leaders in Africa, not only because it creates a system of accountability, but also because it provides a platform for leadership succession. Under the leadership of Pastor Oscar Muriu, for example, the Nairobi Chapel churches have developed internship programs and practicums that provide a blueprint or model for ministry that interns can learn from and apply in other ministry settings. Pastor Muriu has mentored other pastors who have planted churches, including Muriithi Wanjau, the senior pastor at Mavuno Chapel, who himself is now mentoring others. Pastor Wanjau was also identified in our survey as an effective leader in Kenya. It should be noted, however, that of those we interviewed only Oscar Muriu provided a sustained and systematic description of how he mentors others. While all those we interviewed affirmed the value of mentorship, and many told stories of how they had been mentored, it appears that few were mentoring others in as self-conscious, systematic, and sustained a fashion as Muriu.

Embrace of Technology

One dimension of our current global culture is the technoscape. As Appadurai defines it, a technoscape is the "global configuration, also ever fluid, of technology, both high and low, both mechanical and informational, [that] now moves at high speeds across various kinds of previously impervious boundaries" (Appadurai 2002, 51). The embrace and use of information communications technology (ICT) is increasingly valued across higher education in Africa (see Nguru 2012, 65) and is also valued by effective African Christian leaders.

Leaders who used technology tended to be those found in cities or those who worked with youth, such as Diamantino Doba from Angola, who used the Internet and various devices to keep in touch. Other leaders who used technology include Edward Munene and Isaac Mutua of Kenya. Their priority focus on youth led them to embrace ICT. Such leaders work to use television, radio, and Internet-based social media platforms—especially in those regions where the Internet is easily available.

Passion for Civic Engagement

Another aspect of effective leaders is their passion for civic engagement. As authentic leaders, such men and women are "passionate individuals who have a deep-seated interest in what they are doing and truly care about their work" (Northhouse 2013, 258). Leaders we studied justified their commitments to civic engagement by referencing scripture, such as when Dr. Koudougueret framed civic engagement as part of our stewardship mandate: "When God told the first couple to cultivate and keep the garden, it is already the management of what God put in their hands."

Effective leaders are passion-specific about things that transform their communities, and this transformation may be accomplished through a political process. Sometimes the church has given politics a wide berth because it is often associated with partisanship, corruption, and nepotism. Until recently, for example, many church leaders in Kenya would not have

considered running for office. But now some church leaders are choosing
to resign and run for political office with the support of their congregation.
Our data indicates that many of Africa's Christian leaders are hesitant to
take a strong stance on politics except to teach what God wants from leaders and citizens regarding political participation. However, the church is
doing better at addressing politics, and those leaders with the most impact
often steered clear of ethnic and partisan commentary, but rather gave clear
guidelines on what God expects and on how to pick a good leader. Pastor
Dinis Eurico of Angola was known for addressing conflict and corruption in a non-combative manner. He and others drew a clear line between
party politics and political participation—which is a civic duty for all. In
educating the voters, they were able to bring about change in the political
landscape of their country because voters could make decisions based on
Christian values. As Northhouse asserts: "Transformational leaders are
effective at working with people, that is, they are civically engaged. They
build trust and foster collaboration with others" (Northhouse 2012, 200).

ARENAS OF INFLUENCE

"A true leader is able to influence others" (Lunenburg 2012, 5), and
as Hackman and Johnson assert, "Exercising influence is the essence of
leadership" (Hackman and Johnson 2004, 154). Some Christian leaders are
able to influence others in and through prominent religious organizations,
while others are able to exercise this influence in the wider context beyond
such religious confines (Lindsay 2007, 260). As is often said, "Leadership is
influence." Such leadership is exerted in different arenas and tangible ways.

The leaders we studied are making an impact in a wide variety of
arenas, ranging from the development of programs for drug addicts and
prostitutes to education for children and youth, to sex education, to church
leadership development, to combating HIV/AIDS, to women's ministries,
music, business, and church leadership development.

Drug Abuse Prevention

Drug use in Kenya has long been recognized, and although both men
and women abuse drugs, men do so more frequently (Beckerleg et al.
2006, 1037). In 2015, the Government of Kenya ordered its administrative machinery to rid Central Kenya of illicit brews that had become a
menace in the region. In an area characterized by drug addiction among
youth, Cosmas Maina, who himself was formerly a drug user, addresses
problems of drug addiction through two organizations that he founded.
Teens Watch, a community-based organization, utilizes peer educators to
raise awareness of and to work toward harm reduction in drug abuse,

alcoholism, and prostitution. Teens Watch receives funding and support from governmental and other nonreligious sources and thus does not explicitly identify itself as a religious organization or carry out religious activities. Separately, Maina created a parallel, faith-based organization, Set the Captives Free, that explicitly shares the gospel and the need for Jesus, and that uses biblical teaching to encourage full recovery and spiritual restoration. At the time of our interview he had a plan for Set the Captives Free to acquire fifty-two acres of land and was raising funds to build a rehabilitation center for drug addicts. After rehabilitation, the recovered youth will be equipped with work and life skills so that they can be integrated back into their communities.

Children and Youth Education

Children and youth in Africa make up the majority of the population. It is estimated that sub-Saharan Africa will carry "the worst youth bulges" in the world through the year 2020 (CIA Fact Book, 2001). And yet most theological education and pastoral focus relate to adults, although many African Christians are deeply concerned for their strategic role in childhood and youth education. It is, therefore, commendable to see many African leaders expend efforts in nurturing children and youth. For example, Eunice Chiquete is an Angolan seminary lecturer known for her projects focused on the evangelization, discipleship, and education of children and teenagers. In partnership with Christian organizations, Chiquete has coordinated interdenominational projects for thousands of children. Edward Munene from Kenya focuses on influencing young men and women spiritually and socially. He has structured his church in ways that encourage young people, regardless of their religious background, to feel welcome.

Sex Education and Fighting against HIV/AIDS

In the past many Africans would have undergone rites of passage to educate them for adulthood. These would have included sex education, but in the contemporary world this is absent. Africans seldom talk openly about issues related to sex. Thus, young people today acquire their understandings of sexuality from their peers and the media, leading to negative and distorted views of sex and to behaviors contributing to higher rates of sexually transmitted diseases, such as HIV/AIDS. Of all continents Africa has the highest prevalence of HIV/AIDS, decimating many families and leaving orphans in its wake.

While Kenyan schools are tasked with providing sex education, teachers are often not trained for this, and some of them feel uncomfortable teaching on the subject. Thus, when Isaac Mutua, who has a master's degree in community pastoral care for HIV/AIDS from St. Paul's University, developed a curriculum for life skills and sex education, he was addressing a felt need. Students were delighted with his teaching, and schoolteachers were enthusiastic about inviting him to teach in their schools. A significant number of young respondents to our survey identified Isaac Mutua as the non-clergy Christian leader who has had the greatest impact in their community. However, by the time we interviewed Isaac, he reported that for financial reasons as a young father and husband he had needed to take a paying job with a hospital in community health administration. Thus, one of the most popular and influential leadership initiatives emerging from our research turns out not to have been sustainable over time.

Another example of an African Christian leader addressing the AIDS scourge is Dr. Nestor Mamadou Nali from the CAR. He was trained in Canada as a medical doctor and became a founding member of the medical faculty at Bangui, where he served on the faculty and as rector. He has also served as minister for public health in the CAR. In 2010, life expectancy in the CAR was estimated at forty years, as opposed to over sixty years if AIDS were not a factor. In a country and continent where the scourge of HIV/AIDS has been such a menace, Dr. Nali was appointed by his government to lead the fight against this epidemic and to advise the prime minister.

Entrepreneurship

Mr. Evariste Dignito from the CAR is a civil engineer identified as an influential entrepreneur in his country. He is the founder and owner of La Semence (the seed), which is a company that specializes in building and public works. The work he has been doing in that sector has been recognized as excellent and is among those selected by international organizations for public works. He reports that his successes in entrepreneurship as a Christian have encouraged other Christians to realize that they too can create and sustain very successful enterprises. His Christian business specializing in road construction and drainage employs hundreds of people, thus empowering them to provide for their needs in a nation that has been ravaged by war.

Music

Music in the history of humanity has been a significant means of worship, comfort, encouragement, and also serves to shape values. The influence of music is especially pervasive in Africa (Kofi 2003, 8). General

Kianga reports that his childhood participation in choir was one of the things that "influenced my thinking and formed what was later to become my values." Manuel Missa from Angola exemplifies strategic leadership through music. A primary-school teacher by profession, he is currently the lead administrator at a government school. He is a gifted singer and composer of Christian music. In addition to serving in his church as a deacon and Bible-study teacher, he serves as choirmaster of a well-known choir and has taught many young people to sing, including his own family of singers. Despite his age (sixty) and health problems, he continues to serve as choirmaster and expressed a strong desire to complete formal theological training.

Church Leadership Development

Clergy were often centrally involved in church leadership development. For example, Oscar Muriu, the senior pastor of Nairobi Chapel reports that he has a passion to invest "his life into the generations that come after me and to live for more than just my generation." He has developed a program at his church that has trained over five hundred interns for ministry leadership. He has used this leadership pipeline to underpin a significant church-planting movement. Together with Nairobi Chapel's sister churches, they have planted churches in various African and European countries and have sent African missionaries around the world.

Pastor Edward Munene of International Christian Church situated in Mombasa, Kenya, is likewise passionate about leadership development and was rated among the top five in terms of the extent to which he trains leaders. Since his congregation largely comprises people in their twenties and thirties who are "hungry for information," and often seek it on the Internet, his efforts to teach the word of God and to train others make extensive use of digital technology.

Pastor René Malépou, president of Independent Community of Baptist Churches in the CAR, is identified by respondents as having high impact through formal theological education. He has regularly taught in seminaries, such as FATEB, thus helping prepare a new generation of church leaders. Being aware of the divide across denominations in the CAR, he sees himself as working hard to create unity among the churches as he develops leaders through formal theological education.

FORMATION OF AFRICAN CHRISTIAN LEADERS

Childhood homes, educational backgrounds, and broadening experiences have all contributed strategically to the formation of the African Christian leaders that we interviewed.

Childhood Home

The leaders we interviewed grew up in a variety of homes. Alice Kirambi's father died when she was a toddler. Nestor Nali grew up in a Muslim polygamous home, with parents who were morally and ethically strict. General Kianga grew up in a polygamous home, but with a devout Christian mother who insisted her son be a member of three choirs: Sunday School, church, and school. Marie Yakemba also grew up in a polygamous home, but with a grandmother who took a strong spiritual interest in her and encouraged her to become a Sunday School teacher.

Some grew up in homes that were nominally Christian. For example, Oscar Muriu's parents, who were Anglican, would drop Oscar and his siblings at church and pick them up later. The parents would attend church occasionally when there was a major ceremony. Similarly, Evariste Dignito grew up with parents who were nominally Catholic. Both Oscar Muriu and Evariste Dignito would later come to a deep and personal faith.

A number of key leaders were raised in unusually strong Christian homes. In Angola, Dinis Eurico's father was an evangelical catechist, and his mother worked closely with him in ministry. Eunice Chiquete grew up at an evangelical mission station in Angola where her parents were studying Bible. Later she accompanied her parents to Brazil, where they received further theological education. She attended a Christian school in Brazil and thus received Christian training both inside and outside her home. Dr. David Koudougueret grew up with a father that was first a Bible-school student and later a pastor. He spent his early years on a mission station, attending a Christian school, and became good friends with the children of the missionaries.

In many cases leaders named an individual family member as having played a strategic role in their spiritual life. Thus, while Kenyan Professor Esther Mombo's parents were both Christians, the person who most influenced her was the Quaker grandmother she lived with, who lived to the ripe old age of 101. Her grandmother provided a strong female role model, preached in women's prisons, and was a wonderful narrator of biblical stories as well as cultural narratives. Similarly, Marie Yakemba from the CAR came from a polygamous home but lived with her grandmother— who coached and motivated her to become a Sunday School teacher at a young age. For Luisa Mateus of Angola, the primary influence came from her grandfather, the first Bible teacher in their village. He taught Luisa scripture, prayer, and doctrine.

While many of the leaders we examined grew up in families living in rural or village settings, some of the most influential urban pastors grew up in homes situated in urban or city environments—where as children they had greater exposure to modern technology, good schools, quality medical care, and urban infrastructures. Pastor Edward Munene grew up in Athi River town, near Nairobi, and later in Kiambu town, also close to

Nairobi. As a child he recalls watching the *Six Million Dollar Man* and other superhero programs on television. He would tell his parents that when he grew up, he wanted to become a superhero so he could rescue people. This urban exposure was important in his formation as a leader who would later utilize modern technology effectively in training others as leaders.

A majority of the leaders we examined were raised in homes that in comparison with others around them were relatively stable economically—with most leaders mentioning parents who had jobs or ran small businesses. These jobs were in factories, government, teaching, tailoring, bricklaying, and pastoring. Nestor Mamadou Nali's father was a village tailor who provided a "comfortable living for the family." Patrick Nyachogo reports that growing up in a rural setting, he "never lacked for anything." Some had parents who were prominent community leaders (such as General Kianga's father) or prosperous businesspeople (such as Oscar Muriu's father). A surprising number of leaders report siblings who live abroad. Bishop Bosco, by contrast, grew up in the slums of Kibera, and his mother brewed and sold beer for a living.

Educational Background

"Education is the process of socialization through which individuals and groups are guided to become responsible members of society" (Mugambi 2013, 119). Since leaders exercise influence through the social dimension of life, their education is important. The Christian leaders we interviewed had all received basic education and beyond, ranging from post-high-school education to acquiring PhDs. Many of them had several university degrees and were educated both in their countries of birth and overseas.

Three of them had PhDs: René Malépou in theology from the United States of America, Esther Mombo in church history from the United Kingdom, and Adelaide Catanha in psychology earned online from Honolulu, Hawaii, USA. Nearly half had a master's degree or were studying for one in various disciplines. David Koudougueret has a master of art degree in theology earned in the CAR. General Jeremiah Kianga from Kenya, has a master's degree in military arts and science from the United States. Eunice Chiquete, from Angola, has a master's degree in missiology from Brazil. Oscar Muriu, from Kenya, has a master of divinity degree. Isaac Mutua has a master's degree in community pastoral care for HIV/AIDS. And Patrick Nyachogo, from Kenya, was pursuing a master's degree in business administration. Leaders with undergraduate degrees included Evariste Dignito from the CAR, with a degree in civil engineering; Edward Munene, with a bachelor of science degree in agriculture; and Diamantino Doba, from Angola, who has a degree in science. Virtually all leaders interviewed had engaged in at least some post-secondary study. That is, most who were identified as key leaders had a significant amount of formal education. The educational level of the parents of these leaders varied from very little to some who had completed graduate studies.

Broadening Experiences

An African proverb says, "One who is not traveled thinks his mother cooks best." The proverb captures the value of travel exposure among the leaders surveyed. With the exception of two leaders, all had traveled to other countries, most of them to more than one. Angolans most frequently visited other Portuguese-speaking countries such as Brazil. Leaders from the CAR had visited countries where French was spoken, such as France or Canada, while leaders from Kenya had traveled most frequently to the United States, Canada, or the United Kingdom. However, many had also visited other countries in Africa and Asia. The longest reported stay abroad was ten years, with the majority having lived abroad for more than three months.

These leaders' travel is significant for several reasons. First, it enables leaders to build bridges with various stakeholders in resource mobilization. Second, these networks help them to grow professionally. Third, exposure to the rest of the world gives leaders ideas and increases the potential for innovation when creating solutions in their context—since they have seen or have been inspired by other likeminded men and women grappling with similar issues.

CONCLUSION

This chapter has highlighted the qualities, arenas of influence, and formation of effective African Christian leaders. Among the qualities that the study identified are commitment, lifelong learning, mentoring and empowering young leaders, as well as caring and compassion. Thus there are clear qualities that help define an effective African leader; those can be used as criteria in discerning or appointing leaders to serve others. Effective African leaders are having an impact on their communities in specific arenas of influence. Such arenas include, but are not limited to, childhood and youth education, business entrepreneurship, and church leadership development. Effective African Christian leaders are stakeholders with governments and other establishments that address human needs in African contexts. Furthermore, these leaders are role models in their various arenas and can be engaged by other stakeholders in the transformation of other sectors such as education.

The formation of African Christian leaders reflects input from diverse spheres. These include childhood home, educational background, and broadening experiences. A majority of these leaders grew up in homes that were economically stable, and a significant number in unusually strong Christian homes. Many of the leaders received a level of education that went far beyond the basics. A majority of them had traveled to other nations of the world and thus had broad exposure to environments that increased their understanding of a diverse world.

There are several implications to the above findings. First, the leadership attributes that were identified should be employed in leader selection and screening. As with the secular marketplace, effective African leadership is about having the right person in the right job. Therefore, screening leaders for particularly sensitive posts needs to be a priority lest abuse or neglect of a constituent occur because the person appointed was not properly skilled in handling his or her responsibilities.

Second, these characteristics can be intentionally fostered and developed in new leaders, both through leadership training courses and books and through effective mentoring. Feedback from mentors and those being served can be elicited through feedback tools that feature the desired leadership attributes and that point to areas of needed improvement.

Third, African Christian leaders must step outside the church and become part of civil society in order to positively affect their communities. As our research revealed, those leaders who invested in the lives of church attendees as well as those who did not attend church were seen as effective in their ministry. Therefore, something as simple as organizing a monthly cleanup of garbage in the community would go a long way in a continent where waste-management is lacking.

From the study it was also noted that effective Christian leadership required engagement with civil society opinion leaders. Involvement with these types of leaders helps influence the culture in positive directions. However, this cannot be done properly without the knowledge needed to make wise decisions. As part of any leadership development course, good governance using biblical principles should be included. Effective African leaders should know how the system within which they are working operates in order to identify gaps and propose policies that are guided by godly principles.

Finally, effective Christian leaders are those who have been exposed to various social and cultural contexts both in and outside their immediate spheres of influence. Therefore, to be effective, African leaders should value travel and participation in educational forums, such as seminars and workshops. Effective leaders will have reading habits that expose them to the knowledge and insight needed for understanding and engaging their world. They will avail themselves of current technology, will pursue continuous learning, and will make effective use of their "problem-solving toolkit" in ways that are practical, applied, and appropriate for contemporary African contexts.

REFERENCES CITED

Appadurai, Arjun. 2002. "Disjuncture and Difference in the Global Cultural Economy." In *The Anthropology of Globalization: A Reader*, ed. Jonathan Xavier Inda and Renato Rosaldo, 46–64. Malden, MA: Blackwell Publishing.

Aspin, David, and Judith Chapman. 2001. "Lifelong Learning: Conceptual, Philosophical, Values Issues." In *International Handbook of Lifelong Learning*, ed. David N. Aspin, Judith D. Chapman, Michael Hatton, and Yukiko Sawano, 3–34. Dordrecht, Netherlands: Kluwer Academic Publishers.

Beckerleg, Susan, Maggie Telfer, and Ahmed Sadiq. 2006. "A Rapid Assessment of Heroin Use in Kenya." *Substance Use and Misuse* 41: 1029–44.

Blackaby, Henry, and Richard Blackaby. 2011. *Spiritual Leadership: Moving People on to God's Agenda*. Nashville, TN: B and H Publishing Group.

CIA Fact Book. 2001. *Long-term Global Demographic Trends: Reshaping the Geopolitical Landscape*. Central Intelligence Agency.

Clinton, Robert, and Paul D. Stanley. 1992. *Connecting: The Mentoring Relationships You Need to Succeed*. Downers Grove, IL: NavPress.

Gitari, David M. 2005. *Responsible Church Leadership*. Nairobi: Acton Press.

Hackman, Michael Z., and Craig E. Johnson. 2004. *Leadership: A Communication Perspective*. Long Grove, IL: Waveland Press.

Kofi, Agawu. 2003. *Representing African Music: Postcolonial Notes, Queries, Positions*. New York: Routledge.

Lindsay, Michael. 2007. *Faith in the Halls of Power*. New York: Oxford University Press.

Lunenburg, Fred C. 2012. "Power and Leadership: An Influence Process. *International Journal of Business, Management. and Administration* 15/1: 1–9.

Mugambi, Jesse N. K. 2013. "The Future of Theological Education in Africa and the Challenges It Faces." In *Handbook of Theological Education in Africa*, ed. Isabel Apawo Phiri and Dietrich Werner, 117–25. Oxford, UK: Regnum Books International.

Nguru, Faith W. 2012. "Development of Christian Higher Education in Kenya: An Overview in Christian Higher Education." In *Christian Higher Education: A Global Reconnaissance*, ed. Joel Carpenter, 43–67. Cambridge UK: William B. Eerdmans Publishing Company.

Northhouse, Peter G. 2013. *Leadership: Theory and Practice*, 6th ed. London: Sage Publications.

Putnam, Robert D. 2000. *Bowling Alone: The Collapse and Revival of American Community*. London: Simon and Schuster.

Tiénou, Tite. 2008. "The Great Commission in Africa." In *The Great Commission: Evangelicals and the History of World Missions,* ed. Martin I. Klauber and Scott M. Manetsch, 164–75. Nashville, TN: B and H Publishing Group.

Chapter 3

Formation of African Christian Leaders: Patterns from the ALS Data

Wanjiru M. Gitau

How leaders are formed is no doubt a contested concept. While some assume that great leaders are simply born with innate leadership qualities, most who study leadership have concluded that leadership skills and qualities are acquired through social processes, life contexts, and social connections (Avolio, Walumbwa, and Weber 2009; Avolio 2004; Johnson et. al. 1999; Fourie et. al. 2015; Venter 2004; James 2008). Our research with African Christian leaders leads us to the conclusion that leadership formation is an interactive journey between context and relationships in a dynamic journey of growth and maturation. This chapter considers a wide range of influences that constitute the interactive journey that has shaped the individuals that our research identified as having an unusual and significant leadership impact. The analysis examines their lifelong social connections for patterns that prepared them for leadership. Narratives of their lives link the leaders to churches, schools, and other types of community organizations, the activities of which collectively contributed to the development of a leader-like character in them.

PARENTS AND EXTENDED KIN

The first significant influence on future leaders comes from early caregivers. When we asked African Christian leaders about important influences in their lives, more than 70 percent identified a parent or parental figure as having been especially influential. That is, the formation of leaders begins in childhood with their families (Rogoff 2003, 20). Kenyan Judge Onesmus Makau grew up in a peasant family but cites his parents, a proxy grandfather, Mzee Mathuva, and a godly woman, Mrs. Itume, as early influences. General Kianga, a retired army general named his parents and his older brother as positively influencing him, while Esther Mombo's grandmother had an effect on her educational decisions from childhood through her young adult years, including her decision to remain unmarried so as to pursue an independent career serving God.

Literature shows that there is a relationship between family attributes and the choices that children make as they grow toward maturity; family members are seen as templates of ethical behavior, responsibility, and achievement (Madhavan and Crowell 2014). Koudougueret and Nvouni, both named important leaders from the CAR, report that they learned their core values from their fathers, even though teachers later also influenced them. Marie Yakemba, a senior Treasury official in the CAR government and an important leader of women's work, grew up in a Christian family and was deeply influenced by her father, who worked with the missionaries, and by her grandmother, a committed Christian. René Malépou, a lecturer in the CAR and president of Independent Community of Baptist Churches, was raised in a family guided by firm biblical values. He cites his father as his key influence and one of the reasons he is a successful leader today. Adelaide Cantanha grew up in a Christian home in the unstable circumstances of colonial Angola, yet the influence of her parents shaped the leader she grew to become.

Cosmas Maina's father figure was a rather different sort. As a young teen Cosmas Maina would run away from school with his brother and friends and experiment with drugs. While on "the street," they were caught by the 380–pound legendary and notorious police reservist Patrick Shaw (see Smith 2013; Zucchino 1988). He "caned them," gave them tea and bread, took them to visit Starehe Boys' Centre where he served as an administrator, and drove them back to their own school. In the evenings Shaw invited Maina to accompany him in his Volvo to "go around and see what he does, warning people not to take drugs, not to be thieves." Later, when Maina developed his own ministry for drug users, he bought his own Volvo to drive and modeled portions of his ministry on what he had learned from Shaw. For example, he sometimes drives around at night to places where alcohol, drugs, and prostitution might ensnare children so as to find the children and take them back to their parents.

NURTURING ENVIRONMENTS

Another important clue to how leaders emerge is the kind of setting in which they are brought up, schooled, and mature. A nurturing environment raises children's prospects of survival, healthy growth, and entrance into formal literacy, thereby increasing their chances of flourishing in life (Saugstad 2002) and developing leadership capabilities. Good homes are the initial setting where a child receives care, protection, support, and inspiration, and acquires a variety of values from the older generation.

In our interviews a majority of the interviewed leaders pointed to being raised in a home that nurtured their value system in ways that had a direct effect on their leadership strengths. Louisa Mateus is one such example. As a child, despite growing up in a home with limited resources, her parents provided her with love and affection. They encouraged her to value studies, to be content, and to respect others. She credits her success in life to her parents and stresses how proud she is of them.

However, as Chapter 2 in this book points out, good homes do not necessarily mean a stress-free childhood or the absence of exposure to war, poverty, and other family struggles. Marie Yakemba and Esther Mombo were raised by grandmothers in situations where they had to work hard as children to contribute to the family's sustenance, in part because their biological parents were absent. Others grew up in conditions of hardship. Edouard Nvouni, Joseph Kimeli, Judge Onesmus Makau, and General Kianga all grew up under varying degrees of hardship and had to work hard to help their parents meet their needs in between school hours. In some cases hardship seems to have contributed to their growth into leadership as they acquired problem-solving capacities, resilience, and determination to succeed. Judge Makau, for instance, "missed school regularly, looking after my father's cattle. This survival experience molded me to be hardworking and committed to my work. And the struggles of life made me a dedicated Christian."

The role of formal education is discussed in a later section, yet schools offer another nurturing space. A supportive school empowers the child to thrive in school and consequently to progress in society. For instance, the presence of Redeemed Gospel Academy in the Digo community uplifted the whole community. John Bosco started the school when he settled among the Digo and observed the deprivation of the community. To transform the region in a permanent way, he realized he would have to influence a new generation; hence, in 1996 he started the academy, growing it one grade at a time. The school is described as a child-friendly environment, committed to equipping the children holistically. However, it is more than a child-friendly school; it has become the community's focal point, a source of pride to the people as so many of their children have completed primary and secondary education. Teachers from the community use it as a starting point in their own career development before heading to more gainful employment. Musila, the headmistress, says that the school trains not only children but also teachers (on the job). When some leave because the school is not able to pay them competitively, "they start their own schools." They can do this "because the Redeemed Academy has given them experience"; that is, "this school trains not only the children but also the teachers—to be better teachers tomorrow and better leaders tomorrow." What makes this a unique nurturing environment is the challenges they have had to overcome, from religious hostility to endemic poverty that affects the school's finances, sexual exploitation of children through local tourism, and drug abuse. The bishop has collaborated with local leaders to overcome these difficulties and earn respect and protection for the school. Although this school remains basic in its facilities and remuneration of teachers, it has become a nurturing environment for an otherwise marginalized community.

Some leaders pointed out that the school environment was strategic to their formation. Louisa Mateus said that during her secondary schooling in Uige, she created good friendships that gave her fortitude as a student. Nyachogo attributes his passion for community activism, for which he was cited as a significant leader, to the Nazarene University environment that molded his character, competency, and leadership potential. Munene points out that his urban primary school opened up the cross-cultural world to him. Chiquete tells her story in a way that shows she considers school a critical environment for shaping character in children. She and her siblings attended Christian schools. They had Christian teachers. Moreover, the teaching they received had as its base Christian ethics. This environment inside and outside of the home was decisive in forging her character and in directing her life. Currently, she is a teacher at the Higher Institute of Evangelical Theology (ISTEL) in Lubago, where, among other things, she coordinates the Integral Biblical Course to empower others to serve their communities better.

Churches in the African context add value to the life of a growing person in many ways, from being a conduit of essential services to enabling education and, of course, offering a constructive community of friends and respected figures of authority. Churches have been at the forefront of providing education, development, and health services in Africa (Gifford 2009; Gatune 2010). Our research showed that pastors played central roles in the lives of African Christian leaders. Our original survey asked people to identify a Christian outside their immediate family who had the most impact on them (Table 3–1).

	Angola	CAR	Kenya
A pastor	35.4%	50.4%	56.2%
Another church leader	23.2%	25.3%	13.7%
A teacher	8.5%	8.1%	10.1%
An employer	1.6%	2.0%	2.4%
A friend	21.5%	9.5%	15.4%
Other	9.8%	4.6%	2.2%

Table 3–1. Christians Who Most Impacted You (Other than Family)

All of the interviewed leaders were themselves influenced by a church or by church leaders, some of them all the way from childhood through adulthood, although others only as adults. An example is Bishop Bosco, growing up in the slums with an unloving stepfather who mocked his dark skin and called him "the lame one." As a young man he met the bishop of the Redeemed Gospel Church, Arthur Gitonga, who became a "father" to him. Gitonga, he says, "was the one who walked with me in those early days when I was still having those slum attitudes and, you know, that background of a sinner. He is the one who raised me to where I now have Christian leadership qualities in me." Bishop Maisha also describes how an old leader in a Baptist church, Elijah Wanje, "took me as his son," "loved me when I was young and growing up" and "poured a lot of his life . . . into my life. . . . He was always advising me, nurturing me, and helping me to grow . . . until God really brought me somewhere." Maisha concludes that apart from Elijah Wanje, "I would not be what I am today."

In addition to churches other kinds of Christian organizations working with youth offer nurturing environments through ministries designed to engage them in specialized ways. Such organizations do much to help youth to develop selfhood and stronger relationships around a common identity and peer activity (Madhavan and Crowell 2014). Scripture Union, Fellowship of Christian Unions (FOCUS Kenya), and Kenya Students Christian Fellowship (KSCF) in Kenya; Mocidade Para Cristo (Youth for Christ) in Angola; and Campus pour Christ in the CAR, are examples of these. Their activities are structured around large and small groups either at primary or secondary schools (KSCF) or on university campuses. These groups carry out discipleship, evangelism, missions, fellowship and networking, and leadership development, all involving forms of community that nurture leader-like values in participants.

Nurture of another kind comes from organizations specifically dedicated to looking after children and youth. There were many such organizations identified through our research as having an impact. In Kenya, these include Tumaini Children's Home, Upendo Children's Home, Redeemed Academy, Plan International, Nyumba ya Mayatima (House of Orphans), Dorcas Aid International, Compassion International, Baobab Christian Home, and St. Martin's Catholic Social Apostolate in Nyahururu, among others. In Angola, of twenty influential organizations named, six were identified as working with youth in development, poverty alleviation, or education. In the CAR, of twenty-four organizations named as having a significant impact, four (Campus pour Christ, Jeunesse Chrétienne Conquérante, Jeunesse Evangélique Africaine, and Union des Jeunes Chrétiens) were said to be working primarily with youth. What is significant about these organizations is that their activities often create a surrogate family for children and youth, especially in contexts undergoing turbulent change. All these organizations are playing an important role in giving future leaders a place to grow.

LIFE-SKILLS INSTRUCTIONAL PROGRAMS

We found that some of those who grew into important leaders were equipped with, or involved in equipping others with, curriculum-based programs that empowered them with positive life skills. Life-skills instruction empowers youth toward life competency and is especially useful to socially disadvantaged groups (Adams 2011).

Several organizations were cited because their instructional programs, delivered through seasonal classes, seminars, and workshops, offer specific ministry and life skills to youth. The content goes beyond generic skills of leadership. Such instructional programs may focus on the felt needs of specific target groups, or on personal growth, faith building (religious instruction), community organizing, economic empowerment, planning and vision casting, collective action, and so on. These organizations include Scripture Union, KSCF, FOCUS Kenya, National Council of Churches of Kenya (NCCK), Transform Kenya, Departamento de Assistência Social, Estudos e Projectos (DASEP) of Angola's Evangelical Congregational Church, Youth for Christ, the CAR's Ambassade Chrétienne, and Adonai Mission International.

Consider Scripture Union in Kenya. The organization was identified as having a significant impact on schoolchildren in the four- to fourteen-year-old age group. Scripture Union gained entrance into selected public primary schools by adopting the government's Pastoral Instruction Program (PIP). Teachers are encouraged to run this program as an extracurricular activity to teach morality and character among children. However, because teachers are often overloaded with the regular class work, the PIP program was being neglected in most schools. Scripture Union has focused on supporting this program. In the three thousand Kenyan government schools where it has access, out of thirty thousand total, Scripture Union mobilizes, trains, and provides Christian teachers with resources to run programs within the general guidelines of PIP. Using age- and language-appropriate content, Scripture Union adds value to Kenya's formal education by contributing to the moral formation of students and by providing psychosocial support to parents and teachers through the first eight years of schooling. In parts of the country where Scripture Union does not have the capacity to reach schools, it collaborates with organizations that also work with primary-school children, such as World Relief and Catholic Relief Services. Although not every child influenced by Scripture Union will turn into a leader, this model has significant potential for setting up some of the children to be future leaders within the community.

A key factor in the success of lesson-based instruction is the preparedness of teachers. Appropriately trained, properly motivated, and well-supported teachers have a positive impact on children's learning outcomes, including their proficiency in many areas of life (Fredriksen and Kagia 2013). Consider, for example, sex education. In much of Africa in the past, sexuality would have been addressed during traditional coming-of-age rites of passage. However, modern African societies often are reticent when it comes to sexual instruction. Schools are supposed to teach sex education, but teachers seldom are prepared with the specialized knowledge and training needed. Most children get distorted information from peers and media.

One of the Kenyan leaders named as having a significant impact, Isaac Mutua, is a life-skills instructor with a special focus on sexuality. Following his conversion as a teenager, he developed a strong conviction that he should empower children and youth with life values. In the course of pursuing training toward this end, Mutua was introduced to a sex-education program designed to address the escalating problem of HIV/AIDs. During his practicum in primary schools, he designed and taught material based on sexual realities surrounding the HIV/AIDs challenge. Mutua came to understand that rather than merely harangue children into conforming to moral behavior, they required basic instructions about their changing bodies and social environments. He systematized the instruction in formats similar to their school work, but in ways that addressed their challenges, curiosity, and behaviors. His content addressed body image, belonging, friendship, sexuality, and the consequences of sexual behavior. His material has gone a long way to help youth who are otherwise confused by their growing bodies in a changing society. Mutua's friendliness, communication skills, and proficiency in the issues quickly earned him popularity among pupils and teachers, placing him in high demand as a speaker at Kenyan schools. More Kenyan respondents identified him as a non-clergy Christian leader with significant impact than any other.

UNPAID SERVICE TO COMMUNITY

Emerging leaders need opportunities to practice their developing skills before they enter formal employment or become leaders in their own right. Often they undertake various forms of unremunerated service, including volunteering, interning, or short-term service projects. These expand the capacities of the growing leader in a variety of ways. We found that serving without pay for a time was part of the earlier ethos of currently successful leaders. For others, it is a way of life.

Edouard Nvouni was identified as a non-clergy leader having a significant impact because "he has helped to build many buildings for the church and served in leadership in his local church." Nvouni studied civil engineering and became one of the first Africans in the CAR to replace Europeans as a technical instructor. Since 2001, he has worked with Organisation Internationale de la Francophonie (OIF) as the national representative of technical and vocational training. He also represents the CAR in UNESCO. However, among Baptist church members he is known especially for donating his time and architectural skills without pay to building churches. "Everything he acquired as an engineer he has put to the service of building the Baptist Churches of Sapeke (CEBEC), Kembé (UFEB), Kpetené (EEB), Castor (UEB), and Battalion III." It is significant that he has volunteered in church in a variety of other ways since his youth and throughout his time of studies. Similarly, most of the non-clergy leaders we interviewed cite instances in their youth when they were involved in volunteer activities, and even in adulthood most serve in ways that do not cost their communities.

Volunteering puts young, energetic, and unengaged youth to work. In turn, the embodiment of the service ideal allows participants to learn, socialize, discover, and develop their gifts, become integrated into their communities, and resist negative peer influences (Akintola 2011).

The Magena Youth Group in the Kisii area of Kenya began in 2006 after a visiting choir challenged the youth at Magena Seventh Day Adventist church to serve their community. From its origins with six founding members, the group has grown to a membership of eighty youth, most still in high school or college. The group identifies needs in the community and intervenes through service in acts such as repairing houses or caring for the elderly and special-needs children. To raise income for their activities, they plant and sell trees and Napier grass at their church property. The transformation of members of the group has built trust with community members and motivated other churches in the area to begin similar youth groups. These are people to whom greater leadership can be entrusted in the future.

Our research encountered internships as a form of formalized, unremunerated service opportunities in churches and organizations. Nairobi Chapel, Christ Is the Answer Ministries (CITAM), FOCUS Kenya and NCCK in Kenya all have professionally run internships, designed as a one-year leadership development opportunity. Oscar Muriu's church, the Nairobi Chapel, a large middle-class urban church of over three thousand members in Nairobi, uses internships to raise new leaders for the growing church and to plant new churches. Although he does not discount theological training, Oscar sees this apprenticeship model as a more efficient way to meet the needs of fast-growing churches in Africa. His church began to run internships back in 1994. To date, it is said that they have trained more than three hundred leaders. This apprenticeship, "where you walk alongside somebody who is doing it and learn on the job," assumes several things. One is that this was Jesus's way of preparing his disciples to serve. He walked with them for three years, entrusting responsibilities to them by measures. Second, the training occurs in a real-life context; trainees solve real problems. Third, trainees learn alongside a team of peers and mature leaders, which creates room for trainees to learn from senior leaders and for the older to catch the passion of the younger. The younger eventually become the successors. Nairobi Chapel has five large churches in Nairobi that are now planting other churches and training new leaders using this same method.

FOCUS has a comparably structured internship, known as Short Term Experience in Ministry (STEM) which recruits fresh university graduates for a year of apprenticeship to work under seasoned leaders in the organization. For the last forty years FOCUS has developed successful leaders through STEM, with the internship program continually being revised and improved based on experience. Simon Masibo, the general secretary of FOCUS until 2013, served FOCUS for a total of twenty-one years, starting from a STEM staff position. Likewise, the current general secretary, George Ogalo, and virtually all the staff were once STEM interns, graduating to more responsibility by degrees. Well-known ex-FOCUS staff members are serving society in significant leadership positions in Kenya. David Oginde, the bishop of CITAM, a Pentecostal denomination in Kenya that our research identified as having a significant impact, started out serving in FOCUS during his student days. Many of Kenya's thriving church leaders received a similar start. In short, apprenticeships in structured organizations have proven influential in leadership development.

HIGHER EDUCATION

In concert with other factors, higher education is a significant contributor to the formation of Africans who become leaders. Higher education builds on other forms of leadership experience to improve knowledge and understanding, to cultivate relevant skills, to generate knowledge through new research, and to make use of social experiences toward a much more productive life (Teal 2010; Bloom, Canning, and Chan 2006). Formal literacy rates are improving in Africa, up to 70 percent in parts of sub-Saharan Africa (UNESCO 2013), and in countries like Kenya recent economic developments have led to considerable growth in the higher education sector.

All the leaders featured in our interviews have some level of post-secondary education from diverse sources, including local and Western universities, seminaries, and local diploma colleges. Formal education contributes critical elements to leadership strengths. In many cases high levels of education clearly played central roles in positioning individuals for high-visibility leadership positions. Sixty-seven-year-old Professor Nestor Mamadou Nali, a medical doctor from the CAR, was named one of the most influential non-clergy persons in the CAR. He received medical training in Canada, where he lived from 1965 to 1975. Besides his medical practice, he has held other significant roles. These include founding the Medical Faculty at the University of Bangui, appointment to the Ministry of Public Health in the CAR, and leading the fight against HIV/AIDs. In church circles, he is a church deacon, president of the Association of Child Evangelism, President of the Union of Christian Medical Workers, and is on the board of the Faculté de Théologie Évangélique de Bangui.

Adelaide Catanha, ordained in 1978 at a time when the ordination of women was rare, was cited as one of the ten most influential women pastors in Angola. Her formal education includes a science of education degree in psychology from the Instituto Superior de Ciencias de Educacao (Higher Institute of Education, ISCED), a master's degree in clinical psychopedagogy from an online university in Spain (2009), the PhD from Honolulu, Hawaii (2013), and a theological degree. Her work portfolio includes teaching at Emanuel do Dondi Seminary as well as leadership in a variety of venues, ranging from the World Council of Churches to World Prayer Day, to community development through PROVAJE (Abundant Life in Jesus Program), to the supervision of sixteen congregations of the Igreja Evangélica Congregacional. Significantly, "she considers that giving classes in the Theological Seminary is one of the ways to train leaders" and cites more than fifty people in high-visibility positions whom she has trained. Professor Esther Mombo from St. Paul's University, Judge Onesmus Makau, René Malépou, Pastor Dinis Eurico, Edouard Nvouni, and David Koudougueret are other leaders whose leadership positions are based in part on their high levels of formal education.

There are others who are less highly educated, yet who place a high premium on education and are continually acquiring further training, either to increase their chances of finding gainful employment, or to acquire competencies in their current roles. Joseph Kimeli has attended several short courses on leadership, community development, and business management to gain more knowledge and skills in his capacity as a manager of Cheptebo Rural Development Center. Life-skills educator Isaac Mutua attended more than fifteen certificate courses on such diverse issues as professional palliative care, gender-based violence, spiritual formation, leadership and administration, fundraising, chaplaincy, computers, conflict resolution, and several other subjects.

Oscar Muriu, who has global influence in church circles, while conceding that formal theological training has a place when it graduates prayerful men and women "who are seasoned in thinking," nonetheless critiques formal theological education as an inadequate method of developing leaders for the church in Africa:

> Theological College is not Africa's answer to the need of leadership. It will provide some [leaders], but the process is long, and time and resource consuming. . . . Very few African churches and very few African Christian organizations can afford that kind of leadership development.

He then identifies the apprenticeship model (internship) as a more effective model of developing leaders for the church. However, at the same time, Muriu prefers even those who come to Nairobi Chapel for an apprenticeship to be university graduates:

Working with university students is practically helpful because they have been taught to think, are familiar with books and written material, can work with hypothetical logic model so that when you sit down and have a conversation they clue in easily. . . . They understand how to get along, how to make decisions . . . can read books because we are going to require them to read . . . [and] are teachable, are able to look at problems and break them down.

Nairobi Chapel's leadership development process involves a long journey that builds on formal education, and may also include further formal education. It is designed progressively, from a one-year internship, to two years of pastoral training, after which the trainee leader, according to Muriu, may be

sent to theological college for a period . . . because [now] they have enough questions . . . for which they recognize they do not have answers. . . . So they are compelled toward clear theological reflection, not just for the sake of theological reflection but because they recognize they need help.

After theological college, Nairobi Chapel sends trainees for cross-cultural interaction in partner churches abroad. Alternatively, newly minted trainees may be assigned more responsibility in their own churches. What Oscar Muriu is recommending here is that the development of leaders is not just about formal theological education; it should be seen as part of a process matched with other opportunities that involve above all serving in community. Formal education is an integral part of this process, just not the whole.

MENTORING

Mentoring, the close walk between a trainee protégé and an experienced leader (Adair 2009, 98, 105), is often an integral part of other leadership-development factors cited earlier. However, it merits consideration itself, since it is often central to leadership formation, even for those who have already gone through other leadership-formation processes. Across research disciplines mentoring has been associated with a range of positive results for protégés including attitudinal, health-related, relational, and career outcomes (Eby et al. 2008). It has been a significant factor in shaping African leaders of influence.

We found that mentoring was a theme that ran through all stages of the growth of individuals who grew to be leaders, and that it served different functions at each stage. For instance, Isaac Mutua was challenged by Paul Muladi to acquire theological training so that he could be more competent to engage youth. Ron Sonnas coached Edward Munene to focus his energies in a single church rather than pursuing unfocused itinerant ministry. Munene proceeded to plant a church and to focus his outreach on a specific demographic in Mombasa city. Joseph Kimeli was handpicked and coached to run Cheptebo Rural Development Project as a successor to the missionaries at the center.

The training programs of Christian organizations such as FOCUS Kenya, NCCK, Nairobi Chapel, and the CITAM group of churches intentionally structure mentoring into their programs. The very design of these organizations focuses on coaching protégés to learn the ropes of running the organizations through mentored participation so that, in turn, they can lead successfully when left in charge.

OPPORTUNITIES TO LEAD

Creating conditions for young people to emerge as leaders is ineffective unless they eventually are weaned off of dependence on other leaders and are able to solve real-world problems on their own. Strategic opportunities to lead are the fulfillment of the process itself. On the other hand, they trigger further growth in the leader. The resulting impact and visibility are relative to their context, field, and circumstances.

Many of the leaders interviewed in this project began serving as assistants to more visible leaders. When John Bosco relocated to Mombasa, Bishop Kitonga of Nairobi Redeemed Gospel Church recommended that Bishop Lai of Mombasa not allow Bosco to stay idle. "In fact he should be made a deacon immediately." Lai paid heed to Kitonga. "I was pronounced a deacon on arrival in the church, and I was placed in charge of evangelism because I was good at evangelism." In the course of managing Lai's outdoor events, Bosco saw a niche for a church, and eventually a school, among the Digo, and then found ways of overcoming the hostility, hardship, and inadequate resources to become effective in the area. Using a bare minimum of resources, he would go on to grow the church to a membership of over three thousand, build a school, plant over forty churches, and become the regional bishop of over ninety churches. The opportunity to assist an experienced leader coalesced with a recognition of a gap in society. His personal drive, vision, character, and humility set him apart as one of the most influential Christian leaders in the region.

Becoming recognized as a leader of significant impact in one arena doubtless opens doors for other arenas of leadership influence. Moreover, the exercise of leadership in diverse arenas contributes, in turn, toward being more widely recognized as a leader with impact. Dr. David Koudougueret is the pastor of the seven-thousand-member Ngoubagara Baptist Church. Previously he led elsewhere, as the academic dean of FATEB; in the World Evangelical Alliance and the Service Chrétien d'Appui à l'Animation Rurale (SECAAR); and the Union Fraternelle des Eglises Baptistes as general secretary. His leadership acumen has initiated many projects, including a frontier school, health ministry to the "Pygmies," and projects among youth. All these opportunities have turned him into a leader who was rated highly for his leadership.

Opportunity to lead may arise with a sudden need, when one is thrust into an unexpected responsibility but previous experience has prepared one for the moment. Eunice Chiquete led from an early age, offering literacy classes to children from the time she was fourteen years old. Since war-torn Angola had expelled missionaries, Eunice reproduced what her teachers had taught her, instructing the children using coal as chalk and foil as a blackboard. In 1997, Teresa, a woman from Switzerland who ran the radio program *Yeva Ondaka,* invited Eunice to train other children as part of the program. In 1999, this woman was tragically murdered in her residence, and it fell on a deeply shocked Eunice to continue what her mentor had begun. By the age of thirty-five, she held a broad portfolio as a teacher of children, as a theological teacher, as a facilitator of a variety of children's evangelistic and discipleship projects, and as a trainer with 80 percent of the churches in her province of Huila.

CONCLUSION

This chapter tracks the lives of men and women that were deemed influential in their local communities. We found their formation being forged in practical-life worlds, influenced by those who raised and interacted with them through life, what they learned as part of socialization and education, and what kind of leadership exposure they received as they matured. The web of relationships was particularly vital. Researchers observe that much discourse on leadership in sub-Saharan Africa emphasizes characteristics, skills, styles and behaviors of observed (and sometimes dysfunctional) leaders while ignoring the web of relationships, interactions, and unique community contexts out of which leaders emerge (Haruna 2009, Venter 2004). This chapter suggests that if we are to make sense of leadership in African communities and to recommend the formation of new leaders, it is important to take to heart the unique contexts in which people grow and to invest in such contexts toward the formation of future leaders. The African communal ethos of collaboration and cooperation through dependence, interdependence, and learning, caring, giving, and receiving is still effective in much of African life. Participants—at home, at school, in church, in organizations—are the stakeholders in determining what happens in the community, including how leaders are formed and engaged. Seen this way, two concluding observations and recommendations are offered here.

First, leadership development potentially involves a journey of incremental steps commensurate with biological growth, socialization, education, and maturation into responsibility. Growth into leadership is not a one-time activity. It is proportionate with better prospects of nurture, formal schooling and training, apprenticeship, and mentoring. This is a dynamic, iterative process that depends on many incremental investments in a potential leader. The acquisition of each new skill continually revisits and reinforces skills learned earlier and anticipates further learning. The key ingredients are intentionality and consistency on the part of all players. For example, child psychologists suggest that early childhood is the optimum time for teaching foundational values to children, while late childhood and teenage years are most conducive for teaching curricula-based training. Young adults are at a stage of self-discovery for leadership and career trajectories; hence, it is a great time to expose them to experimental responsibilities through internships and mentoring. Some of these stages may be missed altogether, as when children are raised in a troubled home. However, if they receive nurture and instructional content in later years, they can make up for what was missed in childhood and still become leaders. Parents, teachers, church leaders, mentors, youth organizations, and theological educators should be aware of one another's work, at the very least, and should seek ways of collaborating. The influence of each one can reinforce the influence of the others. A good home base that offers security, modeling, and belonging prepares a child to be more competent at school, and therefore likely to be identified as a leader among peers; a church that offers belonging to youth minimizes the chances of negative peer influence elsewhere.

Second, leadership is not irrevocably fixed at birth. If leadership involves the exercise of an observable set of useful skills and abilities that emerge with opportunity and situations (Adair 2009, 7–33), almost anyone can be a leader and, in fact, should aim to be a leader at some level, whether in a small group, family, church, or organization (Kouzes and Posner 1995, 1–2). People may be born with personality traits of charisma, extroversion, and creativity that predispose them to particular leadership roles. However, most characteristics that leaders possess can be, and are, learned, as the word *develop* suggests. Even charismatic persons have to hone critical leadership skills like relational competencies, self-awareness, and technical know-how. Practically, pastors, teachers, youth workers, and educators should design their activities and programs to create every opportunity for every child to grow up believing he or she can make a positive difference in the world, an opportunity to rise as a leader.

In light of the myriad crises on the African continent, principled, ethical, well-trained, and impartial leadership is required to bring about change in the political, social, economic, and cultural life, that is, to transform the continent. Leaders of repute have remarked that Africa needs a cross-sectional leadership revolution among all its inhabitants, from its top leaders to its poorest citizenry (Maathai 2009, 25). This chapter suggests this revolution is possible, by turning every step of socialization into a leadership-development opportunity.

REFERENCES CITED

Adair, John. 2009. *How to Grow leaders: The Seven Key Principles of Effective Leadership Development*. London: Kogan Page.

Adams, Avril. 2011. "The Role of Skills Development in Overcoming Social Disadvantage." Background paper prepared for the *Education for All Global Monitoring Report 2012*. Paris: UNESCO.

Akintola, Olagoke. 2011. "What Motivates People to Volunteer? The Case of Volunteer AIDS Caregivers in Faith-Based Organizations in KwaZulu-Natal, South Africa. *Health Policy and Planning* 26/1: 53–62.

Avolio, Bruce. 2004. *Leadership Development in Balance: MADE/Born*. Mahwah, NJ: Lawrence Erlbaum.

Avolio, Bruce J., Fred O. Walumbwa, and Todd J. Weber. 2009. "Leadership: Current Theories, Research, and Future Directions." *Annual Review of Psychology* 60/1: 421–49.

Bloom, David, David Canning, and Kevin Chan. 2006. *Higher Education and Economic Development in Africa*. Boston: Harvard University.

Eby, Lillian T., Tammy D. Allen, Sarah C. Evans, Thomas Ng, and David DuBois. 2008. "Does Mentoring Matter? A Multidisciplinary Meta-analysis comparing Mentored and Non-mentored Individuals." *Journal of Vocational Behavior* 72/2: 254–67.

Fourie, Willem, Suzanne C. van der Merwe, and Ben van der Merwe. 2015. "Sixty Years of Research on Leadership in Africa: A Review of the Literature." *Leadership* 13/2: 221–51.

Fredriksen, Birger, and Ruth Kagia. 2013. "Attaining the 2050 Vision for Africa Breaking the Human Capital Barrier." *Global Journal of Emerging Market Economies* 5/3: 269–328.

Gatune, Julius. 2010. "Africa's Development beyond Aid: Getting out of the Box." *The ANNALS of the American Academy of Political and Social Science* 632/1: 103–20.

Gifford, Paul. 2009. *Christianity, Politics, and Public Life in Kenya*. New York: Columbia University Press.

Haruna, Peter Fuseini. 2009. "Revising the Leadership Paradigm in Sub-Saharan Africa: A Study of Community-based Leadership." *Public Administration Review* 69/5: 941–50.

James, Rick. 2008. "Leadership Development Inside-Out in Africa." *Nonprofit Management and Leadership* 18/3: 359–75.

Johnson, Andrew M., Philip A. Vernon, Julie M. McCarthy, Mindy Molson, Julie A. Harris, and Kerry L. Jang. 1999. "Nature vs. Nurture: Are Leaders Born or Made? A Behavior Genetic Investigation of Leadership Style." *Twin Research* 1/4: 216–23.

Kouzes, James M. and Barry Posner. 1995. *The Leadership Challenge: How to Keep Getting Extraordinary Things,* second edition. San Francisco: Jossey-Bass Publishers.

Maathai, Wangari. 2009. *The Challenge for Africa*. New York: Pantheon Books.

Madhavan, Sangeetha, and Jacqueline Crowell. 2014. "Who Would You Like to Be Like? Family, Village, and National Role Models among Black Youth in Rural South Africa." *Journal of Adolescent Research* 29/6): 716–37.

Rogoff, Barbara. 2003. *The Cultural Nature of Human Development.* Oxford, UK: Oxford University Press.

Saugstad, Letten F. 2002. "Third World Adversity: African Infant Precocity and the Role of Environment." *Nutrition and Health* 16/3: 147–60.

Smith, David. 2013. "Investigating Patrick Shaw, Kenya's Most Dreaded Cop." *Daily Nation* (March 25). http://www.nation.co.ke.

Teal, Francis. 2010. "Higher Education and Economic Development in Africa: A Review of Channels and Interactions." *Journal of African Economies* 20 (Suppl. 3): iii50–iii79.

UNESCO. 2013. "Adult and Youth Literacy." UNESCO Institute for Statistics. http://www.uis.unesco.org.

Venter, Elza. 2004. "The Notion of Ubuntu and Communalism in African Educational Discourse." *Studies in Philosophy and Education* 23/2–3: 149–60.

Zucchino, David. 1988. "A Kenyan Lawman: Large in Life, Now Larger in Legend." *Philly.com* (March 13). http://articles.philly.com.

Chapter 4

Connected—The Role of Social Capital for Leaders with Impact

Steven D. H. Rasmussen

"Everything works relationally. If you want to impact anything, you have to be face-to-face," said Oscar Muriu, a Kenyan megachurch pastor. In fact, he said he gave me these hours for an interview on his day off only because of our relationship. My own twenty years of experience in East Africa confirm that Oscar Muriu is right. I can get an amazing amount accomplished if I have a relationship—and almost nothing without one.

The insight that social relationships have great value is the basis for social capital theory, which stresses that in any society, positive social relationships involving mutual trust and reciprocal obligation are essential for success and human flourishing (Putnam 2000, 19). Such relationships constitute a sort of capital, a resource that enables significant things to happen. Leaders, to be successful, must be able to draw on, direct, and make use of significant amounts of social capital.

Our survey was intended to identify key African Christian leaders deemed to be making a positive impact. However, our survey simultaneously enabled us to identify those with high social capital. We asked 8,041 African Christians to share who had influenced them the most, and which Christian leaders and organizations they believed were having the most positive impact in their communities. Respondents were asked to rate these leaders on their skills, wisdom, ethical integrity, positive reputation, efficient use of resources, love of and service to others, and their ability to mobilize community members for positive ends. That is, the very criteria that we used to identify strategic leaders for follow-up study also identified them as rich in social capital—as having social trust and the ability to activate relationships on behalf of some shared vision of the Good. From the most well-known, trusted, and respected people identified in our survey, we selected and interviewed a variety of clergy and non-clergy leaders as well as leaders of the most effective organizations. We wrote more than fifty profiles and have attempted to answer the following questions: What can we learn from these leaders and organizations with high social capital? What types of social capital underpins their leadership success? How do they develop this social capital? How do they use this social capital in their exercise of leadership?

COSTS, BENEFITS, AND TYPES OF SOCIAL CAPITAL

Social capital has costs and benefits for the individuals involved, but also for the wider community (Putnam 2000, 20). For example, my interview with Pastor Oscar cost us time but also built our relationship. It also had a cost and benefits for Nairobi Chapel, where he is the senior pastor and I am a member. Hopefully, it benefits you as a reader of this book. Social connections also promote "mutual obligations" and "sturdy norms of reciprocity" (Putnam 2000, 20). These commitments are often with specific individuals. However, they also include more generalized commitments, such as the commitment to help any family or congregation member that is in need. Such norms and repeated interactions produce and demonstrate trustworthiness and encourage more efficient and effective environments (Horsager 2012). Many studies have shown that social capital produces significant positive effects. Putnam, for example, presents evidence in the United States to show that "social capital makes us smarter, healthier, safer, richer, and better able to govern a just and stable democracy" (Putnam 2000, 290).

Scholars have identified three types of social capital, reflecting three types of social relationship. Some relationships are among people who are demographically similar to one another. Rather than being distant or different, these people tend to be "nearby" and "like me" (Lin 2002, 39). They live in the same community, attend the same church, participate in the same social clubs, speak the same mother tongue, have similar lifestyles, and have dense patterns of relationship with one another. Sociologists speak of this form of relationship as *bonding social capital*. Bonding social capital is easy to form, involves high levels of obligation, and offers strong social and emotional support. Relations with family and close friends are part of bonding social capital. Bonding social capital exists within ethnic, religious, linguistic, racial, and tribal groups.

However, the very bonding capital that creates strong in-group loyalties often hinders the development of positive relationships across major social divides. Societies are frequently characterized by deep ethnic, religious, linguistic, racial, or tribal divides around which there is often enmity, prejudice, grievances and grudges, conflict, and violence. Scholars have learned, however, that there are often individuals with strategic relationships that bridge these major "social cleavages," relationships that have socially strategic implications. They identify these relationships as constituting another form of social capital, *bridging social capital* (Putnam 2000, 22). People who establish social ties when they move into a new community or country, when they learn a second, third, or fourth language, or when they work closely with people of other religions or ethnic groups can be said to have bridging social capital. Bridging social capital reduces in-group bias, allows for the transfer of new ideas and resources, builds trust and commitment among groups, and allows for cooperative action across major social divides.

Finally, scholars point out that the world is not only divided horizontally by cultural, ethnic, linguistic, or religious cleavages, but also vertically by enormous differentials of wealth, status, and power. Thus, individuals or churches that are poor and powerless may have extensive social capital with other people or churches that are poor and powerless, but may still be disadvantaged. Their situation is likely to be very different from those that also have social ties of a vertical nature—social ties to individuals or institutions that are rich in material and human capital. Especially in relation to contexts where comparative poverty exists, sociologists emphasize the value of significant relationships of trust and mutual obligation that link people vertically across hierarchies of education, status, power, wealth, and influence (Woolcock and Radin 2008, 432; cf. Brown 2008, 212–214; Priest 2008, 259–261). Where such vertical relationships exist, we can speak of the presence of *linking social capital*. Our research demonstrated that African Christian leaders effectively draw on, and activate, all three forms of social capital.

BONDING SOCIAL CAPITAL

Proverbs like "I am because we are" and "It takes a village to raise a child" express the importance of bonding social capital in Africa. Bonding social capital is critical for emotional, social, and material support (Lin 2002, 41–50). For example, a recent study of 298 primarily poor Kenyan families surveyed them every two weeks for a year about all income and expenses. These households relied very heavily on their bonding social capital. In fact, 27 percent of their income was received from friends and relatives (Zollman 2014, 4). "For large and small needs alike, the two most important strategies for coping with these situations were, first, to ask for contributions from the social network, and second, to borrow from the social network" (Zollman 2014, 28).

Sometimes the bonding social capital that underpins strategic initiatives is ethnic. For example, while the Kenyan Bomaregwa Welfare Association (BWA) meets in a church, receives limited support from it, and has many members who are Christians, its primary social network is clan based. While most of its members live in Nairobi, their social links originate through a clan that occupies five square kilometers in the rural village setting from which they migrated. The original purpose of the BWA was to help one another in the new setting of the city in times of sickness and bereavement. Later BWA members realized that many in their home village were also struggling. So they created a corresponding BWA committee in the village. Their purpose is to promote social cohesion and development. They consider their clan-based unity a key strength and success. They have helped with education, including building a polytechnic school in the village.

Churches also provide many opportunities within the routines of congregational life for people to develop relationships. They teach people to care for others, to be generous, to serve, and to volunteer. They foster values that make people trustworthy and thus contribute to social trust. In short, churches are a significant factor in generating social capital (Cnaan et. al. 2003, 22). A study in rural Tanzania showed that churches contributed to the social capital of Tanzanians more than any other institution and that households in villages with higher social capital were materially more prosperous (Narayan and Pritchett 1999). Our own research consistently gave evidence of this. For example, the Magena Youth Group is part of a Seventh Day Adventist Church in the Kenyan town of Magena. It was founded to help youth grow spiritually and to stay "away from drugs, alcoholism, and immorality." Soon, however, its youth were helping build houses for the elderly, caring for physically challenged children, visiting the sick and aged, assisting those in financial need, and always singing. The group raises funds for all this by planting and selling trees and Napier grass, and by selling compact disc albums of songs that its choir has recorded. The social capital that the Magena Youth Group fosters is within a specific ethnic group (Kisii), a specific town (Magena), and a specific church and denomination (Seventh Day Adventist). Thus, it exemplifies *bonding social capital*—an essential contributor to social well-being for those within these communities.

Our research consistently showed that Christian leaders acquired human and social capital through church life. Pastor Luisa Mateus, from Angola, reports that as a child her participation in choir taught her "unity, love, and respect." At the age of twelve she was made the leader of her youth choir. Today, as a prominent pastor herself, she benefits from a lifetime of accumulating extensive social ties with a wide variety of church-based groups, from choirs to women's groups, men's groups, children's groups, and youth groups. Pastors who are key leaders clearly have dense patterns of social relationship with people who are part of their community, and they are successful as leaders in part because of their ability to capitalize on these relationships to accomplish shared commitments.

Both ethnicity and religion may provide the sense of community and relationship that underlies bonding social capital. Denominations and ethnic groups take the bonding social capital of congregation or family and extend this to a much larger group. One seeks ties, marital and otherwise, within one's group. The advantage is that a person can move to a new city or even a new country and find some of "us" to belong to and be helped by. Interestingly, the boundaries between ethnicity and denomination or religion occasionally coincide. Old missionary comity agreements divided up different mission fields in ways that sometimes coincided with ethnic boundaries. Thus, for example, in Kenya, 72 percent of our 389 Seventh Day Adventist respondents were ethnically Kisii, and 88 percent of the 78 Salvation Army respondents were Luhya. In Angola, 95 percent of the 293 Baptist respondents (Igreja Evangélica Batista de Angola) were ethnically Bakongo, and 92 percent of the 589 Congregational respondents (Igreja Evangélica Congregacional de Angola) were Ovimbundu. This pattern was far less true in the CAR. When respondents were asked to name a pastor they considered to have the highest positive impact, 77 percent of Angolans and 65 percent of Kenyans named a pastor from their own ethnic group. However, only 37 percent of respondents in the CAR did so. This is at least partly because in the CAR the single language of Sango became a core unifying factor across churches and ethnic groups. It is worth remembering that there is not a single Africa, with all countries exemplifying the same patterns.

Churches are unusually good at producing bonding social capital, something that has wonderful benefits but can also have a dark side. Any form of capital, of course, "can be directed toward malevolent, antisocial purposes" (Putnam 2000, 22). However, the very nature of bonding social capital is "inward looking and tends to reinforce exclusive identities and homogeneous groups. . . . By creating strong in-group loyalty, [it] may also create strong out-group antagonism" (Putnam 2000, 22–23). Ethnocentrism, sectarianism, and corruption often accompany bonding social capital, as when ethnic bonding social capital plays a central role in Kenyan governmental corruption, as told in the book *It's Our Turn to Eat* (Wrong 2010). When church and denominational boundaries coincide with in-group ethnic allegiances, the resulting social capital may have doubly unfortunate consequences—as was evident in Kenya's 2008 post-election violence, when some church leaders contributed to ethnic envy and tension. The problem is not bonding social capital per se, but bonding social capital affirmed to the exclusion of bridging and linking social capital. Moreover, since sociologists and political scientists have often associated religion almost exclusively with bonding social capital, it becomes especially important that we consider the role of African Christian leaders in fostering bridging and linking social capital.

BRIDGING SOCIAL CAPITAL

Africa is no exception to the reality that we all live in divided worlds. People are often divided by ethnicity, denomination, and religion. Identity is sometimes infused with historic grudges. To be one of "us," you must not be one of "them." We are "not them." We are better than "them." We remember how "they" have harmed us, stolen from us, ignored us, killed us in the past. Therefore, as good as bonding social capital is, there is a great need for bridging social capital across these various identities and groups. Do the Christian leaders and organizations that we examined contribute to these divides by reinforcing in-group bonding, or do they lead people into building networks, norms, and even trust across such historic divides between groups? If so, how do they build bridges across ethnic groups and denominations? Have some even found ways to bridge the Christian-Muslim gap?

Bridging Ethnic Divides

While some denominations reaffirmed ethnic in-group loyalties and identities, others bridged such divides. In Kenya, both the Anglican Church and the Roman Catholic Church have worked across all ethnic lines, unlike some of the older mission churches. The same is true of many newer churches. After Kenya's 2008 post-election violence there was a concerted effort by numerous organizations and churches to play a role in counteracting the impact of such ethnic allegiances. Transform Kenya was explicitly launched in response to the 2008 post-election violence. For the 2013 election, Transform Kenya advocated prayer and did a sermon series in multiple churches calling people to select leaders on character and skill, not ethnicity. Pastor Oscar Muriu preached that tribe is good, tribalism evil. He told his congregants it would be better to mark their ballot randomly than to vote for someone simply because that person had a last name from their own tribe. Such pastors preached that our deepest identity, grounded in scripture, is not ethnic (Eph 3:19–20; 4:3–6).

In addition to preaching, many of these leaders are building inter-ethnic churches, coalitions and organizations to develop bridging social capital. CITAM and Nairobi Chapel churches, for example, work intentionally to build multi-ethnic congregations with multi-ethnic pastoral staffs.

Bridging Denominational Divides

As mentioned earlier, in Angola and Kenya ethnicity and denomination often coincide, so both countries can divide people based on historic animosities. A fair number of those we interviewed stressed that denominations often contributed to Christian disunity. Eunice Chiquete of Angola expressed it this way, "Another challenge resides in the denominational spirit that still hovers among many denominations—which doesn't encourage cooperation for the expansion of the kingdom of God."

And yet many of the leaders and organizations that we examined have been unusually successful at forging interdenominational bridging social capital.

A key way that Putnam (2000) tracks the rise and fall of social capital in America is through the development of, and participation in, various voluntary groups or organizations. Indeed, those in our study developed bridging social capital across divides by building inter-ethnic and inter-denominational Christian groups and networks. Such groups develop shared rituals, purpose, and group culture through regular meetings and working together faithfully and lovingly. Various kinds of organizations do this, including councils of churches, interdenominational seminaries, and parachurch organizations.

National church councils like NCCK and the Council of Christian Churches in Angola (CICA) have had a significant impact through bridging between denominations nationally. An NCCK leader said:

> Broadly our vision is one church. We are for unity. We believe in what Jesus taught about [being] one. . . . It has been the concern of the country that denominational issues are becoming equal to tribal-ism in the country. So we have been trying to bring down the walls of denominationalism by building bridges through the community. That has been our main focus.

In its thirty-seven years CICA has likewise won trust from its member churches, the Angolan people, Africa, and the world, due to its posture of openness and cooperation with everyone. According to our interviewee, the CICA staff includes all of the main Angolan ethnicities. CICA exem-plifies the role of such organizations. During the fratricidal Angolan war fed by external powers, CICA joined forces with the Angolan Evangelical Alliance, the Roman Catholic Church, and other independent churches to found the Inter-Ecclesial Committee for Peace in Angola (COIEPA). By speaking to the government with one voice representing all churches, they achieved a significant positive impact on behalf of peace.

Interdenominational associations can also have influence through independent ministries that they begin—such as the interdenominational theological schools that we observed in each country. In the late 1970s and early 1980s, the Association of Evangelicals in Africa (AEA), in an effort to provide graduate-level theological education to evangelicals in Africa, started the FATEB for French-speaking Africans and the Nairobi Evangelical Graduate School of Theology (NEGST) for English-speaking Africans. Both of these provide high-quality education with a rich interde-nominational, inter-ethnic, and international mix of faculty and students. The fact that pastors and theological leaders of different denominations, countries, and ethnic backgrounds are trained in the same school, naturally builds cross-denominational relationships among church leaders.

In Kenya, for example, we discovered that many of the leaders of the most impactful Kenyan organizations (such as NCCK, FOCUS Kenya, Daraja La Tumaini) and churches (CITAM, Nairobi Chapel) were NEGST graduates who clearly had broad social ties across denominational lines that were strengthened through their NEGST formation. Alternatively, consider FATEB, which, in our survey, received the highest number of votes as the top Christian organization in the CAR. As told at some length in Chapter 5, FATEB has recently played a unifying and peacebuilding role in the aftermath of the CAR civil war. It was the one institution that was deeply appreciated and respected by virtually all Protestant Christians. When Pope Francis visited the CAR and wished to meet with Protestant leaders, the meeting took place (29 November 2015) at FATEB. In Angola, ISTEL, the only interdenominational theological school in Angola, likewise was named by Angolans as one of the top Christian organizations in Angola. Its interdenominational governing council "represents the Executive Committee of the Angolan Evangelical Alliance and has a national reach." ISTEL partners with many denominations who send students there and also benefit from its graduates. It contributes to cross-denominational ties among church leaders in Angola. Distance and differences are bridged when people study, live, and worship together.

Other interdenominational parachurch organizations foster bridging social capital among future non-clergy leaders. FOCUS Kenya, for example, brings forty-two thousand members together in interdenominational, inter-ethnic Christian Unions in almost every university in Kenya. Weekly worship, Bible studies, and collaborative outreach activities develop bridging social capital among diverse students. FOCUS connects these many campus groups in a national organization. FOCUS is connected to similar groups all over Africa and the world through the IFES, including the Intervarsity Christian Fellowship (IVCF) in the United States. Calisto Odede, who spent decades in FOCUS leadership, has been a featured speaker at the IVCF Urbana Missions Conference in the United States, as has Pastor Oscar Muriu—illustrating the range of social ties fostered. The Kenya Students' Christian Fellowship is another nondenominational organization, in this case focused on young people in more than three thousand secondary schools, while Scripture Union focuses its ministry on young people in roughly three thousand of Kenya's primary schools. Many young people find Jesus, are discipled, and are given opportunities to lead through these groups. Most Kenyan church leaders have been discipled through at least one of these three groups. This builds interdenominational bridging social capital. Similarly, in Angola, Youth for Christ disciples youth from many denominations. Its biggest dream "is to see Angolan churches working together toward the expansion of the kingdom of God."

Many of the leaders identified through our survey serve in interdenominational organizations. Many of the clergy leaders identified in our research serve not only their particular church but also interdenominationally. René

Malépou is currently president of the Communauté des Eglises Baptistes Indépendantes (Independent Community of Baptist Churches) but is also lecturing at the Brethren Theological Bible School, at FATEB, and at the Baptist school that opened two years ago. He is deeply committed to overcoming denominational divides. Malépou asserts, "If we always continue with our differences it will not help our salvation. Our biblical doctrine is more focused on our selfish interests, [and] we will never reach the goal."

Even if not serving interdenominationally, many of the church leaders have interdenominational networks. For example, Edward Munene is planting a church from his Kenya Assemblies of God denomination and went to its denominational school. However, he also keeps in close touch with friends from FOCUS. Some of these are Pentecostal, such as pastors in CITAM. Others are not. For example, he patterns many things in his church after Nairobi Chapel churches and pastor friends—Mavuno Chapel, Simon Mbevi, and Pastor Oscar Muriu.

Munene also builds intercultural bridging social capital in his ministry. He moved from Nairobi to plant a church in Mombasa. He discusses his sermon ideas with non-Christians and revises them according to their input. How did he learn to relate to people different from himself? He mentioned learning from his intercultural relationships growing up in the city of Nairobi:

> From a very early age, one of my best friends was a Ugandan. We used to hang out as three boys. The other one was an Ethiopian. So I grew up, my education was a multicultural setup, which helped me at a very young age appreciate other cultures and be able to realize that we all go through the same challenges regardless of the countries. In standard four my best friend was an Asian guy [a Kenyan of Indian descent].

Munene is a pastor of broad interests. He reports that in the previous year he read 130 books. He blogs and stays in communication with a variety of individuals. All of this contributes to his unusual ability to relate to a broad range of people.

Bridging Divides between Religions

Angola, the CAR, and Kenya are all majority Christian. Both the CAR and Kenya have large minority populations that are Muslim, but the number of Muslims in Angola is small. While a common faith can sometimes create unity among people that are otherwise diverse, religion can also create an identity of "us" against "them." In Africa, Christianity and Islam have provided unity among adherents of each faith, but also hostility against each other. In the last two years in Kenya, tensions between

Muslims and Christians have increased, in part because the terrorist group Al Shabaab has killed over four hundred people in attacks on churches, malls, buses, and a university, most of them on the coast. They claim to be specifically targeting Christians. However, most of these Somali terrorists do not know any Christians. Globally only 14 percent of the members of other world religions know a Christian personally (Johnson et al. 2015). The distance to be bridged is very wide.

In our survey we asked respondents the extent to which their church provided some form of outreach ministry to Muslims. The results are presented in Table 4–1.

To what extent does your church provide outreach ministry to Muslims?	Angola	CAR	Kenya
Not at all	85.8%	59.8%	41.5%
A little	7.5%	20.0%	23.3%
A good bit	3.1%	9.5%	17.1%
Very much	3.6%	10.7%	18.2%

Table 4–1. Church Ministry to Muslims

Most respondents indicated that their churches did little or nothing to focus on Islam. However, approximately 11 percent in the CAR and 18 percent in Kenya indicated that their churches did "very much" in the area of Muslim outreach.

Chapter 5 herein tells the story of how the CAR Christian organizations and leaders have recently been playing pivotal peacebuilding roles across the Muslim-Christian divide. Our interviews in Kenya also revealed an impressive array of ways in which Christians there are building positive relationships and engaging Muslims on behalf of peace as well as Christian witness. For leaders (such as Bishop Bosco) and organizations (such as Mombasa Church Forum, Redeemed Academy, Word of Life) on the Muslim-dominated coast of Kenya, forging trust relationships with Muslim leaders has been a key to success. Cosmas Maina, who received the second highest number of votes in Kenya for a non-clergy leader with impact, has partnered with Muslims to treat drug addicts. The NCCK and Mombasa Church Forum have worked to cultivate Muslim leaders as conversation partners, providing support for Muslim political candidates that exemplify positive approaches to interreligious relations, and partnering with community policing against interreligious violence.

Bishop John Bosco received the highest number of nominations by Kenyan Christians as the pastor with the greatest impact. His intercultural and linguistic skills have helped him develop bridging social capital with Muslims as well as Christians. He grew up in a slum in Nairobi and, after years without a job, he approached his former principal, who remembered him and posted him to teach in Mombasa. He did not know that this man was a Digo Muslim, who was sending him to help his home area. In the fully Muslim Digo area south of Mombasa, when he first attempted to preach, people threw stones at him. However, he learned and made cultural adjustments, becoming less confrontational, utilizing Coastal Swahili in his preaching, and eventually speaking Digo. He noted that the Digo, despite their birth identity as Muslims, and despite their initial desire to burn down his church, were not very religiously observant. He noted that the local schools were "very bad, poor performing schools," and concluded that if he could provide an excellent school that was Christian but would welcome Digo children and help them achieve academic success, the more "serious" parents would bring their children to that school. By creating a "forum where the Christian children can mix with the Muslim children," Muslims will come to "understand that the Christians are not as bad as they have been told by their parents." Bosco reports that his school, the Redeemed Gospel Academy with 350 students has "became one of the best performing schools in the district," with "50 percent of the children, Muslims." Because many Digo children have achieved significant educational success through the school, hostility has dissipated. Local Digo consider the school their own and are not inclined to burn down the very building that also educates their children.

Thus we see that many of these influential leaders and organizations are building, not just bonding, but significant bridging social capital among ethnic, denominational, and even religious groups. They do this by preaching and demonstrating a larger identity, especially as fellow Christians, but even as neighbors with common challenges to Muslims. They are building inter-ethnic churches, networks, and organizations. Interdenominational and/or inter-ethnic councils of churches, schools, and parachurch organizations provide opportunities for shared activities, identity, purpose, norms, and trust. Youth organizations and schools that bring people together from different ethnicities, denominations, and religions build bridges early that sometimes produce lifelong networks. Individual leaders have developed and used these bridging networks. They also have learned new languages and cultures to bridge. By serving Muslims, and then serving with Muslims, warmer relationships and attitudes have been built.

LINKING SOCIAL CAPITAL

People are divided by more than horizontal differences of culture and identity. Our world is full of incredible hierarchies of wealth, status, and power. Within communities sharing a specific socioeconomic location in the hierarchy, there are often tight networks of obligation, trust, and reciprocity, in other words, bonding social capital. However, there are usually far fewer relational ties across the vertical divide of socioeconomic hierarchies.

Thus, the initial position of individuals and their churches within these hierarchies provides marked constraints on the resources available to them. With bonding social capital, norms of reciprocity among the poor give access to the limited resources of those who are likewise poor. Scholars who map relationship networks observe dense patterns of relationship within social groups and within socioeconomic strata, but also note that there are often *social holes* where are there are no network links between groups that are differently positioned socioeconomically. And yet scholars have noted that occasionally there are relationships that cross these socioeconomic divides, helping bring the rich and poor into relationships across the vertical divide. These relationships constitute a different sort of social capital, *linking social capital* (Lin 2002, 69–72: Woolcock and Radin 2008), and allow for significant results especially within the communities characterized by greater poverty. People and organizations that bridge or link across the structural holes between otherwise isolated networks can benefit both groups, helping transmit information and resources across divides, while providing strategic guidance for all who are involved in shared projects (Lin 2002, 57–77). Research has shown that linking social capital can help people get jobs, higher positions, economic advancement, help in family crises, and provide access to education and health care information because it spans vertical divides of "power, influence, wealth and prestige" (Wuthnow 2002, 670).

According to Jean-François Bayart (2000), Africa exists within a world economic order in such a way that Africans achieve leadership success, not only because of downward social ties toward followers, but also upward externally and globally toward those with resources. He sees this *extraversion*, as he calls their efforts to capitalize on global links, as simply part of an exploitive system. But other scholars note that even leaders in America exercise effective leadership through their ability to connect upward to those who steward significant resources (linking social capital). That is, while most scholars of social capital recognize that there may be a "dark side" in the way any form of social capital is used (see, for example, Wuthnow 2002), most also stress that each of the three forms of social capital are essential for positive ends. Moreover, when Christians connect globally within the framework of shared transcendent values, and within the framework of trust and trustworthiness, their collaborative efforts can achieve far more than either partner could achieve without such ties.

Churches help people link. Wuthnow's research demonstrates that "people who belong to congregations are more likely than those who do not to say that they have friends who are political leaders, business executives, or persons of wealth" (2002, 682). Relationships among churches can link people and institutions across bigger gaps, even international gaps. Wuthnow's research (2009) shows how much American churches and their congregants are linked to churches, Christian organizations, and individuals in other countries. Given the distance and difference of most

Africans from people, churches, and organizations with great power and influence, wealth, and prestige; linking capital is especially important. In the past, when compared to other regions, Africans were relatively cut off from one another as well as from international education, economics, and communication. Therefore, international relationships that bridge divides between wealthier and less wealthy countries and churches merit special consideration.

In Africa, global religious networks are often where one finds relationships of trust and commitment that cross socioeconomic lines—relationships that form the basis of coordinated social action. Christianity has great strength both in Africa and North America, but the comparative strength of African Christianity, with its energy, dynamism, and numbers, exists within a radically different socioeconomic space than does North American Christianity, which stewards a vast proportion of global Christianity's material resources. Of course, when governments in Europe or North America wish to transmit resources to places like Africa, their lack of close ties with those most in need means that the resources typically are transferred in ways that invite high levels of corruption and misuse by unscrupulous middlemen. Christians and churches in distant places also sometimes wish to direct resources to and within Africa in ways that foster Christian ends. However, they may lack close relationships and knowledge at the grassroots levels that would give them the ability to wisely administer such resources. African churches, Christian organizations, and Christian leaders, however, tend to foster the values that make for trustworthiness (against corruption), but they also are closely embedded in relationships with those in situations of great need. They are trusted locally. They are contextually knowledgeable. Not surprisingly, even secular governments or aid organizations often find such religious networks (churches, other institutions, and leaders) vastly preferable partners to local nonreligious parties.

Many of the African leaders and organizations we examined seem skillful and comfortable with building social capital across socioeconomic and national divides. How have they developed and used international and intercultural bridging and especially linking social capital? How do they link up and down? How do they accomplish important ends through their links and resource brokering?

Individual Leaders

Individual leaders develop bridging and linking social capital through intercultural and international movement, learning, experiences, and relationships. Overall, the effective leaders we interviewed had extensive inter-ethnic, intercultural, and international experience. Most had lived and/or studied outside their country (in Canada, France, India, Italy, UK, the United States, Brazil, as well as many African countries). Many travel nationally, regionally, and internationally on a regular basis. They overcome distances and differences to expand relational networks.

However, there was variation among the countries. All seven leaders from the CAR, and eight out of the ten leaders from Kenya had acquired part of their training and education outside their own country. Of the six Angolan leaders we interviewed, two had traveled no more than fifteen days in neighboring African countries; three had spent one-and-a-half to six months studying outside Angola (and had also traveled); one had lived and studied eight years in Brazil. The Angolan leaders also had less international and interdenominational social capital. This is particularly true for Protestants. One reason for this is language. Portuguese is less of a global language than French or especially English.

Most Africans know several languages. In addition to a mother tongue (key for bonding social capital), all of those interviewed were fluent in the language of their country's former colonial ruler (which is key for bridging and linking capital). This enabled them to develop social capital across the nation, the region, and the world. Such language proficiency enabled travel, as well as living and studying in multicultural settings. Notably, the majority spent their time overseas in a country where the colonial language was spoken. For example, Kenyans had lived in the United States, UK, or India. Angolans studied in Brazil. The CAR leaders had worked and studied in France, Canada, and other francophone countries around Africa.

Because of the prominence of English in education, and especially Protestant theological education, Kenyan leaders seemed to have more international linking social capital than leaders from Angola or the CAR. And yet a number of those from Angola and the CAR had also learned English, studied in English, or lived in English-speaking countries. For example, Adelaide Catanha has visited Switzerland, the United States, Ghana, South Africa, and Hungary, but has only lived abroad for six months in Kenya while learning English. Even so, after completing her studies in Angola in Portuguese, she studied online for her masters in Spain (Spanish) and the PhD in the United States (English). Speaking the same language as more prosperous British, South African, and North American Protestants makes communication and partnerships easier. It also ensures that such African leaders have a stronger hand when dealing with foreign partners.

Education also plays a key role in developing human capital, as well as bridging and linking social capital. Formal education can expose a person through books, teachers, and fellow students to various people with different perspectives. This develops critical thinking and bridging and/or linking friendships. The very content of education often features cultural and relational skills. Thus, for example, René Malépou of the CAR believes his studies in anthropology have helped him better understand others and prepared him to work with teams and challenging individuals under difficult circumstances—including paternalistic missionaries and pastors fighting for control of limited finances. Similarly, Eunice Chiquete used understandings acquired through missiological studies in Brazil and Angola to be an effective broker who leads across diverse ethnic, denominational, national and socioeconomic lines, and who mobilizes various groups in service of a variety of ministry initiatives. Relationships acquired while in school are sometimes of a linking sort, as when Bosco's former principal helped get him a key job in Mombasa. Not only did many of our leaders study abroad, but many of them studied in African institutions that themselves had global ties. Thus, FATEB, NEGST, and ISTEL all have faculty from abroad, and all have African faculty who have studied abroad. Graduate-level theological education, with its need for libraries, online subscriptions, and computer technology, for example, is always expensive. Almost nowhere on earth are such expenses covered purely through tuition. These African schools thus achieve high-quality educational success in part by cultivating relations with partners abroad who help with educational, technological, library, and other material resources.

Bishop Maisha's ministry benefits from his linking social capital. Having studied in the United States and periodically traveling back and forth, he has built ties with professionals in America and England and has brokered numerous teams of professionals coming to Kenya—doctors, nurses, business people, lawyers, and magistrates. These teams serve in a variety of ways, such as providing medical services or speaking to fellow professionals in hotel venues. When Maisha brought a top police chief to Kenya from the United States, and this police chief offered Kenyan police the opportunity to visit and study in America, this was naturally much appreciated. Moreover, since this visitor explicitly identified himself as Christian when Maisha introduced him to all sorts of high officials, Maisha simultaneously built respect for the impact of his own ministry in Kenya. He developed partnerships in the United States that have enabled him to train church leaders, give scholarships, offer medical care, plant churches, and help orphans and other less fortunate families. In short, Maisha's ministry impact is greatly enhanced by linking social ties both upward and downward.

Similarly, Pastor Oscar Muriu builds bridging and linking social capital. He links partner churches and networks in the United States, Australia, Germany, and India primarily to plant churches together in Kenya and other gateway cities of Africa and to carry out social justice ministries. Nairobi Chapel provides school fees and mentoring for more than three hundred students from poor backgrounds. An assistant pastor has now taken over leading the thousands in the local church so that Pastor Oscar can spend half of his time on travel to connect with global partners and with the sixty congregations that Nairobi Chapel has planted.

Organizations

Effective Christian *organizations* and their leaders also make significant use of linking social capital (as well as bonding and bridging capital), which they use to minister, to build unity and trust, and to access resources: financial, training, skills and advice. They link upward internationally and downward locally to help the less fortunate. St. Martin's has a partner organization in Italy and international interns, but greater influence comes from its thousands of committed local volunteers who work with the marginalized of their communities. In addition to this example, all of the organizations discussed under bridging social capital also pursue linking social capital internationally. For example, CICA and NCCK connect to international bodies like the World Council of Churches (WCC) and to international donors. They also link churches to the government. Government policies have been influenced by the united voice of CICA, NCCK, and the regional Mombasa Church Forum.

We focused our interviews and reports on locally led organizations. Even so, missionaries or other outsiders invested considerable time establishing many of them. Some were international organizations that were founded from outside and retained external connections though they now had local leadership (Campus Crusade, Youth for Christ). Some were still being led by the first African leader they had had, for example, Cheptebo, St. Martin's, Word of Life, Nairobi Chapel, and Tenwek Community Health and Development (TCHD). Others were led by African leaders who had replaced earlier African leaders and thus had long been African led, for example, NCCK, FOCUS Kenya, Scripture Union, and most of the churches. In both cases there tended to be significant ties to international networks and partners. A few were started by locals with good skills at building external connections and trust, such as Alice Kirambi and the Kenyan Christian Partners Development Association. Most of these organizations had long-serving, persevering, committed, trusted leaders who had built bonding, bridging, and linking social capital. Leadership succession is a challenge, including how the successor maintains or develops relational networks and social capital.

TCHD has strong social capital with local communities, churches, the Kenyan government, and international funders. The current Kenyan TCHD leaders praised the previous missionary who trained and worked with them for years, as well as taking each of them on a trip to America to build relationships with donors. While most staff work primarily in the villages, these top leaders spent a majority of their time sharing the TCHD vision with visiting missionaries, emailing reports to sponsoring organizations like Samaritans Purse and PEPFAR (linking up). They have more work now, since they must approach more funders, each of which gives less. USAID was their initial major funder, but they sought other funding agencies because USAID does not allow the use of any of its resources for religious purposes. This conflicted with their own vision of integrating care with Christian faith. TCHD's social capital in the villages also means that villagers often ask newer organizations to cooperate and coordinate with TCHD. Even as they link up and down, TCHD has been putting increased emphasis on encouraging bonding social capital through people-owned processes and working more through churches.

Another pattern is that leaders and organizations serve as brokers, linking people with certain resources to others with needs. These resources or needs may involve deeper understandings of God, literature, education, or a sense of significance/meaning. Non-African missionary founders often used connections from a richer support base back home to benefit the ministry in their new African home, which is what the Italian priest who founded St. Martin's did. However, many of these African leaders use their connections with different people in a richer place to benefit the home area and people where they live and currently serve. For example, Judge Onesmus Makau, and especially his wife, gained international social capital and specific skills while living in the UK. They have used this to start an organization that helps people in their home villages. Her relationships with the women in these groups is equally important (as is the bonding capital between them).

In short, in case after case, we observed that effective African leaders have relationships involving trust and commitment with the local people they lead and serve, as well as with people of other ethnic, denominational, and religious lines. However, it is especially true that these leaders can mobilize joint action on behalf of a vision of the common good, joint action that brings people collaboratively into relationship with one another across marked differentials of wealth, power, and status. It is because of transcendent values that are shared, and because of a sense of partnership in the gospel by the global body of Christ, that these leaders, themselves trusted because of their wisdom and integrity, are able to mobilize and channel significant energy and resources toward the common good. Linking social capital is one essential part of African Christian leadership in the contemporary world.

CONCLUSION

"Invest in Africa! The tigers are now tame, invest in the lions," say the economists. Many have tried to help Africa with donations. Others with more foresight have invested in financial, physical (infrastructure), natural (environmental), human capital (education), and social capital. But of the "big five," the one most valued and used by African leaders and most overlooked by outsiders is social capital. The African Christian leaders and organizations who were studied tend to have modest financial or physical capital but high human capital, and sometimes very high social capital.

African Christian leaders who are recognized to be wise and trustworthy by a wide variety of people are expected to provide leadership and guidance in collaborative endeavors that foster kingdom purposes in Africa. What can we learn from listening to them?

1. *Invest in relationships.* Develop and use bonding, bridging, and linking social capital. Although these easily compete, a complementary combination creates more impact. Investing in family and local churches builds the base and blesses the whole community; however, investing in more difficult bridging and linking social capital is crucial in our divided world.

2. *Invest in human capital through formal education and mentoring.* Make developing social capital a key goal and part of the curriculum. Train in intercultural skills, language learning, and building relationships with those who are different. Such training can help those going from Angola to Brazil, Italy to Kenya, or from a Nairobi slum to the Mombasa coast. It can give skills to relate to paternalistic missionaries or to those from diverse denominations or ethnicities. Encourage study, travel, and ministry in intercultural settings, whether in another nation or in one of Africa's international seminaries. Enable reading and writing through books, email, or social media. There should be no double standard. Both Africans and outsiders need all that is mentioned above. Wuthnow (2009) is right: in our interconnected world, international social capital is important for American and African Christians. We need one another and our shared social capital to build the kingdom of God. We especially need wise linking/bridging people and resource brokers. We need them from every race, nationality, language, and status. It takes many different sorts of links to reach across the immense gaps and disparities in our world.

3. *Invest not only in individuals but in churches and organizations that can create all kinds of social capital.* Strengthen and invest in the bridges and links among these organizations and churches, both nationally and internationally. Language and culture create additional barriers that will take more effort to bridge. We found many links even internationally within Anglophone, Lusophone, and Francophone spheres, but few links between them. Kenyans are much more likely to go to America or Britain than to Angola or the CAR. This leads to significant disparities of social capital. Kenyan leaders had more international linking capital than did leaders from the CAR or Angola. Building linking social capital with Africa's influential Christian leaders and organizations merits investment.

4. *Invest in research.* As anywhere, Africa has its share of ineffective and bad Christian leaders and organizations, as well as good. Research can help ensure that wisdom underpins partnerships. The research methods we used detected and investigated more than fifty amazingly effective and trusted leaders and organizations in three countries. Reports on each of these are now available, and, of course, this book analyzes and presents the results of the research. Expanding this study to the other fifty countries of Africa

could reveal many more locally effective and respected organizations and leaders in which it would be well worth investing.

Without our asking, many interviewees credited the same most important relationship as the main reason for their impact. They gave glory to God. They claimed to be inspired and empowered by Jesus and the Holy Spirit. This research shows that through diverse people God is building God's kingdom and blessing Africa.

REFERENCES CITED

Bayart, Jean-François. 2000. "Africa in the World: A History of Extraversion." *African Affairs* 99/395: 217–67.

Brown, Carl M. 2008. "Friendship Is Forever: Congregation-to-Congregation Relationships." In *Effective Engagement in Short-Term Missions: Doing It Right!* ed. Robert J. Priest, 209–238. Pasadena, CA: William Carey Library.

Cnaan, Ram A. Stephanie C. Boddie, and Gaylor I. Yancey. 2003. "Bowling Alone But Serving Together: The Congregational Norm of Community Involvement." In *Religion as Social Capital: Producing the Common Good*, ed. Corwin E. Smidt, 19–31. Waco, TX: Baylor University Press.

Horsager, David. 2012. *The Trust Edge: How Top Leaders Gain Faster Results, Deeper Relationships, and a Stronger Bottom Line.* New York: Free Press.

Johnson, Todd M., Gina A. Zurlo, Albert W. Hickman, and Peter F. Crossing. "2015. Christianity 2015: Religious Diversity and Personal Contact." *International Bulletin of Missionary Research* 39/1: 28–29.

Lin, Nan. 2002. *Social Capital: A Theory of Social Structure and Action.* Cambridge: Cambridge Univ. Press.

Lindsay, D. Michael, and M. G. Hager. 2014. *View from the Top: An Inside Look at How People in Power See and Shape the World.* Hoboken, NJ: Wiley.

Narayan, Deepa, and Lant Pritchett. 1999. "Cents and Sociability: Household Income and Social Capital in Rural Tanzania." *Economic Development and Cultural Change* 47/4: 871–97.

Priest, Kersten Bayt. 2008. "Women as Resource Brokers: STM Trips, Social and Organizational Ties, and Mutual Resource Benefits." In *Effective Engagement in Short-Term Missions: Doing It Right!*, ed. Robert J. Priest, 209–38. Pasadena, CA: William Carey Library.

Putnam, Robert D. 2000. *Bowling Alone: The Collapse and Revival of American Community.* New York: Simon and Schuster.

Woolcock, Michael, and Elizabeth Radin. 2008. "A Relational Approach to the Theory and Practices of Economic Development." In *Handbook of Social Capital*, ed. Dario Castiglione, Jan van Deth, and Guglielmo Wolleb, 411–38. New York: Oxford University Press.

Wrong, Michela. 2010. *It's Our Turn to Eat: The Story of a Kenyan Whistle-Blower*. New York: Harper Perennial.

Wuthnow, Robert. 2002. "Religious Involvement and Status-Bridging Social Capital." *Journal for the Scientific Study of Religion* 41/4: 669–84.

———.Wuthnow, Robert. 2009. *Boundless Faith: The Global Outreach of American Churches*. Berkeley and Los Angeles: University of California Press.

Zollman, Julie. 2014. "Kenya Financial Diaries: The Financial Lives of the Poor." *FSD Kenya*. http://fsdkenya.org.

Chapter 5

Leadership Responses
during Armed Conflict

Elisabet le Roux and Yolande Sandoua

The experience of violent conflict has been a reality for many countries on the African continent in the past, and several, such as Angola, Kenya and the Central African Republic (CAR), have recent experiences with various kinds of conflict. Angola suffered a prolonged civil war; Kenya has experienced repeated bouts of electoral and interreligious violence; and the CAR is currently in the midst of a serious conflict. In this chapter we focus on the CAR, as it provides a unique and timely opportunity to study how African Christian leaders and organizations are affected by and actively respond to such conflict. The fighting in this country broke out while the ALS research was still in progress, which enabled the researchers to interview many of the same individuals both before and during the conflict.

Some brief background on the conflict in the CAR: The violence that broke out during our ALS research was only the latest in a series of coups and conflicts. Only once did the CAR have a peaceful transfer of power, when it gained independence in 1960 (Herbert, Dukham, and Debos 2013, 2; Carayannis and Lombard 2015). The CAR is a weak state situated in an unstable region. Its concessionary model of politics means that those in power practice exclusionary politics, which makes a lie of dialogue, peace processes, and power sharing (Brown and Zahar 2015, 14; Berg 2008; Zoumara and Ibrahim 2014). Thus, it could arguably have been expected that military opposition to President Bozizé would arise. The Séléka—a coalition of rebel groups—led a violent coup starting in December 2012, which ended with the coalition occupying the capital city, Bangui, ousting Bozizé and installing its own leader, Michel Djotodia, the first CAR leader to come from the largely Muslim northeast (Herbert, Kukham, and Debos 2013, 2–3; Carayannis and Lombard. 2015; Debos 2014). Fighting continued, however, with the Anti-balaka coalition opposing the Séléka. Djotodia resigned and was replaced by Catherine Samba-Panza. Peace has not yet been restored in the CAR.

While our initial ALS research was carried out before the conflict reached Bangui, follow-up interviews were subsequently conducted for purposes of this chapter. These interviews were carried out with the main leaders and organizations targeted in our prior research, but with our focus now on their experiences of, and responses to, the conflict. While we wished to re-interview all leaders and organization staff that we had interviewed the first time around, we were only able to carry out interviews in Bangui, since dangerous travel conditions precluded follow-up research elsewhere in the country. Furthermore, some of the leaders had left the country, and some organizations had closed down. We were able to interview additional leaders to replace those we could not reach.

The following Christian leaders and organization staff were interviewed with a focus on their experiences with, and responses to, armed conflict: Mrs. Marie-Louise Yakemba, a governmental tax inspector who was also involved in two non-governmental organizations, Aglow International and Samaritan's Purse; Dr. David Koudougueret, pastor of the Union Federation of Baptist Churches; Pastor Ferdinand Gregonda, deputy director of Perspectives Réformées Internationales (which has since closed); Mr. Edouard Nvouni, a civil servant and engineer who financially and practically supports various churches; Pastor Rodonne Clotaire, president of the Federation of Brethren Evangelical Churches and also president of GAPAFOD (Action Group for Peace and Training for Transformation), a national NGO. Representatives of several leading Christian organizations were also interviewed, including the managing director of the Voix de l'Evangile radio station; the director of Adonai Mission International (AMI); the director of the Association Centrafricaine pour la Traduction de la Bible et l'Alphabétisation (ACATBA); the coordinator of the Mission pour l'Evangélisation et le Salut du Monde (MESM); the director of the Bible Society in the CAR; and the country director of Campus pour Christ.

In our initial survey the organization that received the highest number of nominations for having the most positive impact was FATEB—The Faculté de Théologie Evangélique de Bangui (Bangui Evangelical School of Theology). Since FATEB subsequently played a central and visible role in Protestant Christian responses to the violent conflict, we chose to focus in some depth on this one organization. The following individuals associated with FATEB were interviewed: Dr. Weanzana Wa Weanzana Nupanga, president of FATEB; Dr. Enoch Tompte Tom, academic dean and director of research; Pastor Matoulou, director of administration; Mrs. Marcelline Rabarieolina, head of the Women's School at FATEB; and Dr. Malépou, a professor lecturing at three graduate schools, including FATEB.

THE RELIGIOUS DIMENSION

In the international press the conflict in the CAR is usually labeled as religious (Onyulo 2015; Vinograd 2015; Al Jazeera and agencies 2015). However, this label oversimplifies and distorts the matter. Understanding the religious dynamic that is present requires an understanding of CAR history.

The precise religious composition of the CAR is contested.[1] However, all agree that the CAR is predominantly Christian, with 10–15 percent of the population being Muslim (Arieff 2014, 2; Brown and Zahar 2015, 15; Kam Kah 2014a, 34). Historically, the northern parts of the country are largely Muslim, and the South, Christian, with rifts between the two (Carayannis and Lombard 2015; Kam Kah 2014a, 34). During the precolonial period Muslim groups raided non-Muslim groups in the South for slaves, resulting in a hostile view of Muslims that lasts until today and which French colonialists tended to encourage (Kam Kah 2014b, 33). Since independence, the Christians in the South have dominated politics, resulting in resentment among many Muslim northerners and the belief that their region is neglected and subject to discrimination (Berg 2008; Kam Kah 2014a).

However, despite the chronic political and economic instability since independence, religion has never been the cause of severe conflict. This is partly because the state has been secular since independence (Carayannis and Lombard 2015; Debos 2014; Kane 2014, 313). However, during President Bozizé's administration religion was used as a political weapon, and the flow of capital and the control of natural resources were directed to the benefit of specific religious groups. Development and the provision of government services were predominantly directed toward Christian communities (Kane 2014, 312). During this period violence against Muslim communities escalated, and anti-Muslim rhetoric was established and maintained by framing Muslims as foreigners (Kam Kah 2014b, 35). The Bozizé administration thus arguably laid the foundation for the religious separatism that ensued from 2009 onward (Berg 2008; Kam Kah 2014b, 35).

It is important to note, however, that the current religious violence in the CAR is not primarily the result of religious differences. The crisis is

---

[1] Some sources argue that indigenous religious groups account for roughly 35 percent of the population; Protestants, 25 percent; Catholics, 25 percent; and Muslims, 15 percent. Other sources argue that the CAR consists of 76.3 percent Christians and 13 percent Muslims. According to the United Nations, 80 percent of the population is Christian. Among these, 51 percent represent Protestant churches and 29 percent, Catholic. The Muslims represent 10 percent, and "animists" another 10 percent (Arieff 2014, 2; Kam Kah 2014b, 34).

indicative of a struggle for political power and also complex tensions over access to and control of resources, control over trade, and lack of national identity (Arieff 2014, 1; Kam Kah 2014b, 35; Boré 2014, 60). Religion has often been used to divide a country for political ends: to either mobilize resistance to political change or to create a movement for such change, or to gain political or economic power (Kasomo 2010, 24; Welz 2014, 604; Zoumara and Ibrahim 2014). For example, following the departure of Hosni Mubarak in Egypt, violence escalated between the Sunni Muslim majority and the Coptic Christian minority. Before Mubarak's ouster, only occasional confrontations occurred. Similarly, the Assad government in Syria used partisan rhetoric to mobilize Syrian Alawite, Druze, and Christian minorities against the mainly Sunni protesters (Kam Kah 2014a, 32).

Religion in the CAR is thus not the source of the conflict, but rather a tool abused by leaders eager for power and spoils (Kane 2014, 314; Welz 2014, 606). The Séléka—often labeled as a Muslim rebel faction—include many nonreligious rebels. More important, only approximately 10 percent of the Séléka are CAR nationals—the rest are from Chad and Sudan (Giroux, Lanz and Sguaitamatti 2009, 13; Kam Kah 2014b, 35). While some of the factions within the coalition state that their goal is to establish an independent Islamic state, the composition of Séléka evidences the error of understanding the conflict and the goals of the movement as primarily religious (Kam Kah 2014b, 35–43).

The Anti-balakas originated as a response to Djotodia and the Séléka coalition that took power in 2013 (Kam Kah 2014b, 36; Vlavonou 2014, 321).The assertion that the Anti-balakas are a Christian response to the Séléka is, on closer inspection, misleading (Tomolya 2014, 466). Anti-balaka ("anti-machete") is a kind of power purportedly bestowed by the charms that hang around the necks of most members (Kam Kah 2014b, 36). While many Anti-balaka members identify themselves as Christian, their featured dependence on traditional animist charms and fetishes distinguishes them from most Christian church attendees. Furthermore, labeling the rebel group as Christian also ignores the fact that many, if not most, of these rebels joined the Anti-balaka for political and economic reasons (Bøås 2014, 4; Giroux, Lanz and Sguaitamatti 2009, 16).

Key Muslim and Christian religious leaders in the CAR decry that the conflict is being labeled religious. Both the Muslim imam and the Roman Catholic archbishop of Bangui publicly oppose the conflict and the religious affiliations attributed to the rebel groups, and passionately plead for religious tolerance. Many religious leaders echo the message that religions should encourage peace, cohesion, and tolerance, and that the current violence is a result of individuals who use religious discourse to further their political ambitions and economic gains (Kane 2014, 314; Kisangani 2015).

It was also the opinion of leaders who were interviewed by the ALS that the conflict did not start for religious reasons. Pastor Rodonne Clotaire argued that it started because of extreme poverty and bad governance. He supported his argument by referring to an NGO project that recruited volunteers to work for approximately five dollars (US) a day. The response was huge:

> Let me tell you that almost all the people involved in the war, carry-ing arms, left their arms to come and work together for survival. The most extreme fighters left their arms where they used to use them, to come and pick up plows and wheelbarrows in order to work. That is to say, this crisis is foremost a crisis of poverty and leadership. In fact, if all these young people succeed in getting jobs, I am sure they will no longer waste their time in armed conflicts.

At the same time Pastor Clotaire recognized that, although the conflict did not start because of religion, it certainly now has a religious dimen-sion. Perceptions have grown that the conflict is a religious one, especially due to media reports, and thus hatred between Christians and Muslims has grown. This perception feeds a cycle of retaliatory violence between Christians and Muslims. On the other hand, in common with other such leaders, Edouard Nvouni is quick to point out that "a true Christian" cannot loot and destroy another's property and states that "these people were not Christians . . . [but rather] bandits that took advantage of the situation to destroy and steal others' belongings."

Many of the key leaders and organizations identified through the ALS are actively addressing the religious dimension of the conflict by emphasiz-ing religious messages of forgiveness and reconciliation and by engaging in interfaith activities. Edouard Nvouni, for example, has counseled young people in his area not to enter the conflict. Pastor Clotaire tells of Christian youth that have lodged Muslims in their houses to save them from being stoned, while Dr. Malépou housed three Muslims himself.

Marie-Louise Yakemba has directly worked with Muslim counterparts for peace and reconciliation between the two faith groups. Both in her NGO work and as part of the Women's Association for Peace, she regularly meets with Muslim women and children. They offer each other mutual encouragement and support, and together they carry out activities in the community. The NGO that she is involved in has also distributed gift boxes to Muslim women and children who have sought refuge at the Central Mosque. Together as Muslims, Catholics, and Protestants, these women are speaking out against the conflict, using various forums, including the radio, to demand that the belligerents stop the hostilities.

Yakemba also actively works for reconciliation between Christians and Muslims through conferences and church services as well as by counseling bereaved families. She shared the following story as an example of the work she now does regularly:

> The Sélékas threw grenades into a church, and four children had their feet blown [off] and amputated. When I went to the hospital to visit them, the doctor told me to work on the parents. He said,

"You who are a Christian, work on the parents of these children to prevent cycles of violence. Because what these children have experienced will continue." An uncle of one of the children became an Anti-balaka because of what happened to his nephew. I ministered to both parents and children, who are now very close to me, and the spirit of vengeance is now going away. The four children with limbs amputated (the youngest nine years old) came to the conference [a conference on reconciliation she organized at FATEB two weeks before the interview] and performed a skit. The one who was eighteen spoke to the people who were there to see what happened to them. He said, "We were also like you, but now parts of our body are cut off. However, we forgive those who did us all that harm." He exhorted the audience also to forgive. It was moving. People in the conference hall cried. The difficult challenge for me is to bring these people to understand that they should let go. They should not exercise vengeance.

Many of these organizations are also involved in interfaith activities. FATEB is part of the Religious Groups Platform, which represents the religious groups of the CAR. The Platform consists of the Catholic archbishop of Bangui, the imam of the Mosque of Bangui, and the president of the Association of Evangelicals in the CAR. In terms of communication with the Anti-balaka, FATEB communicates its ideas and responses to the Platform, which in turn communicates directly with the Anti-balaka and other public groups.

EFFECTS OF ARMED CONFLICT

Armed conflict obviously affects people at the individual level, and Christian leaders are no exception. Pastor Rodonne escaped three kidnappings and was forced to leave his house and seek asylum at FATEB. Dr. Enoch Tompte Tom accommodated family members who were forced to flee other areas in his home, feeding and caring for them while still having to provide for his two sons, who are studying abroad. Dr. Malépou at one point housed seventy-two people, including Muslims.

Caring and providing for others in such circumstances is a heavy emotional burden. Dr. Nupanga, president of FATEB, confessed that he was traumatized by being responsible for the security of the FATEB community and all of the displaced people living there, to the extent that he suffered from insomnia. Mrs. Marie Louise Yakemba was affected similarly when the Anti-balaka killed her nephew. With her family members wanting revenge, she had to counsel them not to avenge the murder, while also having to deal with her own grief.

The conflict has greatly affected the leading organizations identified by the ALS and also the organizations to which the key leaders belong.

The most obvious and direct loss for these organizations has been people. Staff and members have been tortured and died. Pastor Clotaire tells of a bomb that fell on one of his churches on April 14, 2013, killing four people and wounding twenty-seven. In many organizations some staff members have left the country due to the conflict, while others had to be laid off as the organization could no longer afford to pay them. For example, the majority of Campus pour Christ's staff members are now unemployed, while AMI has had to close several mission stations and remove their missionaries.

Significant resources have also been lost. Buildings were destroyed, cars and motorbikes stolen, computers and office supplies looted. The director of Campus pour Christ explains that it lost almost everything: "The furniture, three vehicles, motorcycles, computers, the Jesus' Film equipment, the radio and all the accessories . . . were stolen and the place vandalized." As a result, the group is now in temporary offices located on the FATEB campus, which it is also finding frustrating:

> This forced relocation of the national director of Campus pour Christ in the Central African Republic has had a very terrible impact on our plan of action. The national director shares a small office at FATEB with other services. This change in our initial plan of action has had a negative effect on our lives, institutions, and also churches that are partners of Campus pour Christ.

The financial implications of the conflict have been serious. Many organizations have lost their external funding, with partners refusing or unable to contribute during the conflict, while local financial support has also dried up. The director of ACATBA explains that they have few activities now, as 95 percent of the organization's funding comes from outside of the CAR. Some organizations, such as FATEB, are also facing financial challenges because of the added expenses from their conflict-related humanitarian work. At one point FATEB was accommodating more than two thousand people on its campus and had to provide food, shelter, and support services to all of them.

An obvious result of losing human, material, and financial resources is that all of the organizations have had to cut back on their activities. For example, the Bible Society of the CAR is unable to distribute bibles as planned and has had to limit the number of its literacy classes. FATEB has had to relocate some of its academic programs to Cameroon and has had great difficulty in completing the academic year. Perspectives Réformées Internationale has closed, and GAPAFOD had to suspend the work at its headquarters. Campus pour Christ reports that all its planned projects have failed. ACATBA had ceased its activities in the regions occupied by rebels and is now "forced to stay in one location as if in prison waiting for better days." All of the organizations are frustrated by being unable to implement their planned activities.

RESPONSES TO ARMED CONFLICT

As highlighted in the previous section, the conflict in the CAR, and in Bangui specifically, has severely affected and challenged Christian leaders and organizations. However, the research has also shown that these leaders and organizations have found various positive, empowering responses in this context. The commitment and sacrifice of organization staff and volunteers have been instrumental in enabling positive responses to the conflict. For example, the Voix de l'Evangile radio station's continued existence is due solely to the commitment of its personnel. As the Managing Director explained:

> Talking about material, all the equipment that we have has been provided by us. Every staff person had to bring what they had at home—microphones, cables, and other such items. Even our antennae had not been purchased at the usual price, for a pole costs around 3,000,000 to 4,000,000CFA [approximately US$5,130–$6,840]. In the face of this challenge, the personnel went to the ground and collected iron that served to make the pole. We only paid the manpower with 200,000CFA [approximately US$340].

The director of ACATBA also consistently recognized the commitment of his staff to continuing the work of the organization. Fifty-six of the sixty staff members are still working:

> The people working for ACATBA are not only employees with salaries, but they are first of all missionaries. These are men and women who are committed to the kingdom of God. They contribute to the salvation of souls and the formation of disciples in this country. Therefore, all that happened can be compared to the cross they carry for the realization of this ministry. That is the primary reason the staff is motivated.

Leaders and organizations have responded in various positive ways to the conflict, including humanitarian relief work, partnering with local and international organizations and individuals, carrying out new training and teaching, and engaging in peacebuilding activities, which have resulted in an increase in social cohesion and a deepening of faith.

Humanitarian Responses

Various organizations are involved in humanitarian response activities. Dr. Malépou reports that a Baptist mission station in Bambari sheltered nine hundred people. He had the opportunity to leave the country but refused because he was concerned about the Christians that he would leave behind. Thus, he chose to "suffer together with others, and the Lord has been sustaining us so far." Adonai Mission International has supported widows and has continued with the construction of a school in the hills of the Ndri people. Both the Bible Society and ACATBA launched seminars on healing from trauma. The Bible Society reports that this intervention has been very well received. The Bible Society has also distributed food provided by the Barnabas Fund (an organization based in the United States).

The humanitarian response launched by FATEB was the most comprehensive of all the organizations that we examined. In a very practical way the seminary engaged in humanitarian aid. This was not planned, but came about as a result of the geographic location of FATEB, the secure nature of the campus itself, and the fact that it is a highly respected institution, well-known throughout the CAR.

FATEB was founded in 1977 by the Association of Evangelicals in Africa, to equip men and women for church ministry in central and west francophone Africa. It is often recognized as the leading evangelical post-secondary theological institution in French-speaking Africa. Strategically located in Bangui, its alumni serve in all seventeen sub-Saharan French-speaking countries. The importance and significance of FATEB was implicitly recognized when Pope Francis included a visit to FATEB in his twenty-six-hour visit to the CAR in November 2015 (Sherwood 2015). His address to the evangelical community took place at FATEB.

Figure 5–1. Pope Francis Standing next to Dr. Nupanga Weanzana,
President of FATEB

Displaced people came to FATEB because it is located within a fairly safe area that had less fighting than the rest of Bangui. Furthermore, the entire campus is fenced and has security guards. Thus, people simply came, begged to be let in, and FATEB responded to their cry for help. Not only did FATEB allow people into the compound, but it also provided housing, counseling, and food.

Dr. Tompte Tom was responsible for managing these refugees. He set up a team of people to assist him, and he also consulted with the displaced themselves to see what services and help they required. Regarding housing, all of the classrooms were occupied during the night, with ten to twelve people per classroom. Tents, donated by the Danish Refugee Council, were also set up. FATEB staff who lived on campus took people into their homes. Food was provided, first by FATEB, and later on by international aid organizations, including Tearfund, World Vision, and World Food Program. The Red Cross provided medical support by sending first-aid workers, as did JUPEDEC (a local NGO), which sent medical doctors to give children vaccinations and to provide mosquito nets. Regarding counseling, Dr. Tompte Tom trained his own team members, emphasizing that they must listen rather than ask questions, as traumatized people need to express what happened to them. Spiritual support was also provided in the form of prayer sessions and Sunday services for the displaced. As of December 2015, many of the displaced were still living at FATEB. As Dr. Nupanga explained, "[We] need to recognize that FATEB has become an asylum."

Partnership Activities

As FATEB's humanitarian response highlights, partnerships have been key to enabling leaders to respond positively to the conflict. Various local and international NGOs assisted FATEB in responding to the needs of the displaced that were housed on campus. The conflict situation also allowed FATEB to form new partnerships, in this case with World Vision and Tearfund, and it expects this development to offer other significant long-term opportunities. Other organizations' partnerships have also been key for them to provide humanitarian relief. For example, GAPAFOD, through funding from the Agency for Public Interest Works (a CAR government agency), has been able to provide work and income for 718 youths. Other organizations, such as Campus pour Christ and AMI, have been able to continue their work due to financial support from their international partners. It is also important to note that partnerships with local institutions and individuals have been as important as those with international organizations. The Voix de l'Evangile radio station explained that local pastors have been its biggest supporters:

Our great help and relief during these times of crisis came from pastors that God had set aside for us. The radio station has been working mostly with men of God who believe that God is present and that he has the power to do anything to honor his name. These men of God never cease to give me a piece of advice as the director and also to all the personnel.

Dr. Nupanga emphasized that the conflict also made them recognize the depth and strength of their relationships with their existing partners: "Another positive impact is that FATEB also realized how much its partners were really with her during this difficult period. Some partners reacted spontaneously to send money to buy food; but more importantly, they covered us with their prayers." Many of the other organizations also commented on the importance of partners' prayers. Campus pour Christ, ACATBA, AMI, and Voix de l'Evangile all stated that they relied on partners' emotional support. Pastor Sana of AMI explained: "God did not leave the Central African Republic alone. Many Christians abroad manifested their support through prayers, words of encouragement, phone calls, and emails."

Training and Teaching Initiatives

The conflict has created opportunities for some organizations to engage in training. As mentioned earlier, both the Bible Society and ACATBA are presenting seminars on trauma healing, while Campus pour Christ has facilitated seminars on social cohesion with high-school teachers, university staff, faith leaders, and youth leaders.

FATEB has responded to the conflict by increasing and diversifying the training that it offers. Marcelline Rabarioelina, head of the Women's School at FATEB, explained that the conflict has forced them to reevaluate the ways they have run the school in the past and to become more innovative. For example, while the school used to be exclusively for the wives of the students enrolled at the seminary, it has now been opened to all women from the city. This is a very positive development, as it is now able to train many more women and have more influence in the community.

FATEB itself has always had a Pan-African mandate and vision, but now it has responded to the conflict by accelerating its plans for campuses in other countries. FATEB's Cameroonian campus was opened earlier than planned, and the opening of a Kinshasa campus is now an even greater priority. By having these out-of-country campuses, FATEB can continue teaching even if conflict disrupts the Bangui campus.

Peacebuilding

Leaders and organizations are also actively engaging in peacebuilding. As referred to earlier in the chapter, Marie-Louise Yakemba is involved—

through various NGOs and her personal efforts—in promoting peace, especially through interfaith dialogue. She feels a calling to this, even if it is very challenging and, at times, disheartening work:

> When the events began, especially with the arrival of the Anti-balakas, I was the one on the forefront to speak about peace. Speaking about peace with Catholic and Muslim women and my family was very encouraging to me. Sometimes fear was there. My family told me to be careful. I told them that what I was doing, I was doing it for the glory of God. And if I don't do it, who will? My family could only encourage me and pray for me to continue.

GAPAFOD has been promoting peace through more indirect means. It has been putting stickers in taxis and buses. These stickers proclaim local quotations and proverbs that promote peace, such as "We want peace," "No more war," and "Let's mobilize for peace." Pastor Clotaire said that the feedback has been very positive:

> The feedback from our friends the taxi drivers, and from the inhabitants of different neighborhoods, is really positive. These writings have provoked dialogues among passengers along the way and have allowed some to contribute by giving a piece of their mind on solving the issue of peace in the Central African Republic.

Ulrich Marida, the managing director of Voix de l'Evangile, stated that the radio station is also promoting and building peace. He explained that a radio station has considerable power in a nation. Therefore, he believes that these messages are making a difference:

> We used our power to work on the conscience, the mind, and the hearts of people. The priority today is, first of all, to disarm the hearts, before thinking of a physical disarming and an eventual demobilization. We have integrated into our radio program a civic-oriented broadcast on unity and concord, often emphasizing the Word of God. Even though we are a new radio station, we can assure you that the radio is gaining momentum within the capital, and the echo is quite promising.

Another way in which peace is promoted is through leaders' and organizations' engagement with political and rebel leaders. Dr. Malépou once preached for political officials and Anti-balaka leaders, and once for political officials, including President Catherine Samba-Panza. Campus pour Christ, the Bible Society, ACATBA, and AMI have interacted with Anti-balaka, often evangelizing them. However, Pastor Sana of AMI feels that such work usually has no effect on the rebel group as a whole, because the rebels that the organization interacts with are not the ones with power.

It is thus difficult to engage in constructive discussions on the restoration of peace because they are simply intermediaries.

Social Cohesion

The conflict has also allowed for the development of greater social cohesion within Bangui. Local partnerships have taken the lead in contributing to social cohesion. With FATEB becoming a refuge for the whole city, its relationships with churches were strengthened. Dr. Nupanga argued that "FATEB was the only place where churches, denominations, and congregations could meet and discuss the life of the church." This has meant that the conflict has allowed FATEB to become closer not only to different churches but also to the community in general. Through mutual prayer and encouragement, the sense of community, as well as trust and confidence in one another have been strengthened.

Within FATEB as an organization, the conflict has also led to an increased sense of unity and cohesion. Pastor Matoulou feels that the FATEB staff reacted to the conflict, and the resulting influx of people and responsibilities, in a stellar fashion. This, he argued, is because staff has been acting as a unit and was always willing to listen to instruction. This has meant that the staff has been able to implement all the directives from the administration quickly. The ability to handle these challenges has, in turn, strengthened the sense of being a cohesive team.

Marcelline Rabarioelina affirmed that the conflict has led to increased social cohesion. Through mutual encouragement, especially through prayer, people have supported one another. She feels that in such crisis contexts, unity and community with others are very important. The importance of social cohesion for surviving conflict, and, in turn, the fact that conflict provides an opportunity to develop cohesion, have been the greatest lessons that she has learned.

Due to the conflict, greater interconnection and unity have developed among many churches. Pastor Clotaire explained that in areas where there are many displaced people or areas where churches have been forced to close due to the conflict, people of different denominations are worshiping together. Churches in the CAR tend to protect their denominational borders jealously, and, therefore, this has been an amazingly positive outcome.

As leaders, we have mandated our church leaders in the provinces lodged among the displaced people to collaborate with other religious confessions nearby. As a matter of fact, in the East and Northeast of the country, precisely in the cities such as Bria, Bambari, Batangafo, where all churches are closed, the communities there practiced a kind of ecumenism to keep up their faith. Such a thing is never common in the Central African Republic since we know that our communities are usually narrow-minded, but during the crisis a reconciliation took place and still continues with a very comforting testimony.

Faith Enhancement

The conflict appears to have brought a new awareness of the importance of prayer. In discussing how they were (and are) able to survive the conflict and its resulting challenges, all of the leaders stated that prayer has been their lifeline. Marcelline Rabarioelina stated that, for her, "prayer was of great comfort. Individual prayer, prayer with the team and with other groups was truly one of the first solutions to all of our problems and also in my leadership." This was echoed by Pastor Matoulou and Dr. Tompte Tom. Praying by themselves, with family, friends or colleagues, as well as the prayers of family and friends outside of the CAR, supporting partner organizations, and the faith community in general is what has sustained these leaders and their ministries.

The power of these prayers is testified to by the fact that FATEB was never infiltrated by any rebel groups, and no buildings were damaged. Only one roof sustained slight damage from bullets. FATEB's staff firmly believe that it is God who prevented any campus destruction. In the words of Pastor Matoulou: "When the conflict started, we can assert that FATEB was jealously protected by God. No one was kidnapped or was a victim of pillage, or of any violence. Even our families were protected."

In this way the conflict has enriched FATEB staff's relationship with and experience of God. Dr. Nupanga stated:

> The situation in Bangui allows us to have a good experience with God. We saw how God was really the one who protected us at a moment where there were no police and army; only God protected us. The situation strengthens our confidence in God.

Some of the leaders argue that these renewed and enriched experiences of God are one reason why God allowed the conflict. Dr. Malépou argues that the conflict in the CAR was God's will. As the director of the Bible Society explains, during a crisis people seek God. Thus, the conflict is actually an opportunity for the Bible Society. Pastor Sana, Prophet Wato, and the Director of ACATBA all argue that the conflict is thus actually a good thing, as it awakens people's consciences and leads them back to God.

CONCLUSION

This conflict in the CAR is the latest in a national history that is rife with armed responses to political opposition. However, this conflict is arguably different because it is seen, both locally and internationally, as having religious roots, at least in part. Nevertheless, the religious interpretation is arguably one that has been given after the fact. What originally started as a fight for power and resources is still that, but now it has the added firepower of religious rhetoric and interpretations.

Many faith leaders are working hard to denounce acts of revenge and retaliation and to promote interfaith dialogue and tolerance. On the one hand, this can be seen simply as a way of trying to end the conflict; on the other hand, it can be interpreted as a concerted effort to counter the religious dimension of the conflict. The conflict in the CAR remains, at heart, however, one that is grounded in a battle over power and resources. While the efforts of Christian leaders are much needed and laudable, it is important to note that ending the conflict will also need to rely on finding fair and just means of administering resources. This was not voiced explicitly as a central concern by those we interviewed, although, to be fair, our interview protocol failed to probe explicitly the issue of fairness and justice in governance. Thus, we unfortunately are unable to describe with confidence the extent and the ways in which these leaders might be actively working to address structural issues of fairness and equal access to resources.

The continuing conflict in the CAR is placing a significant strain on the work of the Christian leaders and organizations that the ALS has identified as being influential. Individuals, as well as organizations, have suffered considerable reductions in material, human, and financial resources. Individuals are emotionally drained and traumatized by what they are experiencing. Organizations are frustrated by being unable to implement their planned and mandated activities.

Nevertheless, despite these trying circumstances, leaders, as well as organizations, are responding in many new and positive ways. Leaders, as individuals, are sharing their meager resources and risking their own safety by housing displaced people, including Muslims. Organizations such as FATEB are doing great humanitarian work—housing, feeding, and keeping safe thousands of displaced people. In assisting the displaced population, organizations are assisted by existing and new partners, which provide food or other needed resources. These partnerships provide not only material provision but also emotional and spiritual support. For these leaders and organizations words of encouragement and prayer sustain them, providing strength to continue.

The conflict has also created other opportunities to serve. Organizations are offering new kinds of training or are making their existing training available to other groups and in other settings. They are also engaging in peacebuilding activities.

Unexpectedly and somewhat paradoxically, the conflict has allowed for the development of social cohesion, at least among some groups within Bangui. FATEB has become much more connected to churches and to the Bangui community in general by providing refuge to individuals and organizations. By working together to face various challenges, the staff and volunteers of different organizations are also becoming more interconnected. Churches are becoming more ecumenical, allowing for more cohesion among Christians as a faith group.

The conflict has allowed for an enrichment of faith and relationship with God. In such vulnerable situations leaders have been forced to rely fully on God, and this has led to a deepening of their relationship with God. This is arguably also why so many interpret the conflict as being in the will of God.

Thus, we learn much from looking at how Christian leaders and organizations from the CAR are responding to armed conflict. While such conflict is needless, horrific, and unwanted, good can—and is—coming from it. Through these willing and committed individuals and organizations, excellent work is being done.

REFERENCES CITED

Al Jazeera and agencies. 2015. "CAR's Bangui Tense as Communal Strife Kills Scores." http://www.aljazeera.com.

Arieff, Alexis. 2014. *Crisis in the Central African Republic.* Congressional Research Service.

Berg, Patrick. 2008. The Dynamics of Conflict in the Tri-Border Region of Sudan, Chad and the Central African Republic." Washington DC: Friedrich Ebert Foundation.

Bøås, Morten. 2014. "The Central African Republic—A History of a Collapse Foretold?" The Norwegian Peacebuilding Resource Centre.

Boré, Henry. 2014. "Did You Say, 'Central African Republic'?" *Air and Space Power Journal* 4: 57–67.

Brown, Michael J., and Marie-Joëlle Zahar. 2015. "Social Cohesion as Peacebuilding in the Central African Republic and Beyond." *Journal of Peacebuilding and Development* 10/1: 10–24.

Carayannis, Tatiana, and Louisa Lombard. 2015. *Making Sense of the Central African Republic.* London: Zed Books.

Debos, Marielle. 2014. "'Hate' and 'Security Vacuum': How Not to Ask the Right Questions about a Confusing Crisis." *Cultural Anthropology.* http://production.culanth.org.

Giroux, Jennifer, David Lanz, and Damiano Sguaitamatti. 2009. "The Tormented Triangle: The Regionalisation of Conflict in Sudan, Chad, and the Central African Republic." Center for Security Studies, ETH, and Swisspeace. Working Paper no. 47. http://eprints.lse.ac.uk.

Herbert, Siân. Nathalia Dukham, and Marielle Debos. 2013. *State Fragility in the Central African Republic: What Prompted the 2013 Coup?* Rapid Literature Review. Birmingham, UK: GSDRC, University of Birmingham.

Kam Kah, Henry. 2014a. "History, External Influence, and Political Volatility in the Central African Republic (CAR)." *Journal for the Advancement of Developing Economies* 3/1: 22–36.

Kam Kah, Henry. 2014b. "Anti-balaka/Séléka, 'Religionization,' and Separatism in the History of the Central African Republic." *Conflict Studies Quarterly* 9: 30–48.

Kane, Mouhamadou. 2014. "Interreligious Violence in the Central African Republic: An Analysis of the Causes and Implications." *African Security Review* 23/3: 312–17.

Kasomo, Diane. 2010. "The Position of African Traditional Religion in Conflict Prevention." *International Journal of Sociology and Anthropology* 2/2: 23–28.

Kisangani, Emizet F. 2015. "Social Cleavages and Politics of Exclusion: Instability in the Central African Republic." *International Journal of World Peace* 32/1.

Onyulo, Tonny. 2015. "Christian-Muslim Conflict in the Central Africa Republic Has Refugees Afraid to Leave Camps." http://www.washingtontimes.com.

Sherwood, Harriet. 2015. "Pope Francis Visits Besieged Mosque in the Central African Republic." http://www.theguardian.com/.

Tomolya, János. 2014. "Crisis in the Central African Republic: Is It a Religious War in a Godforsaken Country or Something Else?" *Academic and Applied Research in Military Science* 13/3: 457–76.

Vinograd, Cassandra. 2015. "CARCrisis: UNICEF Says Teens Were Targeted in the Central African Republic." http://www.nbcnews.com.

Vlavonou, Gino. 2014. "Understanding the 'Failure' of the Séléka Rebellion." *African Security Review* 23/3): 318–26.

Welz, Martin. 2014. "Briefing: Crisis in the Central African Republic and the International Response." *African Affairs* 113/453: 601–10.

Zoumara, Babette, and Abdul-Rauf Ibrahim. 2014. "Genesis of the Crisis in the Central African Republic." http://www.pambazuka.net/.

Chapter 6

Word and Deed—Patterns of Influential African Christian Organizations

Nupanga Weanzana

Organizational support is a key element in fostering the training and development of leaders, but organizations also play another crucial role: They provide the institutional framework within which successful leaders accomplish important goals. For this reason it was important that the ALS project include a central focus on Christian organizations.

In our research we asked 8,041 African Christians to identify a "Christian organization, program, or initiative" that they felt had an unusually positive impact in their local area or region (see Appendix B, Q.56). Respondents provided the names of hundreds of organizations. In Kenya the top three answers were World Vision (191), Compassion International (55), and the Red Cross (44). In Angola the top three answers were Mocidade para Cristo—Youth for Christ (57), DASEP—Departamento de Assistência Social Estudos e Projectos (35), and Associação dos Escuteiros de Angola (34). And in the Central African Republic (CAR), the top three were FATEB—Faculté de Théologie Évangélique de Bangui (186), Caritas (185), and Campus pour Christ (161).

We chose initially to consider only the twenty-five organizations in each country that were listed most frequently. It was not possible to do an in-depth study of each, so we worked to filter our lists and carefully select a smaller number that we could focus on in greater depth. Some of the named organizations (such as USAID, the Red Cross, or AMREF Health Africa) did not have explicitly Christian identities and thus did not fit our intended focus. Our questionnaire had asked respondents to provide additional information on each organization, including the focus and nature of its work, and contact information for organization leaders. Respondents also evaluated each organization using a four-point Likert scale (from 1 = "Not at All" to 4 = "Very Much") in terms of the extent to which the organization trains leaders, works wisely in the local context, has a good reputation locally, receives strong support from local churches, and allows women to participate in leadership.

Our senior research team in each country used this information to select a subset of key organizations for further qualitative, follow-up research. Since our focus was on African Christian leadership, we were particularly interested in organizations that were African led, and in studying organizations that were not already well-known internationally. Thus we chose not to do follow-up research on some of the frequently listed and prominent international organizations such as Caritas, Compassion International, and World Vision, which were more likely to have already been studied at length by others (see, for example, Bornstein 2005). We made full use of the information we had collected on each organization to select a subset for follow-up research. We took into account frequency of mention and ratings on various criteria, and also attempted to select a wide range of organization types across different geographical regions. Practical considerations such as the cost of travel for interviewers and whether leaders were available to be interviewed also affected the final selection.

For each organization selected, one to six taped interviews were conducted with organization leaders, and these interviews were subsequently transcribed. Supplementary print information about each organization was also collected. A report following a pre-established protocol was prepared on each of the organizations listed below. Table 6–1 includes information on (1) how frequently each organization was named as having most impact, (2) its rating on the extent to which the specified organization trains leaders, and (3) a composite rating for each (based on the extent to which they have a good reputation locally, whether local churches are supportive of their work, and whether they are felt to work wisely in the local context). Ratings ranged from 1 to 4, with 4 being the highest possible. This research on these specific organizations underpins this chapter.[1]

This chapter draws from interview data on the above thirty-two organizations and seeks to identify several attributes of these organizations that led others to evaluate them as particularly effective. Despite their geographical distance from one another and the very different nature of their activities, there are a couple of broad patterns that most or all seem to share.

POSTCOLONIAL IDENTITY

During the colonial period there were few opportunities for Africans to develop African-led organizations. The Christian organizations that did exist often reflected colonial patterns, with expatriates in leadership. After

---

[1] For the full report on each organization, see www.AfricaLeadershipStudy.org.

Table 6–1. Christian Organizations with Impact

Angola				
Organizations with Impact	**Men-tions**	**Trains Leaders**	**Composite Rating**	**Year of Origin**
Conselho de Igrejas Cris-tãs em Angola (CICA)	25	3.54	3.33	1977
Departamento de As-sistência Social Estudos e Projectos (DASEP)	35	3.53	3.45	1991
Formação Feminina (FOFE)	28	3.05	3.03	2010
Instituto Superior de Teolo-gia Evangélica no Lubango (ISTEL)	11	3.91	3.64	1981
Mocidade para Cristo (Youth for Christ)	57	3.29	3.23	1993
Mulher da Igreja Evangé-lica Reformada de Angola (MIERA)	9	4.00	3.69	2006
CAR				
Adonai Mission Interna-tional	110	3.73	2.99	1996
Ambassade Chrétienne (Radio Evangile Néhémie)	148	3.36	3.12	2001
Association Centrafricaine pour la Traduction de la Bible et l'Alphabétisation (ACATBA)	22	3.48	3.04	1993
Campus pour Christ	161	3.73	3.30	1987
Faculté de Théologie Évangélique de Bangui (FATEB)	186	3.87	3.48	1977
Mission pour l' Évangélisa-tion et le Salut du Monde (MESM)	32	3.35	3.22	1997
Perspectives Réformées	62	3.75	3.27	2002/ 2007

Kenya				
Organizations with Impact	Men-tions	Trains Leaders	Composite Rating	Year of Origin
Bomaregwa Welfare Association	6	4.00	3.83	2010
Cheptebo Rural Development Centre	10	3.25	3.46	1986
Christian Partner's Development Agency	6	3.83	3.61	1985
CITAM (Christ Is the Answer Ministries)	7	3.29	3.70	1959/ 2003
Daraja La Tumaini	15	3.62	3.44	2006
FOCUS Kenya	21	3.89	3.54	1958/ 1973
KSCF (Kenya Students' Christian Fellowship	17	3.86	3.38	1959
Kwiminia Community Based Organization	13	3.62	3.35	2006
Magena Youth Group	16	3.20	3.47	2006
Mombasa Church Forum	10	3.10	2.85	2010
Mothers' Union	24	3.63	3.52	1918
Narok Pillar of Development Organization	11	3.80	3.56	2000/ 2010
NCCK (National Council of Churches of Kenya)	10	3.87	3.61	1966/ 1984
Redeemed Academy	29	3.69	3.60	1996
Scripture Union	32	3.55	3.51	1967
St. Martin's Catholic Social Apostolate	21	3.50	3.55	1997
Tenwek Community Health & Development Programme	13	3.25	3.19	1983
Transform Kenya	15	3.93	3.72	2011
Word of Life	18	3.50	3.40	1971

independence these older structures were often rightly seen as problematic, both because their power structures were not appropriately supportive of African leadership, and because they often had an overly narrow focus on spiritual and religious goals to the exclusion of a more encompassing vision of human flourishing. With independence, initial optimism related to social change focused primarily on new governmental structures. But as political leaders and structures failed to deliver on the promise of a better life (Gifford 1998, 2, 4), it became increasingly common for Africans to found new non-governmental organizations in response to pressing needs. Often African Christians were the ones who developed and led these new organizations.

A majority of the organizations identified as impactful that we studied were either founded after independence or were significantly transformed and reinvented after independence. Only the Anglican Mothers' Union (1918) of Kenya appears to have been organized and retained its identity and organizational structure since colonial days. The three countries where we carried out research gained their independence at different times. The CAR gained independence from France in 1960, while Kenya became independent from the United Kingdom in 1963. Angola gained independence from Portugal in 1975. Most of the influential Christian organizations were founded after the year of political independence, although many have roots in an earlier period. In many respects these three countries can be thought of as representative of much of Africa politically, linguistically, and culturally.

Few respondents named an expatriate missionary organization—such as Africa Inland Mission or World Gospel Mission—as top organizations with impact, even where such organizations have focused extensively on health or education, and even where they have had a long history and continuing presence of missionaries in the country. At the same time, many of the organizations that were named, even if founded post-independence, were nonetheless indebted to such earlier organizations. For example, Tenwek Community Health and Development (TCHD) was founded in 1983 in the context of initiatives supported by the World Gospel Mission. Cheptebo Rural Development Centre (1986) was developed with initial support from the Africa Inland Mission. In Angola, the denomination Igreja Evangélica Reformada de Angola was founded by Archibald Patterson in the 1920s. By 1956, initiatives and efforts to organize women were present, but it was not until 2006 that these prior initiatives finally culminated in the fully official and organized women's society—Mulher da Igreja Evangélica Reformada de Angola. Again, the Kenyan Alliance of Protestant Missions (1918) was a group of expatriate missionary societies that gradually transitioned to include Kenyan churches. Eventually (1966), a new organization was formalized whose constituent members were Kenyan churches, not missionary societies. It is known today as the National Council of Churches of Kenya (NCCK). In the current NCCK, expatriate leaders of expatriate organizations no longer exercise decision-making power, as was the case under the earlier Alliance of Protestant Missions, but rather Kenyan leaders of Kenyan churches. This history represents a common pattern for these organizations.

It should be recognized that several of the organizations listed above, such as Daraja La Tumaini, Word of Life, Mocidade para Cristo, Campus pour Christ, and Perspectives Réformées, are country-specific branches of international organizations. These country-specific branches were founded after independence, and all have local leadership. Thus, they at least partly reflect postcolonial patterns. They also reflect patterns forged in distant places and mandated from abroad. As local branches of international organizations, they often experience significant constraints on local flexibility and decision making. The Kenyan director of Word of Life, for example, openly stated that foreigners had established and mandated patterns that reflected their cultural biases and blind spots, and this created significant challenges for him in his leadership role in the Kenyan context. In the same way that medical instructions sometimes caution, "Do not give the medicine prescribed for you to other persons, even if their symptoms appear similar because it may harm them," organizational structures designed in response to one social context do not automatically work well when exported to a different context—and may even be harmful. Of course, these international organizations allow varying degrees of local flexibility.

Even though only a minority of the above organizations are a local branch of an international organization, they all exist in a globally connected world characterized by great differences of wealth and poverty. As Bowen and Rasmussen demonstrate in Chapters 7 and 4, respectively, the leaders of this kind of organization achieve success, in part, through global social ties and shared resources. And this, of course, leads to other challenges related to interfacing with donors and donor values.

A majority of the organizations listed in Table 6–1 are African led with African identities. For example, FATEB was planned and founded in 1977 by the Association of Evangelicals in Africa with the vision that this seminary would provide quality theological education in Francophone Africa. From the beginning the vision emerged from African theological leaders, and for most of its history it has been African led. Many of the above organizations, from the Mombasa Church Forum to Redeemed Academy, were founded long after independence with African vision and leadership from the very beginning. A variety of African leaders, male and female, young and old, achieved leadership success through organizations that they founded or led. When we asked respondents to name leaders with the greatest impact, these were frequently named.

Most of these organizations exemplified not only postcolonial leadership patterns but also strong grassroots support. They mobilized significant local participation and backing and reflected a communal vision rather than the vision of a solitary individual, a local vision rather than that of distant foreigners. The Mombasa Church Forum was very responsive to local interreligious and political dynamics. Magena Youth Group mobilized youth on behalf of those around them. FOCUS Kenya masterfully drew from its alumni across the country and in different walks of life to mentor students and provided internships in a wide variety of jobs. St. Martin's Catholic Social Apostolate regularly mobilized over a thousand local volunteers to help with programs for those with disabilities or HIV/AIDS and to work for peace.

BROADENED VISION OF HUMAN FLOURISHING

In an earlier era, missionary organizations in Africa often prioritized literacy and basic education, and sometimes had medical ministries. Occasionally, missionaries played significant roles in fighting social injustice (Thompson 2002). Recent research has demonstrated that "conversionist Protestant missionaries" historically had a significant, positive impact on broad social good (Woodberry 2012). And yet it is also true that missionaries in this era often justified educational and medical emphases, or other social involvement, as adjuncts to the true priorities of evangelism, church planting, and church leadership development. Spiritual ends and social welfare were sometimes seen as competing and alternative priorities, rather than as fitting together within an encompassing vision of human flourishing.

People in many African cultures, however, reject any dichotomy between so-called spiritual and physical or social needs. For many Africans the presence of God in their midst should be manifest in a concern for human flourishing that includes health, peace, security, and prosperity.

And yet, during the period of late colonialism and early independence, many Christians in the West, and to some extent in Africa, continued to frame spiritual ends and social welfare as competing and alternative priorities. Christians often insisted that one must choose between prioritizing evangelism or prioritizing social action. An initial turning point for evangelicals came with the 1974 Lausanne Congress on World Evangelization, which affirmed that "word and deed" must go together, that along with gospel communication there must be a concern for social justice, reconciliation, and liberation from oppression. While some continued to use the metaphor of "the seed and the fruit" to suggest the priority of evangelism, Christians increasingly affirmed that the dichotomy between word and deed was not helpful. Finally, in a 1983 consultation of the World Evangelical Fellowship in Wheaton focused on the church in response to human need, a clear statement by an international evangelical body insisted that the dichotomy be rejected. Paragraph 26 of the *Wheaton 1983 Statement* declares: "The mission of the Church includes both the proclamation of the Gospel and its demonstration. We must, therefore, evangelize, respond to immediate human need, and press for social transformation" (Samuel and Sugden 1986). In recent decades holistic or integral mission that brings word and deed together has become the norm for most evangelicals, as evidenced in *Cape Town 2010*.

A majority of the African-led Christian organizations that we examined combine an emphasis on evangelism and Christian witness with a broad range of concerns related to human flourishing. Mocidade para Cristo in Angola focuses on youth evangelism as well as social ministries involving cleanup campaigns, food relief, a hospital, and a psychiatric and rehabilitation center. Association Centrafricaine pour la Traduction de la Bible et l'Alphabétisation (ACATBA) in the CAR focuses on Bible translation along with literacy and community development. Daraja La Tumaini in Kenya combines evangelism with different social ministries aimed at poverty alleviation, counseling, entrepreneurship, and microfinance.

Even organizations that began with a primary focus on evangelism or "word-based" ministries have clearly expanded to combine word and deed. Adonai Mission International in the CAR was founded as a mission organization focused on evangelism and church planting (word). But as it worked with girls whose poverty pressured them into prostitution, the organization broadened its focus to include job and skills training for these vulnerable girls. The Scripture Union in Kenya began with a focus on reaching children and teenagers through biblical literature. However, as it cared for these children and teenagers, their vulnerability to HIV/AIDS became clear, and Scripture Union responded by developing a social ministry focused on HIV/AIDS prevention and intervention. For most of the organizations that we examined, evangelism that proclaims salvation through Jesus Christ was not abandoned, but rather accompanied by social concern for the people to whom the gospel is preached.

Many of the most influential Christian organizations were either founded or revised as a faith-oriented response to very specific local needs. A chance encounter with Thomas, a person living with disability and locked away for his whole life, introduced Father Pipinato to the plight of people with physical challenges in Nyahururu. The need to care for the physically challenged thus became the initial animating vision for founding St. Martin's Catholic Social Apostolate. Interreligious violence and political conflict in Mombasa, Kenya, were the realities that a group of pastors worked to address through their formation of the Mombasa Church Forum. Formação Feminina (FOFE) was founded to educate girls in the context of a war-torn country where girls often had limited opportunities for education and training. Cheptebo Rural Development Centre in the Kerio Valley (Kenya) works to help people deal with insufficient rainfall in this arid and semi-arid region. Through irrigation and agriculture training it improves people's lives by meeting specific needs. Additionally, organizations with prior history revised their priorities in response to the human needs that they encountered. Ambassade Chrétienne in the CAR developed a program to provide professional computer training to teenagers in a country that had a 60 percent unemployment rate. ACATBA prioritized literacy in a country where the rural population is largely illiterate. As a theological seminary, FATEB represents a quintessential "word-based" ministry. And yet, in response to recent crises in the CAR, it has provided protection and care for refugees, leadership in peace initiatives, and training for trauma care. (Chapter 5 herein provides an extended analysis of FATEB's ministry in this crisis.)

Finally, these organizations were largely community based. The focus was not on individuals' well-being in isolation from the community. Rather, individuals were treated within the community context with the goal of flourishing in community. Culturally, this matches the communal characteristic of most African societies, as exemplified in the African ideal of *Ubuntu*—"I am because we are." Without compromising the personal nature of salvation, individuals are always located within their community. The transformation of the whole community was a priority for many of these organizations.

Furthermore, the most influential Christian organizations receive their "moral" support from the community through the contributions and participation of individuals or groups. In the case of Cheptebo Rural Development Centre, the local community gave fifty acres of land to the Centre, clearly showing its perception that this Centre was serving the community. Other organizations reported high numbers of volunteers helping carry out their program. TCHD in Kenya reports receiving 70 percent of its support from the local population, which enables their various schools and health centers to function. These two aspects of community-based organizations are essential for organizational impact and influence. The organization does not pursue the well-being of one individual or one group, but rather the well-being of the entire community. The community needs to achieve some sense of ownership of the organization through direct or indirect involvement in the management and financial support of the organization.

In short, the organizations we examined combine word and deed. They stress reconciliation with God and also with each other. They stress the flourishing of the community. A broad and contextually responsive vision of human flourishing helps define the focus of many of these organizations.

CONCLUSION

This chapter identifies two broad attributes of the organizations we studied. They are characterized first by postcolonial identities and patterns, and second by a broadened vision of human flourishing. This does not mean that there are no lingering legacies of colonialism or new forms of neocolonialism that should be recognized and resisted. Nor does it mean that the holistic mission that characterizes so much of the work of these organizations is always fully balanced with adequate theological underpinnings. While this chapter has stressed that these organizations are contextually responsive to human need, the fact that such organizations often require financial support might also imply that they must be responsive to donor concerns. And naturally this raises other sorts of possible issues (see Chapter 7).

In a globally connected body of Christ, where there are major economic disparities across the world, clearly it will be important for African Christian leaders and the educational institutions that train them to continue to grapple with healthy postcolonial leadership patterns in the modern world. And in a world where Christians are engaged in a broad range of areas focused on human flourishing, it will be important that Christian pastors and theologians adequately underpin this with theological foundations. Seminaries and Bible schools in Africa must not simply replicate the curriculum found in Western theological education, but they must integrate those topics and disciplines (including the social sciences) that will help church and organizational leaders to engage knowledgeably and wisely their own contexts. The curriculum must strengthen the two wings of mission, underpinning ministries of both word and deed. That is, Christians must be trained to articulate the Christian faith and to act wisely in a wide variety of arenas related to human flourishing.

Christian organizations must combine word and deed. They must ensure that theological as well as contextual knowledge underpins the assessments of local needs and prioritized responses. They must work within partnerships that respect the local community and its leaders. Unhealthy colonial or neocolonial leadership patterns must be rejected. Improvisational efforts to address human need must be supported by theological insight and local research. Every project should be anchored in the community and should serve individual as well as communal ends.

The growth of Christianity in Africa has sometimes been characterized as "a mile wide and an inch deep." Africa has often been portrayed as a dark continent without hope, as exemplified in *The Economist's* 2000 cover story entitled "The Hopeless Continent" (May 11). And yet such perceptions are changing, as seen in *The Economist's* 2011 (December 3) cover story entitled "Africa Rising," and repeated in a cover story with the same title in *Time* magazine (December 2012). This chapter reports on the changing face of newly formed or reenergized Christian organizations that are balancing word and deed, presenting the message of the gospel and meeting the needs of the people. This is the new face of a successful Africa and a successful church.

REFERENCES CITED

Bornstein, Erica. 2005. *The Spirit of Development: Protestant NGOs, Morality, and Economics in Zimbabwe.* Stanford, CA: Stanford University Press.

Gifford, Paul. 1998. *African Christianity: Its Public Role.* Bloomington, IN: Indiana University Press.

Samuel, Vinay, and Chris Sugden. 1986. "Evangelism and Social Responsibility: A Biblical Study on Priorities." In *Word and Deed: Evangelium and Social Responsibility* (1986): 199–202.

Thompson, T. Jack. 2002. "Light on the Dark Continent: The Photography of Alice Seeley Harris and the Congo Atrocities of the Early Twentieth Century." *International Bulletin of Missionary Research* 26/4: 146–49.

Woodberry, Robert. 2012. "The Missionary Roots of Liberal Democracy." *American Political Science Review* 106: 244–74.

Chapter 7

African Christian Organizations and Socioeconomic Development

Michael Bowen

How can religious institutions contribute to the promotion of socioeconomic development? In their contribution to the common good, Christian organizations do not exist in a vacuum. Even on the level of religious expression, they are part of a wider group of institutions known as faith-based organizations (FBOs). Julia Berger (2003) defines FBOs as formal organizations whose identity and mission are derived from the teachings of religious tradition and which operate on a nonprofit basis to promote articulated ideas about the public good at different levels. FBOs are often connected with the faith community through personnel and have religiously oriented mission statements (Wuthnow 2004, 2009). Clarke and Jennings (2008) offer a broader definition of an FBO as "any organization that derives inspiration for its activities from the teachings and principles of the faith."

According to Pew (2010), the majority of people in sub-Saharan Africa identify themselves as adherents of Christianity or Islam, and approximately 75 percent of Africans trust their religious leaders. These findings indicate opportunities to leverage the influence of religious leaders and religion in promoting socioeconomic development.

The Millennium Development Goals succinctly articulate the purposes of socioeconomic development: to eradicate extreme poverty and hunger; achieve universal primary education; promote gender equality and empower women; reduce child mortality; combat diseases; and ensure environmental sustainability, among others. This chapter focuses on some of these and derives its themes from the Millennium Development Goals.

In our research we asked over eight thousand African Christians to identify the African-led Christian organizations that they felt were having the most impact on their communities. Based on the frequency with which respondents listed them, we identified several dozen organizations as having significant positive impact. From these, we selected thirty-two for follow-up research, carrying out interviews with leaders and collecting supplementary online and print information on each. One of these organizations (BWA) turned out not to be faith based. Another (CITAM) was more a church than an FBO, and research on a third (FATEB) was not available until after this chapter was completed. Of the remaining twenty-nine, five focused exclusively on spiritual matters, while twenty-four (82.8 percent) focused on one or more socioeconomic concerns. This chapter focuses on those twenty-four organizations.

Our interview data indicates that over half of these FBOs (54.2 percent) provide health services with the same percentage providing income/employment generation services, and also education and leadership development, which, for purposes of this chapter were included only if the education and leadership development focused more broadly on social and/or economic arenas rather than purely spiritual areas. One-third include a central focus on environment and/or agriculture. A smaller number (17.2 percent) prioritize community water provision. Nearly half (45.8 percent) of the FBOs prioritize other social services such as peacebuilding, gender equity, good governance, human rights, service to the vulnerable such as the physically challenged and elderly, drug-abuse awareness and support, training in life skills, or involvement in politics.

Most FBOs that we examined do not limit their focus to a single socioeconomic area. Out of the twenty-four FBOs with a socioeconomic focus, twelve focus on three or more distinct areas. This focus on multiple areas of service may be due to the complementarity of the activities or to the need for a broader scope and impact. Alternatively, this pattern may also be responsive to the expectations of those that fund the FBOs.

OPPORTUNITIES AND ADVANTAGES
IN SOCIOECONOMIC DEVELOPMENT

Christian organizations are moral institutions that foster socioeconomic development. Over time, such organizations earn the trust of communities based on past performance and the teachings and practices arising from their faith. The faith motivation of these FBOs is a driving force in carrying out their development activities and is a response to Jesus Christ's command to serve others, especially the poor and disadvantaged.

Hefferan, Adkins, and Occhipinti (2009) are of the view that Christian organizations bring a distinctive perspective to development by adopting a philosophical approach and contextualizing poverty within religious frameworks. These organizations perceive development as saving people in line with biblical teachings, which goes beyond merely saving them from poverty to saving souls and promoting human dignity. For Christian-based organizations, therefore, development goes beyond material conditions of poverty and extends into the spiritual dimension.

Furthermore, Christian organizations have some advantages over other institutions in bringing about development. Some of these advantages include the ability to mobilize local communities and resources at the lowest level of society. Such organizations often have local and international networks that give them an edge in development activities. Another key opportunity for Christian organizations that engage in socioeconomic development is the trust that society has in them. Such trust is normally earned over a period of operation. Their grassroots presence is another distinct advantage. This enables them to identify accurately community needs and propose appropriate interventions. Below I present each of these distinct advantages, beginning with literature from other scholars and supporting it with data from the Christian-based organizations that we researched.

Mobilization

Christian-based organizations can mobilize resources and operate even at the lowest levels of society with strong links to the grassroots (Lunn 2009). They can mobilize adherents, including those who may feel estranged from secular development programs. An example, in this case, comes from the data collected from one of the organizations. St. Martin's Catholic Social Apostolate is a grassroots religious organization that was established in 1999 near the town of Nyahururu to mobilize and train communities to support vulnerable people in their midst. It started with a program for persons living with a disability. Then it expanded by starting a program for needy children, such as those living on the streets. It expanded yet further with a community program for active nonviolence and human rights advocacy, moving on to develop programs for HIV and drug abuse, and finally, creating a savings and microcredit organization in 2002. St. Martin's focuses on building the capacity of community members so that they can adequately care for the vulnerable among them. The organization enlists and trains over one thousand volunteers annually; they form the core of the community workforce. The St. Martin's approach concentrates on involving the community in finding solutions.

Networks

Many FBOs have an already established long-term presence in communities, giving them knowledge of local contexts and networks. FBOs normally enjoy good domestic and international networks, drawing on the structures and linkages of the religious community to which they belong.

Organization	Health	Environment and Agriculture	Income Generation and Employment	Education and Leadership Development	Water Provision	Other Social Foci
ANGOLA						
Conselho de Igrejas Cristãs em Angola	√			√		√
Departamento de Assistência Social Estudos e Projectos	√			√		√
Formação Feminina	√		√	√		
Instituto Superior de Teologia Evangélica no Lubango				√		
Mocidade para Cristo	√	√				
Mulher da Igreja Evangélica Reformada de Angola	√			√		
CAR						
Adonai Mission International			√	√		
Ambassade Chrétienne (Radio Evang-ile Néhémie)	√		√	√	√	
Association Centrafricaine pour la Traduction de la Bible et l'Alphabétisation				√		√
Campus pour Christ	√			√		√

KENYA							
Cheptebo Rural Development Centre	√	√	√		√	√	√
Christian Partners Development Agency	√	√	√		√	√	√
Daraja La Tumaini			√		√		
Kwiminia Community-Based Organization	√	√	√		√		√
Magena Youth Group			√		√		√
Mombasa Church Forum					√		√
Mothers' Union of Kenya	√				√		
Narok Pillar of Development Organization	√						
National Council of Churches of Kenya			√	√	√		
Redeemed Gospel Academy				√			
Scripture Union							√
St. Martin's Catholic Social Apostolate	√				√		√
Tenwek Community Health & Development		√	√		√	√	
Transform Kenya				√			√
TOTAL	**54.2%**	**33.3%**	**54.2%**	**54.2%**	**54.2%**	**20.8%**	**45.8%**

Table 7–1. Socioeconomic Services Provided by Each Faith-Based Organization

They may also be able to draw on this network for funding and fundraising, making them less donor dependent than other NGOs (Leurs 2012; Pereira, Angel, and Angel 2009). These organizational strengths mean that FBOs can often be uniquely effective on the ground.

An example of an organization with such network strengths is the National Council of Churches of Kenya (NCCK), which has a one-hundred-year history in Kenya. NCCK has sought to make the lives of Kenyans better through programs in the areas of advocacy, justice and equity, poverty alleviation, political mediation, education, and constitution making. This ecumenical organization brings together twenty-seven Protestant member churches, nine fraternal member churches, and six parachurch organizations. NCCK has both national and international partners and networks—some of which are very influential in terms of finances and intellectual resources. These include the East Africa Venture Company, which was incorporated jointly with the Christian Council of Tanzania to publish two Christian newspapers; and the Small and Micro Enterprise Programme (SMEP), NCCK's microfinance organization, which has received recognition and support from USAID. Other NCCK networks and partners include the Christian Churches Educational Association, Christian Health Association of Kenya, Christian Student Leadership Centre (Ufungamano House), Kenya Ecumenical Church Loan Fund, Public Law Institute, and St. Paul's University in Limuru. NCCK is also a member of the All Africa Conference of Churches (AACC), an ecumenical fellowship of churches and institutions working together for the common witness of the gospel. NCCK has a list of about thirty donors; it includes World Vision, the World Council of Churches, UNHCHR, UN Women, USAID, Diakonia, and German GTZ. Given this significant array of global and local networks, NCCK can effectively draw on financial, technical, and human resources to carry out its mandate, even at local and grassroots levels.

Trust

Christian organizations are often trusted and perceived as legitimate and honest (Rivlin 2002). Like the NCCK, CICA (Council of Christian Churches in Angola) is an umbrella organization for many Protestant denominations that has acquired trust as a result of its efforts to bring about a peaceful Angola. During the war in Angola, CICA joined forces with other religious institutions for peacebuilding. CICA wrote guidelines to prepare leaders and communities for the 1992 elections and also prepared a document for peace and conflict resolution. The CICA guidelines and documents were widely used, and their broad acceptance built trust among various political leaders.

NCCK uses the trust it has with the government of Kenya and the public to influence decision makers (including but not limited to politicians) on matters of ethical and democratic governance and policy formulation. Over the years, NCCK has carved out a niche as a respected advocate on behalf of Kenyan citizens on issues of national interest, such as political transitions, insecurity, and the national economy. NCCK played a significant role in contributing to change management in Kenya for the transition toward multi-party politics. This was done through quiet diplomacy and press releases.

Faith Motivation

Christian organizations as part of the broader group of FBOs are seen to have a commitment to serving communities based on their faith motivation (Occhipinti 2013). Consequently, they can tap into and draw on the religiously based commitment and enthusiasm for serving individuals and communities that many people have. FBOs are perceived as distinctive by scholars and donors not only because they draw on shared spiritual and moral values, but because they influence institutions that instill values, such as schools and families (Leurs 2012; Berger 2009). This was seen in the vision and mission of various Christian organizations we examined. For example, the vision of Perspectives Réformées Internationales (International Reformed Perspectives) in the Central African Republic (CAR) is to help men and women be true disciples of Christ, actively engaged in their local churches, and able to influence positively their social environment. In line with its vision and mission, this organization has the following ministries: radio programs, evangelistic crusades, and discipleship programs, all aimed at bringing people to Christ and affecting their lives in a positive way. There is a clear connection between faith and social influence in this organization's vision. A similar vision is seen in the Instituto Superior de Teologia Evangélica no Lubango (ISTEL) in Angola. Its vision is to have trained leaders—servants and disciples—who live and teach sound doctrine, and promote leadership, unity in diversity, and social engagement. ISTEL seeks integrated education where knowledge, character, and abilities are formed for the betterment of society. The outcome has been that many former students of ISTEL are assuming roles of senior leadership in their denominations and communities. Its social engagement is clearly informed by faith grounded in sound biblical doctrine. All the Christian organizations that we examined connect their faith motivation with their engagement in socioeconomic activity.

Grassroots Presence

FBOs often are characterized by independence, flexibility, and creativity (James 2009). This enables them to provide efficient development services, to reach the poorest at the grassroots level, to carry out their work with long-term objectives, and finally, to elicit motivated and voluntary service that encourages civil society advocacy. Religious organizations are often seen as responsive to local needs, flexible, honest, and promoting the development of social capital.

The Kenyan Christian Partners Development Agency (CPDA) exemplifies an organization that has strong grassroots support and mobilization. CPDA was formed by a group of Christians to deal with the effects of drought in Eastern Kenya. It grew from a Christian-based organization in 1985 to an NGO in 1993, with priorities beyond the original focus but based on the needs of the people. Specifically, CPDA has a gender-and-governance program that prioritizes gender concerns within a broader focus on enhancing participatory governance at local and national levels through improved mechanisms and by strengthening the capacities of grassroots communities. Such mechanisms include the strengthening of neighborhood assemblies that act as forums where the community comes together to deliberate on problems and propose solutions. CPDA also has a youth-empowerment program that focuses on governance and leadership development, capacity building for participatory governance, and civic and voter education. All this is carried out at the grassroots level using the participatory development model.

SOCIOECONOMIC AREAS OF IMPACT

The various organizations we examined prioritize several areas of socioeconomic focus that include health, education and training, income-generation activities and employment, poverty reduction, environment and agriculture, and water. These are discussed below.

Health

The World Health Organization (WHO) estimates that 30 to 70 percent of the healthcare infrastructure across the African continent is owned or run by FBOs (WHO 2007). The first census in Africa on the not-for-profit healthcare sector conducted by Uganda in 2001, for example, showed that 70 percent of all private not-for-profit health facilities in Uganda are owned by autonomous dioceses and parishes (Ministry of Health/Uganda Catholic Church 2001). A random sample of government and church dispensaries and health centers in Tanzania showed that church dispensaries provided higher-quality curative care and delivery services, whereas the government dispensaries offered higher quality health education and immunization services to women and children (Gilson et al. 1995). These statistics attest to the important role that Christian organizations play in the field of health.

The data collected from the interviews highlights a Christian organization that is carrying out innovative and extensive health programs in rural Kenya. Tenwek Community Health and Development (TCHD) is a pioneering community-based organization (CBO) that has been in operation since 1983. It is an outreach arm of Tenwek Hospital, earlier registered as a FBO and initiated by the World Gospel Mission in 1961. TCHD was formed in response to an increase in preventable diseases. At the time of its formation, 80 percent of the people visiting the hospital suffered from diseases that were preventable. The organization was formed to implement a community health strategy. Each administrative location was divided into three sub-locations where a husband and wife team were trained for three weeks to provide health services within their village as community health helpers. The mode of operation for each helper was to serve three days each week and reach twenty households under the motto "prevention is better than cure."

The vision of TCHD is to empower communities to be able to identify and address their health needs. Its mission is to serve Christ by facilitating change through community-based health care and appropriate development within needy communities. The organization has expanded by building strong relationships with communities, churches, and other stakeholders such as government departments. In geographical scope the program has expanded into a leading development agency in the South Rift Valley, covering Bomet, Kericho, Narok, Transmara, and Nakuru counties.

TCHD offers various programs including maternal-and-child health care; HIV/AIDS prevention and treatment; food security; and water, hygiene, and sanitation activities. The project has encouraged residents to undertake income-generating activities mostly related to nutrition, that is, kitchen gardens, dairy production, and poultry raising. Bio-sand water filters are also provided in the communities along with construction of twenty-five thousand rainwater tanks and spring-protection activities. The food-security program is enhanced through community food banks. The organization partners with communities for post-harvest food storage and storage of food received from the government. During lean times this stored food is sold to traders at a profit. The organization also runs a dairy-goat project.

Key achievements include a 90 percent reduction in disease incidence, immunization of children and antenatal care through mobile clinics, improvement in nutrition and reduction of nutrition-related infections by 90 percent, and expansion from one to five counties. TCHD has provided a model for other churches. The following churches have adopted this model: Africa Inland Church, Catholic Church, Deliverance Church, Seventh Day Adventist Church, and Full Gospel Church of Kenya. TCHD has spearheaded a people-owned process. It has managed to reach marginalized areas and trained between thirty and thirty-five community leaders in each village. Currently, TCHD has seventy staff, with some of the leaders having served for thirty years.

TCHD has also been able to prevent dependency through community development and gainful-employment projects. Currently, 70 percent of funding is provided by the local community, with TCHD only offering 30 percent of financial support for water and food security projects. In most projects TCHD only assists the community in capacity building. Since 2011, the communities where TCHD operates have been able to develop and own nearly ten projects worth US$690,000. The projects include dispensaries and schools.

Other Christian organizations providing health services include CPDA, Kwiminia CBO, and Narok Pillar of Development Organization, to mention a few. Their activities range from combating HIV/AIDS to creating awareness of and educating on various diseases, sanitation, nutrition, and involvement in health-policy generation.

In our research on Christian organizations deemed to be having an important positive impact, thirteen are involved in health programs. Of these, seven (54 percent) specifically provide services in the field of HIV/AIDS. This emphasis reflects the seriousness of the HIV/AIDS problem in Africa. It further shows that Christian organizations have risen to this challenge and are addressing the problem.

Education, Training, and Leadership Development

Woodberry (2004) points out that education leads to human-capital accumulation, which directly contributes to greater economic growth and development. The value of education has been recognized by many Christian organizations. When the first Christian missionaries came to Africa, they got involved either directly or indirectly in educational projects. The first major impact of Christian activity in sub-Saharan Africa was the introduction of formal education and literacy (Okpala and Okpala 2006). According to Jack Goody (1968), once literacy is introduced into a traditional society, changes occur in thinking patterns that modify the socioeconomic status of the whole society. In sub-Saharan Africa the adult literacy rate stands at 59 percent, with the youth rate at 70 percent (UNESCO 2013). Much work remains in the education sector in Africa.

Data collected from our survey suggest that many Christian organizations are extensively involved in the education sector. That is, indigenous Christian organizations have built on the foundation laid by earlier missionaries and replaced missionary-led educational organizations with African-led ones. For example, Cheptebo Development Centre, one of the Christian organizations we examined, has, in conjunction with the Ministry of Education, sponsored annual motivation talks to national-examination candidates. This sponsorship has reportedly brought about measured improvement in academic performance. Using funding from partners, Cheptebo Development Centre assists in paying school fees for needy students within the community. It also provides university students with internship opportunities in the area of dry-land agriculture and is in the process of starting a college specializing in dry-land farming.

Another example is NCCK, which has established village polytechnical schools that provide skills training to young people who drop out of school. NCCK also offers education scholarships, with more than five thousand students benefitting directly from the awards.

The Redeemed Academy is a school founded by the Redeemed Gospel Church in Ukunda, Mombasa, Kenya. Its primary purpose is to provide low-cost, high-quality education for the local community. It provides education from nursery school to high school for 350 children, at least half of whom are Muslim. The school also provides scholarships for needy high-school students.

Ambassade Chrétienne in the CAR helps youth to obtain professional skills such as computer training, with 232 people trained to date. This FBO also donates computers to schools. CICA in Angola trains personnel in administration, finance, and literacy, while the Department of Social Assistance, Studies, and Projects (DASEP) of the Evangelical Congregational Church in Angola has constructed two boarding schools. Additionally, the Women of the Reformed Evangelical Church of Angola seeks to motivate women to join literacy programs.

In Angola, the organization Formação Feminina trains girls (and more recently boys also) in the area of agriculture, embroidery, decoration, cooking, and home education. The youth are trained in home economics to become productive people in their communities.

Clearly, most of the Christian organizations that we examined have a deep involvement in education matters in their respective countries. This involvement spans the educational spectrum from basic to higher education as well as skills and capacity building.

Income Generation, Employment, and Poverty Reduction

Christian organizations have come to be an integral part of the social reality in Africa, with significant impact on development. Ellis and Ter Haar (2007; 2004) have argued that religion "now forms the most important connection" that "sub-Saharan Africa [has] . . . with the rest of the world." Religion is a central element in the thinking of most Africans, and it is increasingly evident in the public realm and politics. Understandably, attention has been drawn to the need to consider the future of development in Africa within the scope of a wider shift from a narrow economic paradigm to something broader that includes spiritual and religious dimensions.

"Historically, religious groups have provided social services and other community development activities which promote community empowerment" (Littlefield n.d.). FBOs, therefore, are not new in the realm of development. They have been important actors in the social, economic, and political life of developing countries since the colonial period, when they provided educational and health services in conjunction with colonial governments.

The World Bank now recognizes that the war against poverty cannot be won without looking at the spiritual dimension and its many manifestations in religious institutions and movements (Marshall and Keough 2004). The 1995 Beijing Platform for Action (as cited in James 2009) recognizes that religion plays a central role in the lives of millions of women and men. This has led to a positive reassessment of the role of faith in development.

The Nigerian experience has shown that FBOs are important agents of development in Africa (Olarinmoye 2012). Their scope and programming flexibility inspire trust among the communities in which they operate. The state requires the support of FBOs, given the various challenges it faces. Cooperation between the state and FBOs is needed for effective delivery of programs to ensure that development takes place.

The Cheptebo Development Centre runs a conference facility that was built in 1997. It generates funds to run the center and its activities. The center has a capacity of one hundred beds and two conference halls. There are currently thirty-two employees. These employees have several dependents who benefit from the employment created by the center. Additionally, CPDA has empowered youth to be self-reliant and engage in entrepreneurial ventures in Vihiga County. Another Christian organization (Daraja La Tumaini) has established a microfinance scheme that helps its members with startup loans for small businesses. Many local people have started small businesses in slum areas as a result of this endeavor.

Women in the Anglican Mothers' Union form cooperative societies where members support one another in development. The Mothers' Union has presented proposals to donors such as Act Alliance, Action Aid, and World Vision. Funding from these sources is used to improve living standards. Many branches of Mothers' Union have also built parish halls that are hired for a fee, thus generating income. The Mothers' Union has also built Bishops Towers in Nairobi, a building that houses the national office and generates income by leasing office space to many companies.

NCCK has made the lives of Kenyans better through a number of programs. One is SMEP, which is NCCK's microfinance organization. In 2010, SMEP was licensed by the Central Bank of Kenya as a nationwide deposit-taking microfinance agency. Currently, it is being groomed to grow into a full-fledged bank. SMEP is presently running an annual budget of US$22,988,505. NCCK also owns properties in prime locations that include hotels and office space in major towns in Kenya. These properties bring a combined annual income of about USD 6,896,551, allowing

NCCK to employ thousands of Kenyans. Similarly, St. Martin's Catholic Social Apostolate started its Community Program for Savings and Micro-Credit in 2002.

Ambassade Chrétienne in the CAR seeks to alleviate poverty by training women; three thousand had been trained at the time of this research. The organization has created approximately 352 women's associations that manage income-generating micro projects.

Environmental Conservation and Agriculture

According to the 2012 report of the Africa Society, environmental problems constitute one of the key challenges on the African continent in the twenty-first century (Chukwunonyelum et al. 2013). The quality and richness of terrestrial, freshwater, and marine environments have been polluted. Environmental problems have been made worse by rapid population growth, urbanization, energy consumption, overgrazing and over-cultivation of lands.

Chukwunonyelum et al. (2013) suggest that "the environmental crisis facing the African continent is increasingly seen as a crisis of values, and religion, a primary source of human values . . . critical in the search for sustainable solutions." They note that the environment has been created by God to serve our present and future needs and that environmental destruction is partly a result of greed among the ruling elites.

In Africa, Christians are concerned about the environment (Conradie 2007) and ground this concern in a theology of "creation care." However, poverty is a hindrance to environmental conservation. For most of the poor, environmental conservation is seen as a hobby of the rich for their own aesthetic purposes. The rich are sometimes seen as more concerned about environmental resources such as wildlife than about the welfare of human beings. The concern of the poor is that attention to environmental issues will divert resources away from more pressing human needs. This tension needs to be managed.

The literature on environmental concerns sometimes states that religious actors are uninvolved in environmental conservation. However, the All Africa Conference of Churches and some of its member regional councils have hosted several environmentally themed conferences in recent years and have posted a number of declarations (AACC, n.d.). The conference maintains a thematic unit called Climate Change and Care for Creation. This emphasis is fully grounded in Christian theological commitments.

The data collected from the interviews in this study reveal a number of organizations involved in environmental conservation. One of these is the Cheptebo Rural Development Centre located in the Kerio Valley of Elgeyo Marakwet County of Kenya. The place is semi-arid, with poverty levels well over 60 percent. The center has created demonstration units specifically related to environment and agriculture. The concept is that community members will come and learn from the demonstration units within the center and then go back and implement the same technologies on their farms. The center created demonstration units in the following areas: dairy cow and goat units, dry-land farming techniques, drip irrigation, tree nurseries with certified fruit seedlings, beekeeping, orchard farm, poultry unit, conservation agriculture, and greenhouse technology. Cheptebo Development Centre has provided quality seedlings to the community around it. The center has had an impact on people far and wide, with seedlings being sold as far away as southern Sudan.

As a result of the center's demonstration farm, a good number of households have planted mangoes and other fruit trees and receive significant income from these ventures. The area is now greener. As more people grow fruit trees, this will likely change the microclimate within this region. Other households now keep dairy cows and milk goats that are of significant help in pulling the community out of poverty. The number of churches has also increased, as well as membership in those churches.

Water Provision

Allen, Davila, and Hofmann (2006) report that there is a remarkable gap between the poor and the rich in their access to water services. Carrying out a study spanning five cities in the developing world, they found that the poor suffer severe deprivations of water services. This relegates them to alternative water systems that are not safe in terms of health. Some FBOs examined in this study have stepped in to fill this gap and provide water for livestock, crops, and people, especially the poor.

CPDA, one of the FBOs studied, focuses on improving water and sanitation within the communities where it operates. It achieves this through partnering with the population in the promotion of water sanitation and access to clean and safe water. From 1997 to 2009, CPDA constructed over 120 water tanks, protected over 400 springs and constructed 174 latrines to support water and sanitation in Vihiga and Kakamega counties in Kenya. From 1998 to 2003, CPDA supported the construction of fifty shallow wells, eleven water tanks, fifty water troughs for livestock, and ten hand pumps in Machakos County.

Kwiminia CBO constructed thirteen sand dams in 2006 and another thirteen in 2007–8. The group has constructed a total of ten sand dams and has also donated twenty-eight water tanks to schools. TCHD's water programs include the provision of clean drinking water, sanitation, and hygiene. It has provided bio-sand water filters to the community and has constructed rainwater catchment tanks that hold twenty-five-thousand liters of water. It has also protected community springs from pollution. Ambassade Chrétienne in the CAR has dug a water borehole that provides clean water to three thousand people in the community, thus preventing water-borne diseases.

TYPOLOGY OF CHRISTIAN-BASED ORGANIZATIONS

According to Hefferan, Adkins and Occhipinti (2009), there are six ways of categorizing organizations in terms of faith: faith permeated, faith centered, faith affiliated, faith background, faith secular partnerships, and secular. This categorization represents a continuum beginning with those said to be faith permeated to those professing no faith at all (secular). Alternatively, these same authors propose typifying FBOs based on the following aspects: self-description, whether the founder was religious or not, whether staff or volunteers must profess the faith, the source of funding, faith practices within the organization, faith content of the program, and faith symbols. Most of the organizations examined were very clear about their Christian foundations, with a few changing their vision and mission over time. None of the organizations examined claims to be secular, though a few have non-Christian staff. Most of the Christian organizations receive support from and partner with institutions that are not necessarily Christian.

There are many ways to assess the expression of religion related to the provision of social services. Researchers define the span of religious emphasis among FBOs to understand the role of religion as a component of services offered by FBOs. The various typologies share many commonalities with three major assessment categories: expression of religion (see preceding paragraph), organizational control, and program implementation. of religion, and program implementation. Organizational control is examined through funding resources, the religiosity of participants, and definition of outcome measures. Program implementation is examined through the selection of services provided, the integration of religious elements into service delivery, and voluntary or mandatory participation in specific religious activities within the organization and decision-making processes.

The data collected from the interviews shows that the board composition and staff for the organizations we examined in the CAR and Angola are Christian. In Kenya the organizations show a slightly different picture, with four organizations having either boards or staff that are not exclusively Christian. These organizations are CPDA, Kwiminia CBO, Narok Pillar of Development, and TCHD. For example, Narok Pillar of Development reports that some staff are not Christian, but all board members are. Further, the vision and mission of these organizations are more exclusively social compared to those whose board and staff are entirely Christian. Another observation is that those organizations whose boards and staff are not exclusively Christian have an array of international and national secular and Christian donors. The challenge with having powerful non-Christian donors is that their funds come with conditions, and some of these may run counter to the aspirations of a Christian organization, such as winning converts.

TENSIONS AND CHALLENGES IN SOCIOECONOMIC DEVELOPMENT

Maintaining religious identity in the face of powerful secularizing forces is a challenge for Christian organizations (Occhipinti 2013). An organization's mission and vision help maintain a religious identity as well as serving the important function of attracting and motivating employees and volunteers. Religious identity of employees should be nonnegotiable as a way to resist secularizing pressures. Networking among similar organizations with the same beliefs who perform similar work in different locations helps organizations reinforce religious identity through regular contact and interchange of people and ideas. Employees and volunteers express religion through daily activities, and the culture they create can, in turn, influence the sponsoring religious organization. Flexibility and adaptation are very important for organizational survival; however, this flexibility and adaptation can result in organizations retreating from their religious identity.

Two organizations run by the same person, Cosmas Maina, exemplify the tensions present as Christian organizations work with communities. Cosmas Maina works with drug addicts to help set them free from their addictions. To interface with two different sets of stakeholders, he has registered two parallel organizations that serve the same at-risk population: Teens Watch and Set the Captives Free. Teens Watch is a CBO that utilizes peer educators to raise community awareness on harm reduction in areas such as drug abuse, alcoholism, and prostitution. It is not an explicitly Christian organization. And yet Cosmas Maina is convinced that Jesus and the resources provided in the gospel and through the church play a strategic role in turning around the lives of addicts. And so he uses a completely separate and explicitly Christian organization called Set the Captives Free to come alongside these same addicts and provide them with spiritual nurture and care. With the two separate organizations Cosmas can mobilize resources from diverse religious and secular sources and can manage resources separately in ways that are congruent with the nature and values of donors and also foster the well-being of addicts.

Teens Watch has received funding from one non-Christian international organization. The employees and volunteers from Teens Watch move through the streets of Mombasa, Kenya, very early in the morning to locate people on drugs. The employees and volunteers do not preach to these drug addicts, because they are not allowed to do so openly with the funding they receive; the drug addicts have the option of visiting Set the Captives Free where they are taught the word of God. Under Teens Watch the employees go out and supply clean syringes, condoms, and lubricants to sex workers. They also talk to people about sexual and reproductive health and have had the chance to speak to girls who were engaging in bestiality as well as homosexuality. They also reach out to sex workers. They try to counsel them besides giving them money for upkeep.

This particular case is in some senses unique, but it is responsive to tensions that most of these Christian organizations face. On one hand, they would like to serve the community; on the other hand, they do not have the resources. They then approach organizations for support, not all of which are sympathetic to the faith component of their work, and this may actively discourage them from bringing their faith into their service. This tension may be felt not only from donors but also from those being served, who may not be Christian. The expectations of Christian supporters may also complicate matters. Offering condoms and clean syringes may be seen by some Christians as not an acceptable way to serve the community. In fact, churches in Mombasa have refused to cooperate with Teens Watch for this very reason. These are the tensions that Christian organizations will continue to face, and they will need help to navigate these challenges.

CONCLUSION

The data from this study show that most of the FBOs which have a significant impact on the public good also have a socioeconomic purpose. In part because of their spiritual orientation, these organizations are uniquely motivated and positioned to care for societal needs. Indeed, most of these Christian organizations offer health services, income and poverty alleviation programs, education and training, and/or environment and agriculture programs. Half of the Christian organizations interviewed focus on three or more areas of the social economy.

Some of the Christian organizations have forged very close links with government and other agencies in their areas of activity. This creates synergy and ensures broader program acceptance and effectiveness. It is also noted that Christian organizations do not only serve Christians but serve people from other faiths as well.

A number of these organizations evidence an amazing capacity to mobilize people to work and achieve their objectives, with one local organization mobilizing more than one thousand volunteers on a continuous basis. Such organizations have been able to train and motivate these volunteers to provide various services for free. The faith motivation seems to be a key aspect of these volunteers. Many of these organizations have forged wide and deep networks with local and international partners that help them to mobilize financial, technical, and other resources.

Additionally, a number of organizations that we examined have built trust with government, politicians, and other institutions that allow them to play key roles in areas such as peacebuilding. The perception that these organizations exemplify positive values (such as honesty or concern for the poor and needy) and that they contribute to human well-being wins them widespread trust. This trust accords them a public voice, giving them significant influence in various spheres.

In the area of health one organization credibly claims to have reduced the incidence of disease in selected rural areas by 90 percent through a community health strategy. Such models have been replicated elsewhere, with positive effect. Other Christian organizations run hospitals and health centers, and train the population in health-related areas.

Education leads to human-capital accumulation directly contributing to greater economic growth and development. A number of Christian organizations are involved directly or indirectly in educational projects, with some organizations setting up vocational-training and academic-training institutions, while others have provided scholarships to a large number of students.

In the field of income generation, employment, and poverty reduction, Christian organizations have come to be an integral part of the social reality in Africa and are having a noticeable impact specifically in the following areas: employment, entrepreneurial skills, microfinance, fighting discrimination in employment, acquisition of income-generating assets, savings schemes, and social capital through groups.

On environment and agriculture, a number of the Christian organizations have taught the population to plant dual-purpose trees (good for the environment and bearing fruit that can be eaten), set up tree nurseries and dry-land farming demonstration plots, and promote conservation agriculture. As a result of these activities there is a noticeable change in the environment, with the many trees planted likely to change the microclimate. With regard to water, Christian organizations have constructed water tanks, protected springs, installed water pumps, and dug shallow wells, boreholes, and sand dams. Through such combinations of activities clean water is provided to many people in Africa, reducing the potential for water-borne diseases.

There are many tensions that Christian organizations face in the process of serving communities. Their religious identities are a core part of what makes them successful. And yet their religious identities create challenges for them in interfacing with diverse stakeholders, not all of whom share their religious commitments. How such tensions will be addressed in the coming years is an open question that merits further research and reflection.

REFERENCES CITED

AACC. N.d. "Departments and Programmes." All Africa Conference of Churches. http://aacc-ceta.org.

Allen, Adriana, Julio Davila, and Pascale Hofmann. 2006. "The Peri-urban Water Poor: Citizens or Consumers?" *Environment and Urbanization* 18/2: 333–51.

Berger, Julia. 2003. "Religious Nongovernmental Organizations: An Exploratory Analysis." *Voluntas: International Journal of Voluntary and Nonprofit Organizations* 14/1: 15–39.

Berger, Peter L. 2009. "Faith and Development." *Society* 46/1: 69–75.

Chukwunonyelum, Ani Casimir Kingston, Matthew Chukwuelobe, and Ema Ome. 2013. "Philosophy, Religion, and the Environment in Africa: The Challenge of Human Value Education and Sustainability." *Open Journal of Social Sciences* 1/6: 62–72.

Clarke, Gerard, and Michael Jennings. 2008. "Introduction." In *Development, Civil Society, and faith-Based Organizations*, ed. Gerard Clarke and Michael Jennings, 1–16. New York: Palgrave MacMillan.

Conradie, Ernst M. 2007. "Christianity and the Environment in (South) Africa: Four Dominant Approaches." In *Christian in Public: Aims, Methodologies, and Issues,* ed. Len Hansen, 227–50. Stellenbosch, South Africa: African Sun Media.

Ellis, Stephen, and Gerrie Ter Haar. 2004. *Worlds of Power: Religious Thought and Political Practice in Africa.* Oxford: Oxford University Press.

———. 2007. "Religion and Development." *Harvard International Review.* http://hir.harvard.edu.

Gilson, L., M. Magomi, E. Mkangaa. 1995. "The Structural Quality of Tanzanian Primary Health Facilities." *Bulletin of the World Health Organization* 73/1: 105–14.

Goody, Jack, ed. 1968. *Literacy in Traditional Society.* London: Cambridge University Press.

Hefferan, Tara, Julie Adkins, and Laurie Occhipinti. 2009. "Faith-Based Organizations, Neoliberalism, and Development: An Introduction." In *Bridging the Gaps: Faith-Based Organizations, Neoliberalism, and Development in Latin America and the Caribbean,* ed. Tara Hefferan, Julie Adkins, and Laurie Occhipinti, 1–34. Lanham, MD: Rowman and Littlefield.

James, Rick. 2009. "What Is Distinctive about FBOs? How European FBOs Define and Operationalise Their Faith." *Praxis Paper 22.*

Leurs, Robert. 2012. "Are Faith-Based Organizations Distinctive? Comparing Religious and Secular NGOs in Nigeria." *Development in Practice* 22/5–6: 704–20.

Littlefield, Mari B. N.d. "The Impact of Religion and Faith-Based Organizations on the Lives of Low-Income Families." National Poverty Law Center, University of Michigan. http://www.npc.umich.edu.

Lunn, Jenny. 2009. "The Role of Religion, Spirituality, and Faith in Development: A Critical Theory Approach." *Third World Quarterly* 30/5: 937–51.

Marshall, Katherine, and Lucy Keough. 2004. *Mind, Heart, and Soul in the Fight against Poverty.* Washington DC: The World Bank.

Ministry of Health (Uganda) in collaboration with Uganda Catholic Church. 2001. *Facility-Based Private Not-for-Profit Health Providers: A Quantitative Survey.*

Occhipinti, Laurie. 2013. "Liberating Development: Religious Transformations of Development Discourse." *Perspectives on Global Development and Technology* 12: 427–43.

Okpala, Amon, and Comfort Okpala. 2006. "The Effects of Public School Expenditure and Parental Education on Youth Literacy in Sub-Saharan Africa." *Journal of Third World Studies* 23/2: 203–12.

Olarinmoye, Omobolaji Ololade. 2012. "Faith-Based Organizations and Development: Prospects and Constraints." *Transformation: An International Journal of Holistic Mission Studies* 29/1: 1–14.

Pereira, Javier, Ronald J. Angel, and Jacqueline L. Angel. 2009. "A Chilean Faith-Based NGO's Social Service Mission in the Context of Neoliberal Reform." In *Bridging the Gaps: Faith-Based Organizations, Neoliberalism, and Development in Latin America and the Caribbean,* ed. Tara Hefferan, Julie Adkins, and Laurie Occhipinti, 151–64. Lanham, MD: Rowman and Littlefield.

Pew. 2010. "Tolerance and Tension: Islam and Christianity in Sub-Saharan Africa." *Pew-Templeton Global Religious Futures Project.* http://www.pewforum.org.

Rivlin, Benjamin. 2002. "Thoughts on Religious NGOs at the UN: A Component of Global Civil Society." In *Civil Society in the Information Age: NGOs, Coalitions, Relationships,* ed. Peter Hajnal, 155–73. Aldershot: Ashgate.

UNESCO. 2013. "Adult and Youth Literacy." UNESCO Institute for Statistics. http://www.uis.unesco.org.

Woodberry, Robert. 2004. "The Cost of Bigotry: The Educational and Economic Consequences of Restricting Missions." Association for the Study of Religion, Economics, and Culture Conference (October 2004). Kansas City, MO: Unpublished conference paper.

World Health Organization (WHO). 2007. "Faith-Based Organizations Play a Major Role in HIV/AIDS Care and Treatment in Sub-Saharan Africa." *World Health Organization.* http://www.who.int.

Wuthnow, Robert. 2004. *Saving America? Faith-Based Services and the Future of Civil Society.* Princeton, NJ: Princeton University Press.

———. 2009. *Boundless Faith: The Global Outreach of American Churches.* Berkeley and Los Angeles: University of California Press.

Chapter 8

African Women's Leadership— Realities and Opportunities

Truphosa Kwaka-Sumba and Elisabet le Roux

All over the world we find women who have been successful leaders and brought about transformation in their societies; however, this is rarely seen as the norm and often not easily accepted. In much of Africa patriarchal structures and traditions have constrained female leaders. Nevertheless, African women have been and continue to be leaders. Examples include Nzinga Mbandi (1581–1663) who led Angola in resisting Portuguese colonialism and influence (UNESCO 2014). In Kenya, Professor Wangari Maathai (1940–2011) founded the Green Belt Movement and won a Nobel Prize in recognition of her work in environmental conservation. Liberian President Ellen Johnson Sirleaf was the first democratically elected female head of state in Africa. Her Excellency Catherine Samba-Panza in the Central African Republic (CAR) was elected interim president in the midst of the recent civil conflict, in the hope that she would be a leader that could bring peace to the CAR (McGregor 2014).

This chapter discusses seven women identified as being among the most influential leaders in the ALS survey. Through their interviews we learn about African women in leadership—their realities and opportunities. From Angola we interviewed Dr. Adelaide Catanha, Mrs. Eunice Chiquete, and Pastor Luisa Mateus; from the CAR, Mrs. Marie Paule Balezou, and Mrs. Marie Louise Yakemba; and from Kenya, Alice Kirambi and Professor Esther Mombo.

First, we briefly introduce these leaders,[1] and then analyze what we learned. Dr. Adelaide Catanha was identified in our survey as one of the ten most influential pastors in Angola. Dr. Catanha was the second woman to be ordained from the Ovimbundu, one of the three largest ethnic

---

[1] All information pertaining to these women and organizations was current and correct at the time of the research.

groups in her country. She teaches at a theological seminary, is involved in the women's association of her church, and in the survey was rated very highly for the extent to which she trains leaders. Mrs. Eunice Chiquete, a lecturer at a theological institute, was identified as a non-clergy leader with significant impact, noted for her ability to train leaders and for her good reputation. With a master's degree in missiology, she hopes to pursue doctoral studies. Her passion and most of her work are focused on children and children's education. Pastor Luisa Mateus was identified as one of the three most influential pastors from Angola. She is a pastor in the Reformed Evangelical Church of Angola (IERA) and serves as the secretary of its Provincial Synod of Luanda, Bengo, Cuanza Sul, and Cunene.

In the CAR, Mrs. Marie Paule Balezou was listed as a non-clergy person who had greatly influenced others. Originally from Cameroon and holding a master's degree in economics, she is a business woman in Bangui and also has a children's radio ministry. Mrs. Marie Yakemba was another of the most influential non-clergy leaders in the CAR, with a high rating for training leaders. She works for the government as a tax inspector and is also involved in two NGOs: Aglow International and Samaritan's Purse. Additionally, she is a leader in the women's group within her church. She has been to university, with tertiary training in administration, and from 2003 to 2005 she was a national adviser to the transitional government.

Alice Kirambi and Esther Mombo were identified as influential non-clergy leaders in Kenya. Alice Kirambi is a Quaker who formerly worked in the women's department of the All Africa Conference of Churches. In 2013, she ran unsuccessfully for office as women's national assembly representative. Currently, Ms. Kirambi is the executive director of the Christian Partners Development Agency (CPDA), as well as the chairperson of the Western Women Empowerment Network. Esther Mombo is professor of church history at St. Paul's University and, at the time of the study, was also deputy vice chancellor for academic affairs. Furthermore, she is an active member of the Circle of Concerned African Women Theologians.

Additionally, we also considered three organizations that focus on women and were identified by our survey respondents as leading organizations. In Angola, the Women of the Reformed Evangelical Church of Angola (MIERA) was one of the top twenty-five organizations. It is the overarching organization for all women's organizations within the denomination, and its membership is reserved for those thirty-seven years of age and older. It was rated highly in terms of training leaders and for its reputation in the community. Another organization, Formação Feminina, was the fourth most frequently listed Christian organization identified by Angolans as having a positive impact. It was established in 1914 as a center dedicated to training young girls, although in 2011 it began admitting boys. In Kenya, the Mothers' Union was identified as one of the most influential organizations and is the leading women's organization of the

Anglican Church of Kenya. It was started in 1918 by European women in the context of colonization and had a primary focus on families and children. It has evolved and is now open to all women of the Anglican Church. While the Union des Soeurs (Faithful Women and Sisters' Union/ Fellowship) was identified as an influential organization in the CAR, our researchers were unable to conduct in-depth interviews with its staff, so it is not discussed in this chapter.

The ALS questionnaire asked respondents about the extent to which their church provides opportunities for women in leadership. Table 8–1 presents the results from the three countries.

The survey participants noted that there are opportunities for women in leadership in churches. Kenya has the most opportunities available, followed by Angola and the CAR. This chapter discusses these opportunities and limitations in more detail by exploring the experiences of the seven women leaders and the three women's organizations.

Various metaphors have been used to describe the difficult journey that women in leadership face. Commonly used within faith-based literature is the phrase *stained-glass ceiling*. This denotes the existence of a humanly created barrier that prevents Christian women from attaining top leadership within ecclesiastical organizations. This barrier varies in height depending on the church tradition (Stanley 1996; Adams 2007). Our data, however, supports the use of the metaphor of a labyrinth (Eagly and Carli 2007). The labyrinth expresses the idea of a complex journey that is not simple or direct and requires persistence, focus, and awareness. Klenke (2011) also uses the labyrinth metaphor, noting that women leaders in ecclesiastical contexts are faced with religious doctrine and cultural and traditional practices that, in themselves, create hurdles in women's leadership journey. These hurdles are different for every woman leader depending on her context. Nevertheless, Klenke argues that these obstacles can be overcome or circumvented and that doing so is well worth the effort. As the discussion in this chapter shows, this has been the journey for our women leaders.

		Angola	CAR	Kenya
To what extent does your church provide opportunities for women in leadership?	Not at all	10.3%	13.8%	5.9%
	A little	26.5%	31.7%	18.7%
	A good bit	32.8%	29.1%	34.2%
	Very much	30.5%	25.4%	41.2%

Table 8–1. Church-based Opportunities for Women in Leadership

REALITIES

Marginalization and Discrimination

Years of equality and affirmative-action activism have brought about leadership spaces that women can occupy. However, though the opportunities exist, often they are concentrated at subordinate levels while men take up more senior positions (Ngunjiri 2010; Sullins 2000). Research also shows that whereas congregations may give opportunities to women in the church, they resist women serving as pastors (Sullins 2000). Studies on theological education show that historically very few women studied theology because theological education was linked to ordination (Mombo 2008; Oduyoye 1990). Ordination remains a contentious issue. Even in churches where women's ordination is theoretically allowed, implementation varies, and the actual number of ordained women is relatively small (Mombo 2008).

Esther Mombo experienced marginalization from childhood, because she went against the norm by getting extensive education and resisting early marriage. It continued at her first theological teaching position at a theological school in Eldoret. She was treated with suspicion because she was a woman and single. She tells of the reception she received:

> "Bishop Muge gives me this interview, but the council refuses. The council was made of 100% men. So they say they cannot have a woman teaching . . . [because] she is single . . . [and] the students were all men, and they had not agreed on the roles of women's leadership and ordination. But I was not looking for ordination. So Muge tells them, 'I will give you six months [to find] a man [as] qualified as her.' After six months they had not produced anybody, and he needed somebody to teach. So I am invited to come, and I come under a very hostile climate in terms of ethnicity and gender. . . . They are struggling with the place and role of women in the church. Among the issues you would find, for women of my [era] teaching in theological school, was first your place of stay. It was a questionable thing: do they give you a house or a room, or do you live with your family, or are you on your own, and how will they make sure they check on you? I am given to live with a local parish priest. When I come to class, there are five male students and one of them [is the priest in whose house] I was living."

She later left Eldoret to pursue further studies and graduated with the PhD. However, she continued facing suspicion and discrimination even from women in her new position at what was then St. Paul's United Theological College. She describes her experience there:

"Not that it became any easier; the men gave me hell. They would say, 'Nowadays we are being led by a woman.' The challenge was how you were going to be accepted by the people. The women judge you on the way you do not fit the model they know. The men can't cope with you because how can you be with them and above them. . . . How do I convince the secretary that I am just a normal woman like her? Others would say 'I don't like single women because they are a threat to the family.'"

Other women leaders we interviewed have also had multiple experiences of marginalization and discrimination. Eunice Chiquete of Angola notes that as a female leader she faces male leaders' insensitivity, as well as regulations that confine women to certain activities and keeps them from others. For example, women may only teach Sunday School, children, or women; they are not allowed to preach from the main pulpit. Mrs. Yakemba has also experienced her share of suspicion, accusations, and marginalization. At the beginning of her leadership journey she was accused by her denomination of creating a sectarian organization for the purpose of luring women away from their churches. Alice Kirambi, a one-time political aspirant, notes that she had to step out of her comfort zone and had to choose to remain focused and determined even in the face of a patriarchal society and hostility toward women.

Thus, while there are opportunities for women leaders, they also consistently experience marginalization and discrimination, irrespective of what level of leadership they aspire to.

Holistic Approach

It is worth noting that of the seven women leaders identified by the ALS, none exclusively focused on women's issues and women's empowerment. Despite facing gender-based resistance to their own rise to leadership positions, these women have a holistic approach to ministry. Even Esther Mombo, who has continuously resisted and transformed limited and limiting gender constructs, nevertheless states that "any opportunity that I am given I will make sure that I walk with women and the marginalized men" (emphasis added).

Of the top female leaders we interviewed, Esther Mombo most clearly articulated a gender-progressive agenda. From an early age she felt the need to stand up for the rights of women and originally planned to study law because of this. Her experiences of prejudice because she was female and single led her to prioritize the deconstruction and reconstruction of harmful cultural stereotypes and gender constructs, which she has done, not only through her presence as a female theologian, academic dean, and deputy vice chancellor, but also through giving priority to the development of young women. However, as the quotation above shows, her focus is on the marginalized, which sometimes includes men, but which in her Kenyan context is most often women.

Alice Kirambi, although she focused primarily on women's issues at one point in her career, as well as being chair of the Western Women Empowerment Network, is now executive director of CPDA, an organization that focuses on poverty alleviation in general. While one of the organization's seven main focus areas is the promotion of gender equality—for example, implementing the Gender and Governance Project prior to Kenya's 2013 elections—with the help of UN Women, the majority of its activities are aimed at empowering and developing communities in general. This is also the case with Marie-Louise Yakemba of the CAR. While Aglow International, of which she is the national leader, is a Christian women's organization, it also targets men and youth. And through her work with Samaritan's Purse, she assists both female and male children. Thus, although working with women and young girls is a priority for her, it is not her sole focus.

Even though the interviews with women leaders did not explicitly investigate their involvement with and prioritization of women and women's issues, this does not mean that they do not, or did not at one point, focus on such issues. Luisa Mateus (Angola), for example, was the director of IERA's Department for the Society of Women for eight years, while Adelaide Catanha (Angola) was at one point the national general secretary of the Women's Department. At the time of the interviews, though, all of these women identify their ministries as having a general focus, or a specific focus on a group other than women (for example, children, in the case of Eunice Chiquete).

The three women's organizations that were identified as leading organizations—Formação Feminina in Angola, MIERA in Angola, and the Mothers' Union in Kenya—also display a holistic attitude. Formação Feminina is a Dondi Mission Station project that was started in order to train young girls; since 2011 it is also training boys. The 2014 intake included forty-five girls and seventeen boys. MIERA—the women's branch of the Evangelical Church of Angola—has the most explicit women's agenda of the three organizations. While its official agenda is fairly holistic and includes general focus areas such as evangelism and peacemaking, it does prioritize "liberation in the women's sphere." It provides training seminars and theological education for the women members of IERA, which is arguably quite effective, since the organization had a 4.0 rating, the highest rating possible, for training leaders. The Mothers' Union in Kenya, on the other hand, appears not to prioritize women's general empowerment and emancipation from patriarchal stereotypes and restrictions. No mention is made of any activities aimed at the development and empowerment of women in general, and it has a fairly exclusive focus on women's traditional roles within marriage and family life.

Thus, while this was not an issue directly addressed in the interviews, their responses did reveal that these women leaders tend to take a holistic approach to their work. The possible effect of this for women's liberation, in the long run, is something that will be discussed later in this chapter.

Strategic Impact

The ALS survey data shows that, though women leaders are having some impact as clergy, their impact is most strongly felt in non-clergy leadership roles. As Table 8–2 illustrates, the percentage of influential non-clergy women leaders is much higher than influential female clergy leaders. This leads one to assume that the majority of Christian women leaders are finding leadership expression in non-clergy roles. At the same time it should be noted that while survey participants were asked to mention at least one non-clergy woman leader in their list of top three leaders before they were asked to select the single top leader, they were not asked to include a woman in their list of three pastors. Thus, it follows naturally that clergywomen leaders might be expected to be mentioned less often than their non-clergy counterparts.

NGOs and organizations that focus on women appear to provide a more flexible space for female leadership to be accepted and affirmed. Our survey data shows that organizations that focus on women are

	Clergy	Non-Clergy
Angola	10%	25%
CAR	0.5%	35%
Kenya	8%	43.5%

Table 8–2. Percent of Named Influential Leaders Who Are
Female: Clergy vs. Non-Clergy

more likely to have women in leading positions.[2] In fact, many women leaders thrive in the public and non-governmental sectors. For example, Mrs. Yakemba—who was opposed by her own denomination—served as an adviser to the national government. In the current war in the CAR she has served a pivotal role leading peace and reconciliation talks that cross the religious divide. Professor Esther Mombo has also found alternative

---

[2] Angola—$t(1781) = 5.898$, $p<.001$; CAR—$t(1580)=2.479$, $p<.05$: Kenya—$t(2794) = 4.558$, $p<.001$.

spaces of influence, in particular through resource brokering. She used her network of external church funding agencies to get funding for what was then St. Paul's United Theological College. Moreover, she secured PhD sponsorships for her predominantly male colleagues, thus increasing the number of PhD staff, which in turn was instrumental in having the college accredited as a university. Through resource brokering of this nature Professor Mombo became known as "the face of St. Paul's," and it was probably a deciding factor in appointing her as director of international relations and alumni. This position depends on and utilizes her global, external networks.

Professor Mombo's role in resource brokering affirms Kersten Priest's (2015) argument that women leaders are increasingly finding leadership expression outside the church by leveraging the "care work" they are doing and by using their networks to raise resources. In this way they increase their leadership influence and visibility, and as a result, their leadership has become accepted and even affirmed within the church.

Their leadership is not necessarily valued, however, on par with that of male leaders. When we consider the ALS survey data, we see a pattern emerging where respondents evaluate the influence of women leaders and organizations that focus on women, in comparison to male leaders and organizations more broadly, as more local than national. Non-clergy women leaders are rated as mostly having a local impact, especially within homes and families. Similarly, organizations that focus on women are also seen as having a high impact on homes and families.[3] Other areas of impact included education, health, and, particularly in the CAR and Kenya, conflict resolution.

Additionally, survey respondents judged organizations that focus on women as less likely to have a good reputation in the community.[4] Thus the ALS survey data has, in two instances, provided perplexing data on the impact of women's leadership. First, it shows that women's organizations are seen as having a local impact while not having as positive a reputation as other organizations. We would have expected that since households are the ones that receive benefits from these organizations, these women's organizations would have a good reputation. Second, while women's leadership is seen as having an impact at a local level, and men as having more national and international impact, in the CAR and Kenya male leaders are perceived as having more wisdom and knowledge of the local context than female leaders.[5]

A possible explanation for these puzzling data sets is explored by Prime, Carter, and Welbourne (2009). They note that gender constructs influence how men and women are evaluated in terms of leadership. People's gender

---

[3] $t(1183)=2.949$, $p<.01$; $t(1970)=3.11$, $p<.01$; $t(3215)=3.411$, $p<.01$; $t(3280)=3.03$, $p<.01$.

[4] CAR—$t(1603) = 3.218$, $p<.01$; Kenya—$t(2804) = 4.004$, $p<.001$.

[5] $t(1911) = 3.535$, $p<.001$; and $t(3106) = 3.16$, $p<.01$.

perceptions distort how they see male and female leaders, which in turn means that they evaluate the two using different standards. Studies such as those of Eagly and Mladinic (1994) and Eagly and Karau (2002) suggest that women leaders are at a disadvantage because the leadership ability of men is often evaluated based on a lower standard compared to women. Eagly and Mladinic (1994) show that people can be biased in evaluating women leaders, especially where they seem to be taking leadership in an area that would have traditionally been considered male. Furthermore, Eagly and Karau (2002) show that due to role incongruity it is more difficult for women leaders to be accepted and achieve success. Although our study did not explore the extent or reasons for these perceptions of male and female impact and reputation, our women leaders have testified to the difficulty of having their leadership accepted.

Education

All seven female leaders have some form of tertiary education. Esther Mombo and Adelaide Catanha both have PhDs; Eunice Chiquete and Marie Paule Balezou have master's degrees; and Luisa Mateus, Marie Louise Yakemba, and Alice Kirambi have all done some form of tertiary education. Furthermore, nearly all of the leaders (male and female) identified in the ALS are well educated. All have received basic education, almost half have master's degrees or are studying for one, and three have PhDs (see Chapter 2). While this confirms that education is important for leadership development, it shows that African women also face structural barriers to attaining leadership positions. And women tend to receive less education than men in two of the three countries where our research was conducted.

As Table 8–3 shows, in all three countries women are less likely than men to be literate. Whereas in Kenya the margin is very small, in Angola and the CAR there is a gap of 21 percent and 27 percent, respectively. With literacy being the foundation of education, being illiterate removes the possibility of any form of formal education. Although literacy rates vary by country, in all three women's rates are lower than men's. Thus, in these three countries, fewer women have the necessary building blocks for education than men.

	Total literacy	Male literacy	Female literacy
Angola	71%	82%	61%
CAR	37%	51%	24%
Kenya	78%	81%	75%

Table 8–3. Literacy Rate by Country (UNESCO: Institute for Statistics 2015a)

	Percent of enrolled primary school students who are female	Percent of enrolled secondary school students who are female	Percent of enrolled tertiary school students who are female
Angola	39%	39%	27%
CAR	43%	34%	27%
Kenya	50%	48%	41%

Table 8–4. Enrollment Rates (UNESCO: Institute for Statistics 2015b)

This gap between male and female becomes wider when one looks at primary, secondary, and tertiary school enrollment. Table 8–4 shows the percent of enrolled students who are female at the different education levels.

In both Angola and the CAR fewer girls than boys are enrolled in primary school. Only 39 percent of those students in Angola are girls, and 43 percent of those in the CAR. Kenya is the exception, where there are as many girls as boys enrolled in primary school. At the secondary-school level the ratio of girls to boys remains largely unchanged; however in the CAR, the percent of girls' enrollment drops to just 34 percent. At the tertiary level there is a greater disparity between women and men in Kenya, where women drop to 41 percent of students enrolled. In Angola and the CAR, the percent of women enrolled is far lower in tertiary school—only one in four students enrolled at that level of education is a woman. What this shows is that gender inequality in education is present in all three countries, with the greatest disparity evident in Angola and the CAR. The lack of literacy and education is an inhibiting structural factor for women's leadership. We would expect this to be a greater barrier in those countries where the difference in education is more marked. Although Kenya needs more women in tertiary education to achieve parity with men, efforts like Esther Mombo's are most needed in countries like Angola and the CAR where women's education falls so far behind that of men.

OPPORTUNITIES

Prioritizing Women's Writing

An interesting finding of the ALS study concerns the reading patterns of African Christians (see Chapter 10 herein), particularly as it relates to women. Forty-two percent of the Kenyan respondents were female, but only 12 percent of respondents nominated a favorite author that was female. Even among female respondents, only 19 percent named a favorite

Name of Favorite Female Author	Percentage of Female Respondents Naming this Author	Name of Favorite Male Author	Percentage of Female Respondents Naming this Author
Karen Kingbury	100	Joel Osteen	58
Francine Rivers	100	Max Lucado	50
Stormie Omartian	100	Dax Heward	50
Rebecca Brown	75	TD Jakes	48
Joyce Meyer	71	Myles Munroe	24

Table 8–5. Favorite Authors of Female Respondents

female author, while only 7 percent of the male respondents named a female author.

The gender of nominated authors was statistically related to the gender of the respondents. However, it is also true that female respondents tended to name favorite authors, male or female, who write about the realities of women. Thus, while women respondents provided a small proportion of favorite author nominations for many of the male authors, they constituted a high proportion of those nominating certain male authors who write extensively on the realities of women.

All of the women leaders strongly affirmed the importance of reading and writing and said that they regularly read their bibles plus other materials. Dr. Catanha of Angola notes that she likes books that influence her, and she buys books for her spiritual and intellectual growth. Mrs. Marie Louise Yakemba of the CAR states that she is interested in books written by the chairwoman of AGLOW International because of their usefulness to women. Pastor Luisa Mateus also likes to read, especially African authors, and says that "people die, but the works remain." Mrs. Marie Balezou of the CAR regularly reads books that help her to discover more of God, as well as books that tell the story of how God influenced a person to become a role model.

Despite the women leaders' affirmation of the importance of writing, very few of them have written published works. Professor Mombo and Mrs. Marie Balezou of the CAR have published. Esther Mombo has written widely—books; book chapters; and journal articles on gender, and gender and theology. Mrs. Balezou's book on helping Christians change a failure mentality, however, was withdrawn after publication because it had too many errors. All the other women leaders expressed a wish and intent to write. Marie Louise Yakemba notes: "Frankly, I have the intention to write. I have ideas, but I have not started writing. I would like to write about myself, about what I was before becoming what I am today." What this means is that although women are rising to the leadership challenge, they are not passing on critical information about how to navigate successfully the labyrinth and become successful female leaders. This limits the reach and impact of their leadership.

The dearth of African writers on African realities was a common finding with all the ALS leaders, not just women. Arguably, though, the need for women leaders to write, especially on women's issues and realities within the African context, is great. Such writings could provide signposts on how to navigate the African leadership labyrinth. Priest, Barine, and Salombongo (Chapter 10) provide several reasons why there is a shortage of African writers (not just African women writers) and what can be done to change this. One of the key findings was related to the low quality of writing and publication. Mrs. Balezou's book, which had to be withdrawn due to errors, illustrates this point. Therefore, there is a need for capacity development for writing and publishing women leaders. If women are more likely to read authors who write about women's realities, especially if the authors are women, it is imperative that women leaders write more. It will be more than a legacy; it will be a way of extending influence and impact across the continent and beyond.

There is an increasing call for African Christian women leaders to tell their stories. Among other reasons, this is so that the role of African Christian women can be heard about and known in church history, providing role models for future generations of girls and transforming lives and societies in Africa (Phiri, Govinden, and Nadar 2002).

Prioritizing Mentoring

Leadership development is essential to ensuring the continuity of good leadership. Our survey shows that, statistically speaking, there is no difference between the extent to which female versus male leaders develop other leaders.[6] However, much of this leadership development takes the form of training in both formal and informal settings like workshops, conferences, and seminars. Allio (2005, 1072) posits that although this kind of leadership development is important, it may not produce effective leaders. Leadership is developed through deliberately performing acts of leadership. Studies show that mentoring is particularly important and is seen as a critical factor in increasing women's leadership confidence and assumption of more responsibilities (Dahlvig and Longman 2010; Lafreniere and Longman 2008).

---

[6] ALS Survey, Question 23: "Who of the above three pastors would you say is making the most significant impact," is followed by questions about that person's gender/sex and capacity to develop others as leaders (Q 24 and Q 29). In both Angola and Kenya there is no statistically significant difference between male and female.

Female leaders themselves see mentoring as a powerful leadership development tool. Professor Mombo notes that mentoring is the "single most powerful vehicle for transferring learning and life experiences. It takes different forms but is crucial to the leadership development of a younger generation." Mentoring, if structured well, can be a powerful tool because it provides a context in which mentees can practice their leadership and get feedback, the opportunity for growth, and exposure to real-life situations. Professor Mombo mentors female theological students not by doing mentoring purely as general group guidance, but rather by focusing on the individual needs and social location of each mentee and, based on that, she maps out each one's specific developmental needs. She carefully takes into account whether the student is single, married, widowed, disabled, or HIV/AIDS affected, and she focuses on different issues with each one. For example, in mentoring single students, her focus is to create a sense of community and to affirm their capabilities and gifts; when mentoring married women, she assists them in finding a voice in their patriarchal societies (Mombo 2013).

Whereas all the women leaders and organizations are involved in leadership development, Professor Mombo appears to be the only one who prioritizes mentorship and has a clear and structured approach to it. Yet all of these leaders had mentors who played a key role in their life. For example, Mrs. Marie Louise Yakemba (CAR) stated that what she learned from her mentor, Julienne Kette, helps her in her ministry today. Kette was head of Maison Dorcas and always called on Yakemba to assist her in organizing conferences. Through that, Yakemba learned skills and gained confidence. Eunice Chiquete (Angola) also states that her mentor, a missionary from Switzerland named Teresa, played a decisive role in her life. Teresa had moved to Angola to work specifically with children and coordinated an evangelical children's radio program. Eunice met her in 1997, when Teresa invited her to train other children as part of the program. In 1999, this missionary was tragically murdered, and Eunice, though deeply shocked, was given the responsibility of continuing with the programs and maintaining what her mentor had begun. Eunice states that "Teresa's life left a mark forever on my life."

Women's organizations also do not sufficiently prioritize mentoring. The survey data shows that women's organizations in Kenya and the CAR are less likely to be seen as helping train leaders than are other organizations.[7] While the Mothers' Union from Kenya states that as part of its recruitment for leadership, its female leaders train and mentor other women, mentorship is not one of the organization's explicit goals, and there is apathy to a large extent among the younger women. This could effectively be addressed by intentional mentoring, which could bridge the gap between the older and younger women as well as assure continuous strong leadership.

---

[7] t(2778) = 2.437, p<.05; Angola = no differences; CAR t(1576) = 5.284, p<.001.

A further reason for the importance of mentoring in organizations is that women's organizations are more likely to have women in leadership.[8] Yet having women leaders is only helpful if they are good leaders. Therefore, as part of developing and growing women's leadership in Africa, it is imperative that female leaders (both within women's organizations and as individuals) intentionally mentor other women, especially on how to navigate the maze. As Professor Mombo notes, "Mentoring means transferring professional knowledge, technical expertise, and organizational awareness and, as a result, the student (read mentee) is more motivated, productive and innovative" (Mombo 2013).

Direct Approaches

Africa has had its fair share of injustices, of which gender inequality is but one. Thus, priority is often given to addressing injustices like colonial oppression, racial discrimination, and tribal marginalization, rather than gender inequality. These multiple areas of oppression lead to compartmentalized struggles for freedom, and often women's rights are neglected to focus on other issues (Rao 1995, 172).

The impact of Esther Mombo's actions, however, argues for the importance of prioritizing gender equality and directly confronting patriarchal, marginalizing systems and structures. Esther's struggle for female ordination within the Eldoret Diocese illustrates this well. During this time she was consistently marginalized, impeded, and restricted because of being a woman. However, Esther did not fight merely to overcome how she was personally disparaged and restrained, but also to address the restrictions that women in general face, exemplified by the issue of ordination of women within the diocese. She fought for women's ordination for years, and the first woman was finally ordained in 2002. However, this woman was not Esther. She has never been ordained. Yet she saw that the system was unfairly marginalizing women, and she fought to change it.

Thus, we argue that it is important for women leaders to include activities and strategies that strive to address directly and transform patriarchal systems and structures. Even though women leaders are, merely through their presence and activities as leaders, contributing to the gradual deconstruction of limiting gender roles, it can be questioned whether this by itself is enough. Briefly discussing the difference between liberal and radical feminist approaches can serve to illuminate this point.[9]

---

[8] $t(2794) = 4.558$, $p<.001$ (Kenya); $t(1781) = 5.898$, $p<.001$ (Angola); $t(1580) = 2.479$, $p<.05$ (CAR).

[9] These approaches typify two different ways of overcoming restrictive gender roles. Note that the leaders discussed in this chapter have not identified themselves with either of these terms. However, by using feminist terminology, we draw on the work of Sylvia Tamale, noted Ugandan feminist, who argues for the importance

Liberal feminism argues that women should free themselves from restrictive gender roles, but that they should do so within existing societal structures and systems (Haralambos and Holborn 2013, 106). Radical feminism, on the other hand, argues that gender equality cannot be achieved within the existing patriarchal societal system and that patriarchy thus has to be abolished (Rowland and Klein 1997, 11, 12). Liberal feminist approaches are arguably easier to implement, as they allow individuals to continue to conduct their business because they are not demanding reform of the cultural status quo. Yet, whether genuine empowerment for all women is possible with such an approach can be questioned. Maybe a more radical approach, or at least a combination of radical and liberal approaches that actively seek to transform the structures and systems that are restricting and inhibiting women and women's leadership, is needed to ensure that every subsequent generation of women need not again negotiate the same complex labyrinth.

Signposting Alternative Routes

The women leaders discussed in this chapter have all shown alternative ways of negotiating the labyrinth and achieving leadership positions. Esther Mombo attained the PhD and became an academic leader, and she has fought for and achieved women's ordination without herself becoming ordained. Marie Louise Yakemba has achieved leadership positions and influence within the community and country by working within the Civil Service and for various NGOs. Alice Kirambi has chosen to focus on poverty relief and development from within the non-governmental sector and has become a leader with noted international partners and funders.

The routes that these leaders took were very much influenced by the contexts within which they found themselves, something that is very apparent when one looks at the Angolan female leaders. It is notable that all three of these Angolan leaders have positions that are traditionally considered male. Dr. Adelaide Catanha is a pastor and a lecturer at a theological seminary; Luisa Mateus is a pastor and secretary of a Provincial Synod of IERA; and Eunice Chiquete is a lecturer at a theological seminary. It appears that Angolan women are more able to achieve traditionally male roles within the church and theological institutions compared to their CAR and Kenyan counterparts. This assumption is supported by the survey data, where 10 percent of the pastors who were identified as most influential in Angola were female, while only 0.5 percent of CAR's and 8 percent of Kenya's most influential pastors were female. The reason for this is arguably the forty-year civil war in Angola, for armed conflict offers the possibility

---

of using the term *feminism* and feminist terminology within an African context, to avoid "apathetic reluctance, comfortable complacency, dangerous diplomacy and even impotence" when engaging with women's rights (Tamale 2006, 39).

for transformation of gender roles, which in turns allows more freedom and personal agency for women. In conflict settings societal gender roles and restrictions are less enforced, and women are allowed to engage in new roles (Sideris 2000, 44; Gardam and Jarvis 2000, 30; Puechguirbal 2010, 180). As discussed in Chapter 9, for the church in Angola this has meant that women have been allowed a more central role within the church, religious leadership, and education.

While the previous section highlights the need for a more concerted and direct approach to gender equality and women's empowerment in order to strengthen women's leadership in general, one must also give recognition to alternative ways and contexts in which leadership can be achieved. In negotiating the labyrinth women have made use of alternate routes and have drawn benefit from the varied and challenging contexts in which they find themselves. In order to give recognition to the legitimacy and value of these alternative routes, "signposting" should occur. In other words, as was done through this ALS study, these stories should be captured and communicated to others. Every new female leader should not have to negotiate the labyrinth by herself, but should be able to see what those who have gone before her have done in order to follow these signposts if they are useful in her situation.

Informing women and the community in general about the alternative routes, and the legitimacy and value of these routes, can be done in various ways. What has been highlighted by the ALS study is the importance of writing and mentoring, and these are untapped resources for the empowerment and leadership development of women.

CONCLUSION

This chapter has looked at seven of the individual women leaders and three of the women's organizations identified in the ALS survey as having great impact. In exploring these leaders' and organizations' experiences and priorities, we have learned about the opportunities and limitations that African women leaders encounter.

We found that female leaders are often discriminated against and marginalized, both within the church and in society in general. The ALS survey data show that people see women leaders and organizations as having a less positive reputation than male leaders and organizations with a general focus, and posits the possibility that people tend to evaluate and judge women leaders more harshly than their male counterparts. Nevertheless, they continue to concentrate on serving the community in general, including men. Female leaders and women's organizations tend to have a holistic focus. With this community focus it is arguably logical that the impact of female leaders and women's organizations is felt at a local rather than national and international levels. Christian women leaders also tend to turn to alternative leadership positions, such as resource brokering, when they are denied ecclesiastical leadership positions.

Education was revealed as a structural barrier to women attaining leadership positions. Education, particularly tertiary education, was identified as an important indicator for leaders, yet women in all three countries are less able to start on the educational ladder, as they have less access to primary-level education.

Through studying these realities and the ways that female leaders have overcome them, we have identified four means by which women's leadership can be facilitated and supported.

First, they must be encouraged and supported to write about leadership and their leadership experiences.

Second, mentoring of women leaders by women leaders must be prioritized, for women can learn much from others who have faced the same challenges.

Third, we offer the possibility that a somewhat more radical feminist agenda can affect greater change for women in general and not only for female leaders. The story of Esther Mombo shows us how directly confronting patriarchal oppression can lead to structural changes that free women and open up opportunities for them.

Fourth, an opportunity is linked to the fact that many women are denied traditional leadership roles within ecclesiastical circles and thus find alternative avenues and ways of being leaders. These alternative roles and avenues should be signposted for subsequent women leaders, thus enabling easier negotiation.

The reality is that, as other studies have also shown, women in leadership face considerable resistance in the churches, communities, and societies that they serve. Nevertheless, what the ALS survey and the subsequent study of leaders and organizations show us is that African women leaders are overcoming these challenges and having an impact. They are able to negotiate the labyrinth, a complex journey requiring persistence, focus, and tenacity. Much can and should be done to make the labyrinth less daunting. The challenges that they face make it even more laudatory that these women are willing to take on the challenge and come out on top.

REFERENCES CITED

Adams, Jimi. 2007. "Stained Glass Makes the Ceiling Visible: Organizational Opposition to Women in Congregational Leadership." *Gender and Society* 21/1:80–105.

Allio, J. Robert. 2005. "Leadership Development Teaching Versus Learning." *Management Decision* 43/7–8:1071–77.

Eagly, Alice Hendrickson, and Linda Lorene Carli. 2007. *Through the Labyrinth: The Truth about How Women Become Leaders*. Boston: Harvard Business Press.

Eagly, Alice H., and J. Stephen Karau. 2002. "Role Incongruity Theory of Prejudice towards Women." *Psychological Review* 109/3:573–98.

Eagly, Alice H., and A. Mladinic. 1994. "Are People Prejudiced against Women? Some Answers from Research on Attitudes, Gender Stereotypes, and Judgments of Competence." *European Review of Social Psychology* 5:1–35.

Gardam, Judith, and Michelle Jarvis. 2000. "Women and Armed Conflict: The International Response to the Beijing Platform for Action." *Columbia Human Rights Law Review* 32/10:1–65.

Haralambos, Michael, and Martin Holborn. 2013. *Sociology: Themes and Perspectives*. London: Collins.

Klenke, Karin. 2011. *Women in Leadership: Contextual Dynamics and Boundaries*. Bingley: Emerald Group Publishing Limited.

Lafreniere, L. Shawna, and A. Karen Longman. 2008. "Gendered Realities and Women's Leadership Development: Participant Voices from Faith-Based Higher Education." *Christian Higher Education* 7/5:388–404.

McGregor, Jena. 2014. "For the Central African Republic, Hope Takes Female Form." *Washington Post*. January 23.

Mombo, Esther. 2008. "The Ordination of Women in Africa: A Historical Perspective." In *Women and Ordination in the Christian Churches*, ed. Jan Jones, Kirst Thorpe, and Janet Wooten, 123–43. London: T and T Clark International.

———. 2013. "Mentoring Younger Scholars in Theological Education." In *A Handbook of Theological Education in Africa*, ed. Isabel Apawo Phiri and Dietrich Werner, 853–57. Pietermaritzburg, South Africa: Cluster Publications.

Ngunjiri, W. Faith. 2010. *Tempered Radicals and Critical Servant Leaders*. Albany: State University of New York Press.

Oduyoye, Mercy. 1990. *Who Will Roll the Stone Away? The Ecumenical Decade of the Churches in Solidarity with Women*. Geneva: World Council of Churches.

Phiri, A. I., D. B. Govinden, and S. Nadar. 2002. "Called at Twenty-seven and Ordained at Seventy-three! The Story of Rev. Victory Nomvete Mbanjwa in the United Congregational Church in Southern Africa." In *Her Stories: Hidden Histories of Women of Faith in Africa*, ed. Isabel Apawo Phiri, Betty Govinden, and Sarojini Nadar. Pietermaritzburg, South Africa: Cluster Publications.

Priest, Kersten Bayt. 2015. "Breaking through the Stained-glass Ceiling: Christian Women's Short-term Mission Travel and the Emergence of Grassroots Leadership and Resource-Brokering." Andrews U. Swallen Lectureship (unpublished).

Prime, J. L., N. M. Carter, and T. M. Welbourne. 2009. "Women 'Take Care,' Men 'Take Charge': Managers' Stereotypic Perceptions of Women and Men Leaders." *The Psychologist-Manager Journal* 12:25–49.

Puechguirbal, Nadine. 2010. "Discourses on Gender, Patriarchy, and Resolution 1325: A Textual Analysis of UN Documents." *International Peacekeeping* 17/2:172–87.

Rao, Arati. 1995. "The Politics of Gender and Culture in International Human Rights Discourse." In *Women's Rights, Human Rights: International Feminist Perspectives*, ed. Julie Peters and Andrea Wolper, 167–75. New York: Routledge.

Rowland, Robyn, and Renata Klein. 1997. "Radical Feminism: History, Politics, Action." In *Radically Speaking: Feminism Reclaimed*, ed. Diane Bell and Renate Klein, 9–36. Melbourne: Spinifex Press.

Sideris, Tina. 2000. "Rape in War and Peace: Some Thoughts on Social Context and Gender Roles." *Agenda: Empowering Women for Gender Equity* 43:41–45.

Stanley, Susie C. 1996. "The Promise Fulfilled: Women's Ministries in the Wesleyan/Holiness Movement." http://www.wesleyanholinesswomenclergy.org.

Sullins, Paul. 2000. "The Stained Glass Ceiling: Career Attainment for Women Clergy. *Sociology of Religion* 61/3:243–66.

Tamale, S. 2006. "African Feminism: How Should We Change?" *Development* 49/1:38–41.

UNESCO. 2014. "Women in Africa." http://en.unesco.org.

UNESCO Institute for Statistics. 2015a. *Education: Literacy Rate.* http://data.uis.unesco.org.

UNESCO Institute for Statistics. 2015b. *Education MetaData: Percentage of Female Enrolment by Level of Education.* http://data.uis.unesco.org.

Chapter 9

Empowering Leadership—A New Dawn in African Christian Leadership

H. Jurgens Hendriks

Christian leadership in Africa has been influenced significantly by several factors, among them African chiefdoms, cultural patriarchy, the remnants of the colonial master-servant model, and later Western rational thought patterns and Western religious models (Adeyemo 2006, 546). Contemporary Christian leaders in Africa face a crisis of sorts in their attempts to identify and adopt the best model of leadership that will inspire others and serve the best interests of those they lead.

This crisis is not new. Jesus's disciples struggled with similar issues when James and John asked Jesus if they could be seated at his right and left hand when he ruled. The other disciples heard about this and were upset. Jesus responded in words that summarize what this chapter is about: "You know that those who are regarded as rulers of the Gentiles lord it over them, and their high officials exercise authority over them. Not so with you. Instead, whoever wants to become great among you must be your servant, and whoever wants to be first must be slave of all. For even the Son of Man did not come to be served, but to serve, and to give his life as a ransom for many" (Mark 10:42–45, NIV). The issue Jesus raised here was also recognized as particularly relevant in Africa by Gottfried Osei-Mensah in his 1990 book *Wanted: Servant Leaders: The Challenge of Christian Leadership in Africa Today.*

This chapter draws on recent research carried out by a team of researchers with the Africa Leadership Study (ALS) among more than eight thousand Christians in three countries: Kenya, Angola, and the Central African Republic (CAR). One aim of the research was to explore the leadership styles exercised by those whom respondents identified as influential. Many of these leaders were facilitating social change in their communities while exemplifying new patterns of "servant leadership" (Osei-Mensah 1990; Greenleaf 2007). They fostered downward empowerment while still winning respect and influence and exemplifying the power of basic biblical principles in their lives.

Are there lessons on serving and empowering leadership that one may learn from these leaders? How do they understand their leadership style, and what does such leadership entail? Who or what influenced them to adopt a leadership model that runs contrary to what is more commonly practiced in their environments?

Below is a short introduction to the concept of empowering servant leadership, followed by selected examples of the ways in which such leadership is formed and by a summary of some characteristics of this leadership as identified by participants. To remain faithful to the data, these examples are for the most part given in narrative form as expressed by participants.

SERVANT LEADERSHIP AND A NEW DAWN IN EMPOWERING LEADERSHIP

In *Whose Religion Is Christianity?* Lamin Sanneh points out that the postcolonial expansion of Christianity in Africa took place under African leadership. "Africans stepped forward to lead the expansion without the disadvantage of foreign compromise. Young people, especially women, were given a role in the church" (Sanneh 2003, 18). And yet the continuing legacy of colonialism is all too often evident in leadership patterns that are exploitive and self-serving. Those who study leadership in contemporary Africa suggest that power-hungry, exploitive leaders are often the order of the day (Castells 2000, 82–128).[1] However, our ALS research suggests that another model of empowering servant leadership is also present in Africa.

What exactly does the concept of empowerment mean, particularly within the context of leadership? According to theology and development expert Naas Swart, "The term empowerment literally means that people are given power. It refers to a process in which people achieve the capacity to control decisions affecting their lives" (2006, 220). Empowerment thus enables people to define themselves and to construct their own identities.

The phrase "downward mobility," according to Henri Nouwen (1989; 2007), refers to empowering those with less access to power. As such it constitutes a way of serving others (Beck 2013). Theologically speaking, the life of Christ epitomizes downward empowerment. Gorman (2009, 16–17) uses the term *kenosis* (Phil 2:7) in this regard and explains "Paul's master story" as portraying Christ's self-emptying or self-lowering in becoming human and serving humankind. This downward movement also serves

---

[1] Well-known sociologist Manuel Castells stresses that the plight of Africa is linked to the rise of global capitalism. Many factors play a role in the economic woes of the continent, but the role of "predatory states" and "predatory rule" aggravates matters (2000: 95–99). William Easterly, for example, draws attention to the link between colonialism and the new imperialism (2006: 269–305).

as an illustration of authentic Christian identity as well as of Christian leadership. In his extensive work on Christian leadership Nouwen called for downward mobility (1989; 2007) as a way of exercising authority/leadership in a manner that is contrary to the more usual upward-bound race of the elite toward honor and power. Downward mobility and empowerment are signs of leadership integrity, of putting the other before self.

TOOLS FOR EMPOWERMENT TOWARD SERVANT LEADERSHIP

The following sections focus on various ways in which African Christian leaders empower others through their leadership, as well as how others have empowered them.

Empowerment through Education

The role of education in empowerment cannot be overemphasized. "An empowered teacher is pre-eminently able to develop learners' potential optimally," says educator Arend Carl (2012, 1). Most of the prominent Christian leaders identified in the ALS research were mentored toward obtaining a good education. Education helped them to achieve their goals and, as Christians, to have an impact in all walks of life, whether in agriculture, education, public service, or church ministry. What made a difference in their lives was that these leaders all discerned a clear calling from God to serve and to use their positions of influence to empower others. They exemplified servant leadership in action. Their call shaped their identities and eventually also those of others. From a theological perspective one may call this a *Christian identity*, since at least something of the likeness and image of Christ was reflected in their lives and deeds. Some examples of Christian leaders who were empowered by education and who worked toward the empowerment of others through education are presented below.

Many Kenyans identified Bishop John Bosco of the Redeemed Gospel Church in Kenya as an influential pastor. A single mother raised him in Nairobi's infamous Kibera slum. From the age of eight, Bosco attended primary school and later the Kiambu Institute of Technology, where he enthusiastically studied construction. The skills he acquired opened many doors for him while serving in Mombasa. Here he noticed that men sent their wives and children to other towns to get an education. Being skilled in construction and having received "on the job" theological training, his ministry of empowerment began by building a school, the Redeemed Gospel Academy. In the interview with the principal of the Redeemed Gospel Academy, it was reported that the school has one mission and one purpose only, namely, "to offer quality education to all children regardless of their race, religion, or socioeconomic background." The school is situated in an area that is predominantly Muslim and Digo.[2] In the interview with Bosco himself, he refers to the fact that "half the students are Muslim, and they are all doing Christian religious education in school." This school has become one of the best performing private schools in the district. The principal of the school was able to share many examples of learners who attended this school and subsequently, based on their test results, were able to attend "some of the most prominent national high schools in Kenya."

Bosco's type of leadership is empowering servant leadership. It serves as an example of the fact that education empowers. In the interview Bosco shared that his entire family contributed financially to building projects toward achieving the goal of providing education and training. Bosco warns younger leaders against the danger of a false gospel and materialism "where God wants one to get rich quickly, drive a good car and have a big house." At the time of the interview, Bosco's leadership not only had an impact on education but also was reflected in the forty Redeemed Gospel Churches planted in Kwale County in Kenya.

Another Kenyan example is theologian Esther Mombo. Mombo faced the challenge of poverty and gender prejudice and resisted cultural pressure toward early marriage. She eventually received the PhD and became the first dean of students and later deputy vice chancellor of academic affairs at St. Paul's University in Limuru. In her interview Esther told how she used each position to empower the disadvantaged and to create opportunities for her students. During her tenure at St. Paul's University, for example, Esther faced stiff opposition from conservative quarters because she was neither ordained nor married at the time of her appointment. However, with the support of the principal and student body, she became the first dean of theology, thus leading the way for other women. At that stage studying theology was linked to ordination, but under her leadership, this changed. The result was a steep increase in the number of theology students. Even more significant, the number of female theology graduates at the university increased from five in 2000 to thirty-five in 2012. The glass ceiling of gender prejudice was cracking (Mombo and Joziasse 2011).

During the research project Angolan interviewees rated education as very important. Five of the six Angolan Christian leaders interviewed received theological training. The sixth, Manuel Missa, a sixty-year-old schoolteacher and catechist, lamented the fact that he could not study theology due to sickness and civil war. In a country wracked by decades of civil war these six leaders of faith, with firm convictions and clear values, stand out as beacons of hope. They all value theological education, all exercise leadership in church settings (as pastors, Sunday School teachers, choir leaders), and all play significant empowerment roles as mentors. Pastor Dinis Eurico is a case in point. Having served as a senior government

---

[2] Read about the Digo people at http://en.wikipedia.org/wiki/Digo_people and http://joshuaproject.net/people_groups/11557/KE.

official during the civil war, he left his job in 1987, studied theology, and then began ministering as a pastor in 1992.

Another interviewee, Adelaide Catanha, in 1978 became the second Ovimbundu woman to be ordained and subsequently devoted her life to theological education. Finally, interviews with representatives of key Christian organizations in Angola indicated that their staff members widely shared the conviction that theological empowerment of ordinary people was essential. Empowerment was clearly viewed as a holistic activity in these interviews. As such, education and training in different skills are seen as part and parcel of being a church and bringing hope in difficult times.

Three of the Christian leaders interviewed in the CAR obtained their doctorates (two PhDs, one MD) in the Netherlands, Canada, and the United States. Most of the CAR top leaders who we interviewed had studied abroad, and all had extensive global exposure and connections. The CAR reports illustrate how education empowers people to change church and society for the better.

David Koudougueret completed the PhD at Leiden University. Later he was appointed academic dean and dean of research and publications at the Faculté de Théologie Évangélique de Bangui. As a researcher in the field of Bible translation, Koudougueret built an international network. He served as a missionary among "the Pygmies" and among Fulani people. He currently serves as a pastor in a congregation with more than seven thousand members. From the interview conducted with him, it is clear that he believes the message of the gospel should empower and motivate Christians to serve God and neighbor in all walks of life—social, political, and economic.

Professor Nestor Mamadou Nali, a medical doctor, is also a fellow of the Royal College of Surgeons of Canada, head surgeon at Bangui's Hôpital de l'Amitié, former dean of the Medical School, and rector of the University of Bangui; he served as the CAR's minister of health from March 2003 to June 2005. Throughout his career, Nali played a significant role in rebuilding his country's collapsed public-health infrastructure. This included setting up regional pharmaceutical depots, allocating resources for community health centers, and launching the National Sanitation Programme to provide new norms and standards for best practices. Nali is equally active in the church, having served as president of the Association for Child Evangelism, president of the Union of Christian Medical Workers, and board member of FATEB. He is active in working for church unity, which he believes is his biggest challenge in the CAR.

A final example from the CAR is civil engineer Evariste Dignito. Dignito worked for several companies, but then started his own business. He has served his country in many ways, including draining land and constructing roads. At the same time he served as coordinator of cell groups in his local church and as the vice-president of an orphanage.

In concluding this section, it is significant that the interviewees, with their various walks of life, involvement in the education of others, and styles of leadership, often use terminology that refers to the kingdom of God (Mark 1:15). That is, they do not focus purely on the spiritual and salvific part of the gospel, but on being "a blessing to the world" (Gen 12:1–3). Dignito explains his mission as "to do good work to glorify God." Nali says: "We need to bring the Christian worldview to the political arena. Politics is life." These leaders envision a state of affairs where justice and peace reign and where God is obeyed.

Empowerment through Exposure

The CAR leaders mentioned in this chapter include a doctor, an architect, an engineer, a business woman, and a government official. They all have had an impact on society with their gifts and leadership. Interviews with these individuals highlighted the connection between international exposure and effective service in their communities (Chapter 4). Through international exposure these leaders developed a broader frame of reference that helped them to think "outside the box" and to discern and address pressing societal needs in their countries.

A Kenyan illustration may help to clarify this point. When pastors Bosco and Munene were called to serve in Mombasa, it was their first real encounter with Islam. Nairobi and Mombasa represent different worlds. Not being caught in the Mombasa "box" of assumptions about Muslims, Bosco and Munene saw opportunities, and they reached out to Muslims. According to Munene, "Regardless of what people say [about] an Islamic city, they were people just like everywhere else who needed Jesus as their Lord and Savior." Their exposure to a different context was thus eventually translated into the empowerment of congregation members and served as an example to them to do likewise.

Empowerment through Choirs/Music

Music has traditionally played a significant role in most African cultures. The role of music has changed throughout African history and continues to transform as new ideals and genres emerge. Music serves various functions in African societies and is used by people of all ages in many different ways. No wonder that in Angola, for example, music serves as a means of choice toward empowerment.

The frequent references to the role of choirs and how development as leaders went hand in hand with being part of a choir or taking leadership in choirs are quite remarkable in the data. In essence, leadership, especially servant leadership, is more of an attitude than specific knowledge. One cannot acquire this kind of leadership merely by following a particular academic curriculum. It is not program driven but needs to flow from deep inside a person like a fountain that flows from an underground reservoir. The yearning to belong and to share, to harmonize, and to enjoy the beauty and message of a song illustrates the deep relationship-based community awareness that makes choirs so much a part of African life. "I am because you are" may easily be translated to include "we are because we sing" and "we believe because we witness to what we sing."

Four of the six Christian leaders interviewed in Angola explicitly mentioned the influence of choirs on their lives and ministry. One example is Manuel Missa, mentioned fourth among non-clergy leaders with significant impact. The report describes this sixty-year-old teacher and headmaster as a choir director, "a singer as well as a religious music composer." Missa claimed that singing qualified him as a leader. In every community or church where he has gone, he has been recognized as having this gift.

Diamantino Laurindo Doba was also listed by Angolan respondents as a non-clergy leader with high impact. From his Sunday School days, he sang in choirs, became a choir leader, and developed as a leader in youth work serving and empowering others through choirs, choir festivals, and youth programs. Currently, he is national director of the IERA Youth Department, coordinator of the Evangelical Regional Choir of Luanda, and adviser to the IERA Executive Committee.

Angolan respondents identified pastor Adelaide Catanha as one of the most influential pastors in Angola. In her interview Catanha also refers to the important role that choirs, and her participation in them, played in her spiritual formation. The same is true of the influential pastor Luisa Mateus, who even met her pastor-husband in a choir. Her whole family remains involved in choirs, and she explains that choirs imbued her with many positive values, including an appreciation for unity, love, and respect among choir members, treating them as brothers and sisters.

Three CAR leaders, René Malépou, Marie Louise Yakemba, and David Koudougueret, also mention the importance of choirs. Koudougueret is described as "a gentleman who spent all his life in the church: choir, youth group, [and] the Young Christian Union. . . . Thus, he was shaped by the church." In Kenya, choirs are also mentioned. General Jeremiah Kianga "grew up having membership in the Sunday School choir, school choir, and church choir." Clearly, choirs are a medium of leadership development and empowerment.

Empowerment through Prayer

In reading the ALS reports, one is struck by how often prayer is mentioned. Two CAR leaders, Yakemba and Nali, for example, emphasize the importance of prayer in addressing the dire political situation in their country, while engineer Dignito refers six times to the role of prayer in his family's decision making. The Angolan interviewees all mention prayer and share a clear sense of the integral and empowering role of prayer in their lives, especially in circumstances related to the drawn-out civil war. Eight Kenyan reports also referred to prayer. John Bosco stresses how important prayer is for anyone ministering in the difficult context of Mombasa: "If you are here, and you are playing games, you will be finished. Your ministry can't go anywhere. So prayer is needed, serious prayer, consistent prayer."

These leaders had firsthand experiences of being confronted with realities where their resources to cope were no longer able to address the challenges. This is where they needed to step out in faith and trust, putting their very lives in God's hands. Prayer is another example of a haven that provides, in this case, spiritual security.

Empowerment through Mentoring

Empowerment does not happen only through formal education. Mentors, too, have unique abilities to guide and empower people, and this can also happen within the context of education. According to the Global Survey on Theological Education (2011–13), the integrity of senior leaders is seen as the most important element in determining quality in theological education. Mentors are respected for their uncompromising, value-based lifestyle (Tutu 1999). They set an example of self-sacrificing service through which they empower outstanding leaders.

The mentors mentioned in the ALS research all excel in wisdom, in faith-based values, in integrity, in having a clear identity, and in the ability to empower and to journey with their "students." They base their role as mentors on their Christian convictions and faith. Most of them received theological training that shaped their views and sense of vocation.

Well-known Ghanaian scholar Kwame Bediako (1992) helped Africans to see the importance of African identity and of having African mentors. African mentorship is related to a combination of family, faith, and social responsibility. A high percentage of the leaders interviewed mentioned the role of a father, a mother, or a grandmother in their own lives. Family, in particular, is of paramount importance in most African cultures, and the interviews also illustrated this.[3]

With regard to mentorship, the ALS study found that Christian faith forms the ethical basis for the trust between, and the motivation behind, the relationship between mentor and mentee. It also found that mentors' attitude and mentorship styles were based on a respect for the dignity and the potential of fellow human beings. A good example is the way in which Esther Mombo respected the students at St. Paul's University and helped

---

[3] For the role of family in the formation of leaders, see also Chapter 3 in this book.

those in need—both women and men. She exercised authority in collaboration with colleagues "and involved the student body in decisions." The report mentions that she is known for her "soft touch for the low cadre support staff." This attitude of respect for someone else's humanity and talents often results in a lasting relationship in which a mentor resumes responsibility for guiding a mentee, even though doing so requires time, energy, and resources. Judge Onesmus Makau, a first-generation Christian from a peasant family, is another Kenyan example of Christian mentorship in the ALS research. In his interview Makau mentioned the skill of mentoring and the strength of empathy in mentoring when describing how he mentored two junior barristers who got promoted to magistrate level.

The characteristics of a good mentor that were identified in the research are especially well illustrated in the relationship between Kenyan mentee Edward Munene and two of his mentors, Catherine Njoki and Pastor Ron Sonnas. Pastor Munene described the relationship as very personal, empowering, guiding, and built on mutual respect. Njoki and Sonnas noted his leadership potential, and mentored and empowered him by trusting him and by creating opportunities for him to use his exceptional talents.

CHARACTERISTICS OF SERVANT LEADERSHIP

Accessibility and Empowerment

Successful mentors and leaders have the distinction of being accessible. Accessibility provides the womb in which servant leadership can grow and develop. The mentor is accessible for those who are suffering, in need, or in doubt, and for those who need guidance. Mentorship is a process of leading and teaching by example in an interactive and personal way.

Edward Munene clearly articulates this principle: "God has called me to be a servant, and I need to be available to the people I am reaching. I mean, if you send me a Facebook message, I should be able to reply." Munene illustrates his argument with some examples. A husband contacted him on Facebook about a looming divorce. He immediately responded and found a way to help. A lady who wanted to commit suicide because of an unwanted pregnancy responded to his blog. He answered her via the blog, followed up the case, and eventually through family reconciliation helped resolve the problems. Munene is a pastor, and one way in which he remained accessible was through social media, although not in the way social media often functions, as the creator and builder of his own image. The examples Munene gives show the extent to which he follows through on the calls for help of those who contact him and how he gets involved in their lives and pain. His availability as well as his commitment to take and accompany people in need on a journey is truly exemplary: "I began searching the Bible to work for a solution and realized Jesus never sent us out to make converts, he sent us to make disciples. So I began to make disciples. . . . I began to teach the Word so that I can reach the world."

Munene and his wife started their ministry in Mombasa in 2008 during the time of Kenya's post-election violence. In the absence of outside help they were forced to develop their local leadership team. They started as a team of two and reached out primarily to young people from all walks of life in the area. Since then, through discipleship, internships, and teaching Munene estimates that they have developed roughly two hundred leaders. Many of these subsequently pursued Bible School training and even master-level studies in Christian leadership and theology.

Throughout this chapter the word *mentor* has been used, but in biblical terms *discipleship* describes much the same phenomenon.[4] One of the important principles in mentorship clearly seen in the life of Edward Munene is constantly giving power away. Furthermore, the young converts and those discipled by Munene followed their calling in a variety of walks of life, not only in church-related venues. These were truly instances of spreading the light and of being the salt of the earth. In fact, from the interview it is clear that Munene's goal was not focused on the church as such. Munene developed an effective system of growing and multiplying leaders without the need for a centralized institutional or hierarchical structure and process. It did, however, result in the congregation sending people into the world who are equipped to make it a better place by living a moral and principled life in whatever occupation they pursue. The congregation was challenged and discipled to reach out to the world and to make disciples, but in a distinctly missional and not purely bureaucratic ministry. In no way did bureaucratic issues overshadow or hamper the prerequisites of spiritual maturity and a disciplined life. One indeed finds in this a sense of disciplined but challenging freedom to go where the Spirit leads in this suffering and broken world where there is more than enough rescue work to be done.

When John Bosco was asked why he thinks people identified him as an influential pastor, his hesitant reply was that perhaps it was because people know that when they approach him with a problem, he will try his utmost to help, whether the request comes from a born-again believer or not. Furthermore, he says that his own background of growing up and being familiar with life in crowded slums taught him the value of neighborliness and the importance of helping others. How, then, he asks, could he not help others, even those from the Muslim community? This became especially crucial when Bosco moved from Nairobi to Mombasa, from a situation with religious freedom to an area where Christians were at risk. Once in Mombasa he again settled in one of the poorest areas. With little outside

---

[4] Two classical books on discipleship that describe Munene's sentiment are Robert E. Coleman, *The Master Plan of Evangelism* (Old Tappan: Revell, 1963) and Alexander B. Bruce, *The Training of the Twelve* (Grand Rapids, MI: Kregel, 1971).

support Bosco worked among people not held in high esteem by anyone. Furthermore, the population in these areas was in constant transition. Because of poverty, people move on as soon as they have been equipped and empowered. He estimates that church members usually stay in the area for two to four years before they move on. Bosco reported that he had trained hundreds of leaders in his leadership-training institute, including several prominent pastors. It is, therefore, not surprising that respondents in the ALS rated him highly for his ability to train leaders—3.84 out of 4! With pastors like Bosco, who lead by example, who serve and empower people and communities, and who are accessible to them, it also comes as no surprise that the Redeemed Gospel Church is growing at a remarkable rate in the Kenyan coastal region. However, servant leadership and the empowerment it entail come not only with opportunities but also risks.

Toward Servant Leadership and the Ability to Identify Opportunities and Risks

Servant leadership develops when mentors and institutions have faith in younger people to help them identify challenges and opportunities. Esther Mombo's grandmother "encouraged her to dream a better life" and protested when her father wanted her to be committed to an arranged marriage. John Bosco mentioned how his mentor Dr. Lai offered him opportunities "to serve in greater capacities." Catherine Njoki recommended that her mentee Edward Munene be allowed to deliver the sermon when a preacher failed to turn up for a worship service. Such encouragement decidedly influenced these leaders' lives. Many influences, from choirs to youth groups to international friendships, affected David Koudougueret, eventually moving him from civil engineering to the pastorate. Louise Yakemba, a senior CAR treasury official, told of her grandmother's influence as a committed Christian in guiding and encouraging her educational pursuits. Yakemba also mentions the role of the choir of which she was a member and the advice of mentors that led her to study, thus laying the foundations for her future as a prominent female leader in the CAR. Importantly, while still young these leaders not only responded to the challenges presented by their mentors, but also took advantage of the opportunities presented to them. This of course also involved taking risks, especially the risk of failure.

The road toward becoming a servant leader that empowers others requires safe havens that provide stability and security when there are risks involved. A typical haven is a sound family background.[5] Of course, a good education and financial stability also play a role. But perhaps the biggest single haven that these Christian leaders share is their faith in Jesus

---

[5] This also forms the theme of other chapters in this book (see Chapters 2 and 3).

Christ. Spiritually, this implies a radical identity transformation: turning from self to Christ.

Specific experiences influenced the lives of these leaders and, though fraught with risk, often served as turning points in their lives. These leaders embraced a new vision and mission, as shown in the examples presented above. In the CAR, David Koudougueret, who was studying civil engineering with government sponsorship in Canada, tells how his life was influenced by the church and the "brethren" so that he eventually became a well-qualified pastor. He made brave decisions, took risks, but could do so because of the haven offered by the support of his church.

Edward Munene mentioned the support and friendship he experienced at school from friends from a variety of cultural backgrounds: a Ugandan, an Ethiopian, and an Asian. "This helped me at a very young age to appreciate other cultures." Munene also mentions that he grew up in a Presbyterian church where 70–80 percent of the congregation was older, but he testifies that he was "saved" at a youth camp of this Presbyterian Church. Three months after he gave his life to Christ, a preacher did not turn up at a scheduled youth rally, and Munene was given the opportunity to preach and teach. After that he was in touch with several youth groups that created opportunities for him to do the same and to thus cross boundaries. His biggest challenge, he recounts, came when he started an International Christian Centre in Mombasa in 2008 "from scratch." To move from Nairobi to Mombasa was quite a boundary to cross, a risky undertaking, specifically with regard to his and his family's security. Munene explains:

> We came with my family, and we began services just during the post-election violence. At some point, I actually thought I had come at the wrong time. But beginning then, what we realized is that God had brought us to a city that is needy in so many ways. Regardless of what people say [about] an Islamic city, they were people just like everywhere else who needed Jesus as their Lord and Savior. What the post-election violence did, what has been a benefit for me today, is not many people wanted to travel to other cities away from where they were born. For example, people who were working in Nairobi did not want to leave and go to work elsewhere.

The ability to take risks and cross boundaries is linked to having sound safe havens, foundations, or platforms from which activities are launched. Munene had family and a measure of financial security. He also had good mentors and a sound education. Most outstanding, however, was his clear sense of purpose based on a conversion experience that confirmed his passion to help people (he often used the word *rescue*). He also uses the opportunities that present themselves in his ministry, one being social media. The average age of his Mombasa church members is thirty, and

Munene uses the opportunities offered by social media (Skype, Facebook, Twitter, and so on) to minister to them.

Breaking free from established cultural patterns, taking the risk in crossing old boundaries, is illustrated by Munene when he was asked to name factors that helped him to empower others.

> One is my ability to continue to raise leaders, because if I don't keep giving away the things that I do, I will not be able to keep doing the things that I should do. You know as a leader there are things that only I can do but there are things I'm doing right now that somebody else can do, so I need to keep on finding the things that somebody else can do, and I give it away as I raise leaders. So my leadership development critically impacts what I have been able to do.

Dinis Eurico was rated the pastor with the most significant impact in Angola. He is president of the Igreja Evangélica Sinodal de Angola (The Synodal Evangelical Church of Angola) and teaches at a seminary. He became widely known across Angola through his involvement as a Christian broadcaster, and his Christian educational programs on the radio are popular. However, Eurico's leadership and the respect people have for him has a deeper foundation. As mentioned above, he served in the former communist government's Ministry of Internal Trade and was to be promoted to an influential post (implying financial security and other benefits). However, when he sensed God calling him to pastoral ministry, he took the risk and resigned to serve his people as a pastor. This relinquishment of power appears to have won him respect and credibility with many.

To relinquish power is certainly a difficult challenge for African leadership. People commonly assume that this leads to powerlessness. But in Christian terms the relinquishing of power often leads to places and positions where God can entrust even more challenging responsibilities. The lives of both Munene and Eurico testify to this.

SERVANT LEADERSHIP AND THE ABILITY TO NAVIGATE THE CHALLENGES OF EMPOWERMENT

Nothing defines the servanthood of Christ more than the cross. Angolan leaders and organizations testified to the hardship of forty years of independence and civil war, but also to the growth of the church. In the crucible of those forty years, leadership and faith matured. The testimony of Eunice Chiquete, a young girl during the war, serves as a good illustration. She tells how her parents (her mentors) stuck to their calling to minister and educate while so much around them was laid waste in aerial bombardments. The prophetic voices of the contemporary CAR leaders do not go unnoticed in that society. The Esther Mombo story testifies to the fact that the cultural gender bias against women remains a lifelong challenge, a constant cross to carry. However, nothing highlights and sharpens the integrity, faithfulness, and reliability of a leader more than dealing with difficulties like these.

Difficult circumstances, therefore, often play a crucial role in the formation of servant leaders. Leaders are molded by the challenges they face. The obstacles and dangers that confront them test their character and form their faith. Again, the example of Kenyan Bishop John Bosco looms large. When Bosco started serving in Mombasa, with its large Muslim presence, he only had two regular attendees at worship services; there was not a single Christian church in the area. At the time of the interview church attendance was about three thousand. The congregation included people from diverse backgrounds (despite only ten-to-twenty cars in sight). The two armed police officers on guard at these services serve as a silent testimony to the threat of religious violence, a perennial threat that has affected his leadership.

Bosco and his family took on a tremendous challenge. Nothing came easily. It took years, and they lived for long periods without any regular income. They faced these obstacles in faith, in prayer, and with hard work. However, it did not go unnoticed. Bosco was identified by more Kenyans than any other as an influential pastor with positive impact.

One of the effects of the war in Angola was that there was very little national or international financial support for church ministries. Thus, the Angolan interviewees refer to the fact that their primary support was local, and in the case of the six leaders usually came from their own or family resources. The conduct and character of these leaders testify to their calling, faith, and integrity. Thus, people respect and trust them, and follow their example.

Another obstacle to leadership in a continent with few doctors, hospitals, and clinics is medical problems. Manuel Missa had two nearly fatal motorcycle accidents, as well as other health problems. In their testimony about their father, Missa's children mention the nine years in which he was sick: "we have seen mother carrying our father on her back and taking him to the health post." Like all people, leaders are often tested, but their perseverance testifies to their faith and their commitment to their dreams, and as such distinguishes them as leaders.

In the first section of this chapter we looked from a more theoretical perspective at the meaning of servant leadership, empowerment, and downward mobility as central concepts. In the second and third sections, a selection of "tools" for use in empowering leaders toward servant leadership was discussed, as well as selected characteristics of empowered servant leadership. These two sections moved away from theoretical reflections and made use of the data generated by the ALS, especially by referring to the lives and work of influential Christian leaders in Angola, Kenya, and the CAR. One aspect that these examples showed is that, as was suggested at the beginning of this chapter, "empowering servant leadership is not extinct in Africa."

CONCLUSION:
SERVANT LEADERSHIP AS A NEW DAWN THAT BRINGS HOPE

In Mark's Gospel, Jesus is reported saying: "You know that those who are regarded as rulers of the Gentiles lord it over them, and their high officials exercise authority over them. Not so with you. Instead, whoever wants to become great among you must be your servant" (Mark 10:42–43, NIV). Over and against the many instances of predatory rule on the African continent, our ALS research demonstrated that many Christian leaders in Africa exemplify empowering servant leadership.

We found two leadership concepts that played a crucial role: empowerment and downward mobility. Empowerment enables people to define themselves and to construct their identities and future. Downward mobility is the opposite of the typical upward-bound race toward power and honor. For Christians, the best way to explain it is to say that it follows the model of Christ's self-emptying or self-lowering in becoming human, in serving humankind, and in sacrificing his life in service of the world (Phil 2:6–8). Herein lies a strange paradox: It is by giving power away, serving and empowering those who are in need, that true leadership blossoms and, paradoxically, receives power and honor.

This chapter told the stories of influential Christian leaders. In every case education played a key role in their formation. In almost all cases the church and theological training in one way or another played a significant role. Thus, the education process went hand in hand with spiritual attributes like faith and calling, service, sacrifice, and especially, prayer. In contexts of poverty, war, and uncertainty, educated leaders were the ones who could make a difference and who brought both relief and hope.

Family and mentors clearly also played a crucial role in the formation of leaders while the role of choirs and music helps one to understand something of the African soul. This yearning to belong and share, to harmonize and enjoy the beauty and the message of the song, illustrates the deep relationship-based community awareness that makes choirs so much a part of African life. *I am because you are. We are because we sing.* Another factor that played a role was accessibility, and it can be seen as a natural inclination in a relation-based community.

The formation of servant leaders who empower their communities began with creating opportunities for them. They had the freedom to take risks and were given exposure, thus helping them to get "out of the box" and cross boundaries. Challenges, however, needed to be balanced by the security of faith communities, prayer, the trust of mentors, and the necessary means to reach out.

In short, the integrity of leaders is recognized by their willingness to serve, to give power away, and to sacrifice through servant leadership. "When things fall apart" (Achebe 1999), these leaders stand firm because of their faith and commitment, empowering and creating beacons of hope.

REFERENCES CITED

Achebe, Chinua. 1994 [1958]. *Things Fall Apart*. New York: Anchor Books.

Adeyemo, Tokunboh. 2006. "Leadership." In *African Bible Commentary*, general editor Tokunboh Adeyemo, 546. Nairobi: World Alive.

Beck, Richard. 2013. "Downward Mobility." Blogspot entry. Experimental Theology website. Based on Henri Houwen's *The Selfless Way of Christ*. March 19. http://experimentaltheology.blogspot.com/2013/03/downward-mobility.html.

Bediako, Kwame. 1992. *Theology and Identity: The Impact of Culture upon Christian Thought in the Second Century and in Modern Thought*. Oxford: Regnum.

Carl, Arend E. 2012. *Teacher Empowerment through Curriculum Development—Theory into Practice*. 4th ed. Cape Town: Juta.

Castells, Manuel. 2000. *End of Millennium: The Information Age—Economy, Society, and Culture*. Volume 3. 2nd ed. Oxford: Blackwell.

"Global Survey on Theological Education" (GSTE). 2011–13. World Council of Churches. http://www.globethics.net/web/gtl/research/global-survey.

Gorman, Michael J. 2009. *Inhabiting the Cruciform God: Kenosis, Justification, and Theosis in Paul's Narrative Soteriology*. Grand Rapids, MI: Eerdmans.

Greenleaf, Robert K. 2007. "The Servant as Leader." https://greenleaf.org/what-is-servant-leadership/.

Mombo, Esther, and Heleen Joziasse. 2011. *If You Have No Voice, Just Sing! Narratives of Women's Lives and Theological Education at St. Paul's University*. Limuru, Kenya: Zapf Chancery.

Nouwen, Henri J. M. 1989. *In the Name of Jesus: Reflections on Christian Leadership*. New York: Crossroad.

———. 2007. *The Selfless Way of Christ: Downward Mobility and the Spiritual Way of Christ*. Maryknoll, NY: Orbis Books.

Osei-Mensah, Gottfried. 1990. *Wanted: Servant Leaders: The Challenge of Christian Leadership in Africa Today*. Achimota, Ghana: African Christian Press.

Sanneh, Lamin. 2003. *Whose Religion Is Christianity? The Gospel beyond the West*. Grand Rapids, MI: Eerdmans.

Swart, Ignatius. 2006. *The Churches and the Development Debate: Perspectives on a Fourth Generation Approach*. Stellenbosch: SUN.

Tutu, Desmond M. 1999. *No Future without Forgiveness*. New York: Doubleday.

World Health Organization. 2006. "Professor Nestor Mamadou Nali: Medicine Is a Lifelong Religion; It Is a Calling." Heroes for Health in the Central African Republic. http://www.who.int/world-health-day/previous/2006/car/nali/en/.

Chapter 10

Reading and Leading— Challenges for African Christian Leaders

Robert J. Priest, Kirimi Barine, and Alberto Lucamba Salombongo

AFRICAN CHRISTIANS AS READERS

As people of the Book, Christians often place a high value on reading. While in earlier eras elites in much of the world monopolized literacy in service of status and power, Christians have often been at the forefront of educating the masses for literacy. Protestants especially have placed a strong emphasis on allowing everyone to read the Bible and interpret it competently. Wherever such Christians have been influential, this value has positively influenced education, literacy rates, the publishing of reading materials, and reading itself (Woodberry 2012, 249–51). And yet scholars have largely failed to study the reading patterns of global Christians and to consider what those patterns tell us about world Christianity. This chapter is intended as a first step toward researching and analyzing these patterns and considering how an understanding of these patterns might be helpful for those involved in writing, publishing, and disseminating Christian materials today.

The three countries that were examined are majority Christian.[1] The World Christian Database reports adult literacy rates of 57 percent for the Central African Republic (CAR); 70 percent for Angola; and 72 percent for Kenya. While each country is multilingual, we carried out research in the official language of Angola (Portuguese), in both official languages of

---

[1] Angola, with a population of 14 million, is roughly 60 percent Roman Catholic and an additional 28 percent Protestant. The CAR, with 4.5 million, in its last census was half Protestant and 29 percent Roman Catholic. Kenya, with a population of 43 million, is roughly half Protestant and a quarter Roman Catholic.

Kenya (English and Swahili), and in French for the CAR.[2] The question-naire was administered to Christians only, and largely targeted those who were literate and thus had more formal education than average, and those who were active in their churches.[3] Nine percent of our respondents were pastors.

African communities, it is often said, need to cultivate a stronger reading culture (Chakava 1996, 34; Otike 2011, Commeyras, and Mazile 2011). However, our survey results provide evidence that many African Christians read quite a bit. One-third of the respondents indicated they had read at least six books in the last year, with 60 percent of pastors reporting they had read at least six. This can be compared to Pew results showing that half of American adults had read five or fewer books in the previous year (Pew 2014). That is, while African Christians read books at lower rates than Americans do, the difference is less than one might expect. African pastors read books at higher rates than the adult US population as a whole.[4]

In our interviews many influential African leaders reported being avid readers, often pointing out the books in their offices or libraries and re-porting plans to collect and read more. Pastor René Malépou, president of the Communauté des Eglises Baptistes Indépendantes in the CAR, for example, pointed to the disorder among his office books as evidence of his frequent use of them. He reported that he regularly wakes up at midnight and reads till 4 a.m. Pastor Dinis Eurico of Angola, radio preacher and national president of the Igreja Evangélica Sinodal de Angola, reports read-ing the entire Bible each year. He reads a wide variety of books by African and American Christian writers, including books by Nigerian theologian Tokunboh Adeyemo and Ugandan Bishop Festo Kivengere, both of whom he considers himself privileged to have met. Twenty-six-year-old Kenyan environmentalist Patrick Nyachogo reports that he reads a minimum of one book per month, mostly by African authors. Chinua Achebe's *Things Fall Apart* is a favorite.

---

[2] While Sango also is an official language of the CAR and is widely spoken, French is the language of schooling, and thus the CAR Research team decided that French would serve for our purposes.

[3] Fifteen percent of Kenyan respondents were pastors (13.2 percent) or de-nominational leaders (2.1 percent). In the CAR, 12.7 percent of respondents were either pastors (9 percent) or denominational leaders (3.7 percent). And just over 4.6 percent of Angolan respondents were either pastors (4.2 percent) or denomi-national leaders (0.4 percent).

[4] Survey results also showed that more than half of the respondents indicated that they read the Bible daily, with three-quarters indicating they read the Bible at least once a week. By comparison, roughly 21 percent of self-identified Christians in the United States read the Bible daily and 50 percent at least weekly (Barna Group 2014, 11).

Various leaders reported reading in their area of expertise. For example, medical professor Nestor Mamadou Nali of the CAR reports that he reads technical literature related to his specialty as a professor of medicine but also reads on the topic of leadership. Civil engineer and business owner Evariste Dignito of the CAR reported reading primarily books on civil engineering but also the Bible, where he especially enjoys the historical books of Kings and Chronicles. Architect Edouard Nvouni (the CAR) reads technical literature in his field but also Christian literature more broadly and the Bible. Reading, he says, helps him develop intellectually. General Kianga of Kenya indicated that he likes to read about other African leaders like Julius Nyerere and Nelson Mandela. The forty-year-old Cosmas Maina, founding director of Teen's Watch, an organization serving at-risk drug and alcohol addicts as well as prostitutes, reads widely both on the Internet and elsewhere. He reports that he almost exclusively reads sources written by non-Africans because he cannot find African authors addressing the topics of drug addiction, community action, and harm reduction that are his focus.

Leading pastors often stressed the importance of broad reading to their ministries. For example, Assemblies of God Pastor Edward Munene of Kenya said, "I have a statement I love saying to myself, that if I am not learning, I am not growing. And if I am not growing then I am dying." He reports that he set himself a goal for 2013 of reading 130 books, a goal he achieved. Pastor Oscar Muriu of Nairobi Chapel said he regularly asks other pastors to recommend books he should be reading. He intentionally recruits pastoral interns who are university educated and "who have a love for books"—which he sees as a critical pastoral attribute in the modern urban world. His reading, he reports, is increasingly oriented toward books focusing on leadership, ministry, and the specific questions he needs to address in his preaching. Bishop Bosco of Kenya indicated that he reads as part of sermon preparation and listed as favorites Dag Heward-Mills of Ghana, David Oyedepo of Nigeria, and John C. Maxwell of the United States.

Some African Christian leaders we interviewed highlighted the cost of books and stated that they thus preferred using a computer or cell phone to read resources on the Internet, often for free. Patrick Nyachogo points out, for example, that Joel Osteen's books are expensive, but that he is able regularly to read free short postings on Osteen's web page. In each country over 20 percent of respondents indicated that they read the news, articles, or books on their cell phone every day. And yet over half of respondents reported at least occasionally purchasing books at local Christian bookshops.[5] In all three countries African Christians read using a combination of print and electronic resources.

---

[5] In Angola, 57.5 percent; in the CAR, 56.8 percent; and in Kenya, 72.1 percent.

FAVORITE AUTHORS OF AFRICAN CHRISTIANS

One of the items on our survey asked: "If you have a favorite author, what is his or her name?" While 3,614 respondents provided an answer to this question, many answers were illegible, incomplete (using only a first or last name), or referenced an author of a book of the Bible. Some provided the name of a Bible translator/translation (Louis Segond in the CAR, João Almeida in Angola). Furthermore, many names appeared only once or twice, proving difficult to identify. By limiting the analysis to author names showing up three or more times within a single country, we were able to determine the identity of each named author. This gave us a manageable and yet sufficiently large data set for analysis. The data in this chapter refers to eighty-eight names identified by Kenyan respondents as favorite authors, forty-four names by CAR respondents, and thirty names by those in Angola (see Appendix B, Q.93). At one end of the continuum are authors who received only three votes. At the other end we find 162 entries by Kenyans identifying Ben Carson, a retired African American neurosurgeon from Johns Hopkins, as their favorite author. Table 10–1 provides the ranking of the top names in each country, beginning with names mentioned most frequently. (If two names are listed an equal number of times, they are given the same numerical ranking.)

Angolan favorite authors included the poet and first president of Angola António Agostinho Neto (#1); a psychiatrist (Augusto Cury #8); musicians such as Irmã Sofia (#5); the poet Luís Vaz de Camões (#23), as well as other literary figures; novelists; and pastors. CAR favorites included the fiction author Ahmadou Kourouma (#5); the film director and producer Ousmane Sembène (#8); ethnologist and writer Amadou Hampâté Bâ (#8); folklorist and poet Birago Diop (#33); along with other literary figures, novelists, and pastors. Kenyan favorite authors included a historian (Assa Okoth, #32); a political scientist (Ali Mazrui, #56); a former politician (Miguna Miguna, #22); a former criminal (John Kiriamiti, #20); a theologian (John Mbiti, #26); and various other literary figures, novelists, and pastors.

In all three countries prominent literary figures whose works were not religious or Christian were also included in the top names given. Often these were authors from their own country. Thus, CAR respondents identified two local literary figures, Pierre Sammy Mackfoy (#1) and Étienne Goyémidé (#2), as their favorite authors. Angola respondents identified two Angolan literary figures as their favorite authors, António Agostinho Neto (#1), and the white Angolan writer "Pepetela"—Artur Carlos Maurício Pestana dos Santos (#2). Slightly lower in the rankings Kenyans noted Kenyan literary figures Ngugi Wa Thiong'o (#3), Wallah Bin Wallah (#14), Ken Walibora (#17), Francis Imbuga (#30), Grace Ogot (#48), and Marjorie Oludhe Macgoye (#70). Kenyans also identified top African literary figures from other countries as favorites, including Nigerian Chinua Achebe (#4)

Angola	CAR	Kenya
1. António Agostinho Neto	1. Pierre Sammy Mackfoy	1. Ben Carson
2. Pepetela	2. Étienne Goyémidé	2. Joel Osteen
3. John Maxwell	3. Zacharias Tanee Fomum	3. Ngugi Wa Thiong'o
4. Rebecca Brown	4. Billy Graham	4. Chinua Achebe
5. Irmã Sofia	5. Ahmadou Kourouma	5. John C. Maxwell
6. Canguimbo Ananas	6. Alfred Kuen	6. Joyce Meyer
6. Luís "Aires" Samakumbi	6. Paul Mbunga Mpindi	6. Rick Warren
8. Augusto Cury	8. Amadou Hampâté Bâ	8. T. D. Jakes
8. Billy Graham	8. Camara Laye	8. Ellen G. White
8. Oscar Ribas	8. Ousmane Sembène	10.Myles Munroe
11.Silas Malafaia	11. Silas Ali	11. David Oyedepo
11. Penelas Santana	12. Léopold Sédar Senghor	12. William Booth
13. Tim LaHaye	13. Aimé Fernand David Césaire	12. Dag Heward-Mills
14. Augusto Chipesse		14. Wallah Bin Wallah
14. Rick Warren	14. Albert Camus	15. Sidney Sheldon
14. Wanhenga Xitu	14. Victor Hugo	16. John Stott
17. Bambila (Manuel Simão)	14. Martin Luther King	17. Nancy Van Pelt
	14. David Oyedepo	17. Ken Walibora
17. Jaime Kemp	14. John Stott	19. William Shake-speare
17. Fritz Laubach	19. Jean Jacques Rousseau	
17. Lor Mbongo	20. David Yonggi Cho	20. John Kiriamiti
17. Joyce Meyer	20. Tommy Lee Osborn	21. Said Ahmed Mo-hammed
17. Mike Murdock		

Table 10–1. Favorite Authors by Country

and Tanzanian Said Ahmed Mohammed (#20). Respondents from the CAR identified leading literary authors from other African Francophone nations, such as Ahmadou Kourouma (#5) from Côte d'Ivoire, Camara Laye (#8) from Guinea, Amadou Hampâté Bâ (#8) from Mali, and Ousmane Sembène (#8) and Léopold Sédar Senghor (#12) from Senegal. Respondents from Angola mainly chose literary figures from Angola, including Oscar Ribas (#8) and Penelas Santana (#11), but also mentioned some from Brazil (Augusto Cury, #8) and Portugal (Luis Camões, #23). Of course, literary figures from outside Africa also made their appearance in these lists: for Kenyan respondents, William Shakespeare (#19) and C. S. Lewis (#38); for respondents from the CAR, Albert Camus and Victor Hugo (tied for #14), Jean-Jacques Rousseau (#19), Emile Zola (#28), and Jean-Paul Sartre (#33). In all three countries novelists that we might not consider literary figures were mentioned as favorites: in Kenya, Sidney Sheldon (#15), John Grisham (#22), Francine Rivers (#32), Danielle Steele (#38), James Patterson (#41), Robert Ludlum (#58), Karen Kingsbury (#58), Dan Brown (#70), and J. K. Rowlings (#70).

A surprisingly high percentage of favorite authors were ordained pastors and preachers, many of them megachurch pastors. In Kenya, favorite pastoral authors included Joel Osteen (#2), John C. Maxwell (#5), Joyce Meyer (#6), Rick Warren (#6), T. D. Jakes (#8), Ellen G. White (#8), Billy Graham (#25), Kenneth Hagin (#26), John Mason (#26), Benny Hinn (#32), Max Lucado (#32), Bill Hybels (#41), Mark Finley (#58), John Hagee (#58), John Piper (#58), Juanita Bynum (#70), and Robert Schuller (#70) from the United States. Favorites from Nigeria included David Oyedepo (#11) and Chris Oyakhilome (#32); from Ghana, Dag Heward-Mills (#12); from the Bahamas, Myles Munroe (#10); and from Great Britain, William Booth (#12), John Stott (#16), Derek Prince (#45), and Charles Spurgeon (#48). Kenyan pastors included John Mbiti (#26), Joe Kayo (#32), and Simon Mbevi (#48).

Angolans also identified pastors as favorite authors, including Angolans Augusto Chipesse (#14) and Joaquim Hatewa (#23), a Roman Catholic priest. Angolan favorite pastoral writers from the United States included John Maxwell (#3), Billy Graham (#8), Tim LaHaye (#13), Rick Warren (#14), Joyce Meyer (#17), Mike Murdock (#17), Jaime Kemp (#17), and Benny Hinn (#23). From Brazil, we find Silas Malafaia (#11), and from Great Britain, John Stott (#23).

CAR respondents identified favorite pastor-authors from France, Alfred Kuen (#6) and Henri Blocher (#22); from Switzerland, Jules Marcel Nicole (#22) and René Pache (#28); from Cameroon, Zacharias Tanee Fomum (#3); from the DRC, Paul Bunga Mpindi (#6); from the CAR, David Koudougueret (#33); from Nigeria, David Oyedepo (#14) and Emmanuel Eni (#33); from South Korea, David Yonggi Cho (#20); from China, Watchman Nee (#28); from Great Britain, John Stott (#14), Derek Prince (#22), and Charles Spurgeon (#33); and from the United States,

Billy Graham (#4), Martin Luther King, Jr. (#14), Tommy Lee Osborn (#20), and Bill Bright (#33).

For authors who are ministers, one variable that sometimes affected who was considered a favorite author was denominational affiliation. Some leading ministerial authors (Billy Graham, T. D. Jakes, John Maxwell, Joyce Meyer, Myles Munroe, Joel Osteen, John Stott, Rick Warren) are read widely across denominations. For others, there is a much closer tie to a particular church. Thus, in Angola all fourteen nominations of Luís Aires Samakumbi came from his own denomination Igreja Evangélica Congregacional de Angola. In the CAR, fourteen out of the fifteen nominations for Silas Ali came from his own denomination, Communauté des Eglises Apostoliques en Centrafrique. In Kenya, 74 percent of Ellen G. White's fifty votes came from fellow Seventh Day Adventists; 76 percent of Nancy Van Pelt's seventeen votes also came from fellow Seventh Day Adventists; and all thirty votes for William Booth came from members of his own Salvation Army. Similarly, in Kenya, Ghanaian Pastor Dag Heward-Mills and Nigerian pastors David Oyedepo and Chris Oyakhilome were cited largely, though not exclusively, by members of their own church associations (Redeemed Gospel Church, Winner's Chapel, and Christ Embassy).

According to J. Kwabena Asamoah-Gyadu, a leading scholar of African Christianity, in some of these large, prosperity-oriented churches pastors regularly turn their sermons into books and expect all leaders in their church associations to read what they write while sometimes discouraging followers from reading the writings of others. In such settings reading is intertwined with a certain sort of spirituality and is a function of people's relationship with their spiritual leader, who is understood to mediate spirituality and success. What the top leader writes is sometimes treated as an "enchanted word." By reading this word, followers are "soaking in the anointing."[6]

READING PATTERNS IN A GLOBALIZED WORLD

One of the most obvious observations from the data about book authors and their readers is that we are operating in a globalized world. Table 10–2 provides information on the percentage of readers in each of the three countries (Angola, the CAR, Kenya) that identified a favorite author from specific countries of the world and shows the national languages of the authors' countries of origin.

The following observations are based on Table 10–2:

1. African Christians are reading and appreciating authors from all over the world. While a slight majority (57 percent) of Angolans have a favorite author who is Angolan, only 26 percent of respondents from

---

[6] Personal communication, June 22, 2014.

National Language	Authors' Nationality	Authors' Language	Kenya Favs.	CAR Favs.	Angola Favs.
English	Bahamas	English	2.8%	—	—
	Canada	English	0.3%	—	—
	Ghana	English	2.0%	—	—
	Kenya	English/ Swahili	19.2%	—	—
	Nigeria	English	9.7%	2.6%	—
	South Africa	English	0.2%	—	—
	Tanzania	English/ Swahili	1.1%	—	—
	United King-dom	English	6.8%	3.7%	1.1%
	USA	English	56.4%	11.6%	29.4%
French	Cameroon	French	—	6.6%	—
	Central African Republic	French	—	26%	—
	Côte d'Ivoire	French	—	5.7%	—
	Democratic Republic of Congo	French	0.5%	4.4%	1.4%
	France	French	—	15.5%	—
	Guinea	French	—	4.4%	—
	Mali	French	—	3.8%	—
	Martinique	French	—	3.6%	—
	Senegal	French	—	6.8%	—
	Switzerland	French	—	2.0%	—
Portuguese	Angola	Portuguese	—	—	57.4%
	Brazil	Portuguese	0.3%	—	8.2%
	Portugal	Portuguese	—	—	1.1%
Other	China	Chinese	0.3%	0.9%	—
	Germany	German	0.5%	0.7%	1.4%
	South Korea	Korean	—	1.5%	—

Table 10–2. Percentages of Readers Naming Favorite Authors according to Origin

the CAR identify a favorite author from the CAR and only 19 percent of Kenyans favor a Kenyan author.

2. Language affects global flows of influence through writing. Fully 98 percent of Kenyans identify a favorite author from a nation where English is the national language, although it should be noted that some Kenyan favorite authors write in both English and Swahili (such as Ngugi Wa Thiong'o). In the CAR 79 percent of respondents name an author from a nation where French is a national language, and in Angola, 67 percent name an author from a nation where Portuguese is the national language. English-speaking authors seem to have an advantage concerning the translation of their works, given that English books have been translated into Portuguese or French and read in Angola and the CAR more frequently than French-language or Portuguese-language authors are translated and read in English by Kenyans.

3. There is a significant presence of favorite authors from the United States across all countries; with 12 percent in the CAR, 29 percent in Angola, and 56 percent in Kenya.

4. There is a strong interest in writings by African authors. Fifty-nine percent of Angolans, 60 percent of respondents in the CAR, and 33 percent of Kenyans identify a favorite author who is African.

THE FOCUS OF BOOKS BY FAVORITE AUTHORS

If we examine the focus of books written by favorite authors, some of these are novels situated in African settings, such as Chinua Achebe's *Things Fall Apart*, Elechi Amadi's *The Concubine*, Ousmane Sembène's *Les bouts de bois de Dieu* (God's bits of wood), and Ngugi wa Thiong'o's *The River Between*. Others are novels written by non-Africans and without an African focus, such as John Grisham's *The Firm*, Robert Ludlum's *The Bourne Identity*, and Sidney Sheldon's *Nothing Lasts Forever*.

Many of the favorite authors write books focused in practical ways on achieving financial success, such as Napoleon Hill's *Think and Grow Rich* or Robert Kiyosaki's *Rich Dad, Poor Dad*. In the rapidly changing socioeconomic order of our respondents, with radically new social patterns shaping mysterious new patterns of wealth and poverty, respondents clearly have a deep concern for understanding how to negotiate this world successfully. Of course, the accompanying strong interest in prosperity theology that some of the authors exemplify (T. D. Jakes, Joyce Meyer, Joel Osteen) raises important questions about whether people's appropriate concern for thriving in the modern world is informed and guided by theological wisdom that truly contributes to healthy human flourishing.

Other favorite authors write motivational and self-help books. These include Stephen Covey's *The Seven Habits of Highly Effective People*; John Mason's *An Enemy Called Average*; Joyce Meyer's *New Day, New*

You; Pepe Minambo's *Inspired for Destiny;* Erick Opingo's *You Were Born to Be an Answer to Your Generation;* Joel Osteen's *Your Best Life Now: Seven Steps to Living Your Full Potential;* Robin Sharma's *The Greatness Guide;* and Rick Warren's *The Purpose Driven Life.* Various favorite authors write books providing guidance on being an effective leader, such as Bill Hybels's *Courageous Leadership;* John Maxwell's *The Twenty-one Irrefutable Laws of Leadership;* and Myles Munroe's *Becoming a Leader.* Again, it makes sense that in a rapidly changing world, and in regions where Christianity's growth rate has outstripped its supply of mature leaders, and where many of our respondents are playing leadership roles in church and society, authors who write about leadership would prove attractive.

Many favorite authors focus on women, such as Joyce Meyer's *The Confident Woman,* or T. D. Jakes's *Woman, Thou Art Loosed.* Others focus specifically on men, such as Myles Munroe's *Understanding the Purpose and Power of a Man;* and Simon Mbevi's *Dad Is Destiny.* Family dynamics are also often featured by favorite authors, such as James Dobson's *Dare to Discipline;* Steve Farrar's *Point Man: How a Man Can Lead a Family;* or Stormie Omartian's *The Power of a Praying Wife.* Marriage shows up as a frequent theme as with Nancy Van Pelt's *Highly Effective Marriage.*

While 42 percent of our Kenyan respondents were female, only 12 percent of Kenyan respondents nominated a favorite author who was female, with 19 percent of women naming a female author and only 7 percent of male respondents doing so. Many favorite authors were nominated primarily by female respondents—Karen Kingsbury (100 percent), Francine Rivers (100 percent), Stormie Omartian (100 percent), Rebecca Brown (75 percent), and Joyce Meyer (71 percent). In these cases the gender of nominated authors correlated with the gender of the respondents.[7] However, it was also true that women named authors, male or female, who write about realities for women, as favorites at high levels. Women provided none or only a small proportion of favorite author nominations for many of the male preachers—Benny Hinn (0 percent), Reinhard Bonnke (0 percent), John Piper (0 percent), John Stott (15 percent), John Maxwell (17 percent), Billy Graham (18 percent), Chris Oyakilome (20 percent), Myles Munroe (24 percent). However, they constituted a high proportion of those nominating other male preachers: Joel Osteen (58 percent), Dag Heward-Mills (50 percent), Max Lucado (50 percent), T. D. Jakes (48 percent). At least some of those authors focus their writings on realities related to women. In our interviews with women leaders they often named female authors for whom they had an appreciation. For example, teacher and school chaplain Mrs. Nelly Owilla of Kenya listed four favorite authors that are female, Margaret Ogolla, Grace Ogott, Carol Mandi, and Terresia Wairimu, along with three that are male, Reinhardt Bonke, Joel Osteen, and Chinua Achebe. Angolan pastor Adelaide Catahna reports being particularly affected by *Women at the Top* by Diane Halpern and Fanny Cheung.

---

[7] $X^2(1, N=1465) = 47.33, p<.001.$

Again and again, in the books written by both religious and nonreligious writers, themes of power, success, and human flourishing make their appearance against the backdrop of struggles with painful childhoods, poverty, and the challenges of modern life. Exemplars of success against such a backdrop are particularly attractive—as with the top Kenyan favorite, Ben Carson. A high proportion of these authors, quite apart from their writing, are successful and/or famous in some arena of life. Some, such as the Nigerian prosperity pastors David Oyedepo of the Winner's Chapel and Chris Oyakhilome of Christ's Embassy, are extremely wealthy.[8]

FAVORITE CHRISTIAN AUTHORS

The prominence of influential preachers, especially megachurch pastors, among favorite authors bears special notice. For Angolans, this includes John Maxwell, Billy Graham, and Rick Warren; for CAR respondents, David Yonggi Cho and David Oyedepo; and for Kenyans, Joel Osteen, T. D. Jakes, Myles Munroe, Chris Oyokhilome, Robert Schuller, Rick Warren, and Dag Heward-Mills. Nearly one-third of CAR and Angolan respondents and half of Kenyans identified a preacher/pastor as their favorite author. Part of the reason for this is doubtless because these individuals' institutional base, sometimes in a large megachurch, and often with a television presence, positions them as successful and thus worth learning from. However, unlike seminary professors, who tend to teach and write in ways oriented toward academic criteria, highly successful pastors have achieved their positions by their ability to speak to broad audiences. Furthermore, the very structure of the megachurch as a modern phenomenon involves a concentration of resources and access to large audiences. These factors give the megachurch pastor an ideal launching platform for publishing success.

In Kenya denominational affiliation was significantly related to whether the respondent's favorite author was African or not. Roman Catholics were nearly twice as likely to list a favorite author from Africa as from elsewhere. By contrast, Anglican, African Inland Church, and Pentecostal respondents were more than twice as likely to name a favorite author from outside Africa.

One notable finding from our research is that a significant proportion of respondents identified a favorite author who explicitly writes with a Christian voice/viewpoint. Thirty-eight percent of respondents in the CAR, 53 percent of Angolan respondents, and fully 65 percent of Kenyan respondents identified a favorite author whose writings are explicitly Christian.

---

[8] Oyedepo's net worth has been estimated at US$150 million and Oyakhilome's at US$30–$50 million (Mfonobong Nsehe [contributor], "The Five Richest Pastors in Nigeria," *Forbes* [June 7, 2011]).

However, the authors they identify as favorites are much more likely to be Christian if they are American than if they are African.[9] When respondents identified a favorite author from the United States—88 percent of the time in Kenya, 94 percent of the time in the CAR, and 100 percent of the time in Angola—this author was explicitly Christian. However, when naming a favorite from their own country, they were only explicitly Christian 27 percent of the time in Angola, 3 percent of the time in the CAR, and 11 percent of the time in Kenya.

In our survey we found that African Christians read relatively few authors who are neither African nor Christian (9.7 percent). That is, our respondents do not widely read European and American authors who write in a secular voice. They identified a high percentage of their favorite authors as African (41.6 percent) and a high percentage as Christian (58.2 percent). However, the degree of overlap between the two was low, with relatively few respondents (9.5 percent) identifying favorite authors who were both African and Christian.

THE NEED FOR AFRICAN CHRISTIAN WRITERS

If Tim Stafford is correct in his claim that the strength of a "national church is in direct proportion to the strength of its body of local Christian literature" (quoted in Jewell 2009), then this situation should be a matter of concern. Senegalese poet Birago Diop has argued that "truth depends not only on who listens but on who speaks" (cited in Julien 2014, 209). If we understand Diop as writing about the subjective plausibility and relevance of truth, then the one who speaks (and writes) is as important as the one who listens (and reads) if readers are to grasp, appreciate, and meaningfully apply any articulated truth to their lives. Again and again, African Christian leaders that we interviewed signaled their unhappiness with the minimal availability of quality publications by African Christian authors. Such leaders often mentioned both the breadth of their reading and their stated preference for African authors. For example, Dr. David Koudougueret of the CAR reads "African," "Asiatic," and "American" literature but reports being more attracted to books by "African authors because they express African realities." Denominational leader René Malépou calls on

---

[9] In the CAR, when an author from a non-African country is named as favorite, 63 percent of the time the author is Christian, but when an author from an African nation is named, he or she is Christian only 22 percent of the time. In Angola, when an author from a non-African country is named as favorite, 87 percent of the time the author is Christian, but when naming an author from an African nation, the author is explicitly Christian only 29 percent of the time. In Kenya, when an author from a non-African country is named as favorite, 87 percent of the time the author is Christian, but when an author from an African nation is named, he or she is explicitly Christian only 21 percent of the time.

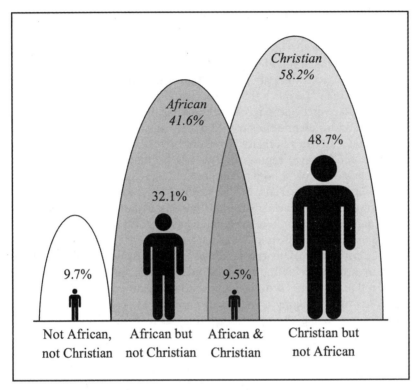

Figure 10–1. Identity of Authors that African Christians Say Are Their Favorites

African theologians to leave an inheritance, not of "old cars or houses," but of "books to read"—something he believes the African church needs. The leading African organizations identified and studied in our survey sometimes stressed this value. For example, in the 2012 Strategic Plan of the Angolan Instituto Superior de Teologia Evangélica no Lubango, the lack of availability of contextual literature is identified as a significant threat to healthy theological education. The stated solution was to "incentivize Angolan theologians to write articles and books"; to "promote a seminar on how to write books"; and to translate and publish writings focused on African contexts into Portuguese for availability in Angola.

Many of the Christian leaders we interviewed indicated that others had encouraged them to write, believing that their stories would be of interest or that their contextual wisdom would be more helpful than what was written by foreigners. Many had written theses or dissertations. Others (such as Alice Kirambi, executive director of Christian Partners Development Agency) had written proposals or reports for donors. Some, such as Cosmas Maina, had prepared pamphlets to copy and hand out, or have posted their writing online. Several reported having unpublished manuscripts in hand. However, relatively few had published, and what was published does not appear to have been widely circulated.

A fair number of the top leaders interviewed indicated a desire to write and had taken initial steps toward this end, but they also expressed a measure of uncertainty about how to proceed. Kenyan General Kianga reports that many people have approached him to write his memoirs, but he has not consented, although he is "thinking about it." He worries that he never kept a journal and thus would not be able to be precise or accurate. Furthermore, Kenya's Security Act would restrict what he could report. Bishop Bosco (Kenya) reports that he has begun work on five different books. He has people who have offered to help, and he has been collecting bibliographic materials, but he has not yet published. He feels time commitments and financial restraints limit opportunities. Ideally, he would like to gain a platform on television. He wants to devote the next decade and a half to writing. Bishop Maisha (Kenya) reports that he is preparing an office with a library featuring key people and authors God has used in Africa in different fields and that he would like to begin writing. He would like to tell his story but would also love to write about the experience and challenges of developing a successful ministry. He is currently finalizing plans for organizing and registering a magazine in Nairobi.

Pastor Oscar Muriu (Kenya) expressed the desire, in the "third season" of his life, to be a sage and available "to the younger generation but not necessarily face to face or physically, but more in the sense that I can write. . . . I can be available and accessible to them, but I'm not the one running around." However, he reports struggling with writing, with busyness, with feeling inadequate, with feeling that he thinks best by speaking in social settings (rather than isolating himself to write), and with wondering how he might work with others to get his ideas in print. Patrick Nyachogo, a twenty-six-year-old Kenyan environmentalist and business leader, has published online articles and is writing a "motivational book based on the biblical life of Joseph" oriented toward addressing the gap between getting a degree and getting one's first job. It was unclear whether he had a publisher lined up. Seminary professor Eunice Chiquete of Angola plans to write a book based on conversations with girls and focused on realities in the lives of girls and women. However, she is unsure who will publish it. Isaac Mutua, a forty-two-year-old Kenyan teaching sex education (and about HIV/AIDS) in Kenyan schools, received the highest number of nominations for the most influential non-clergy leader in Kenya. He had written up his sex-education materials and shared some of these with our research team, but clearly he had little idea how to go about exploring publishing possibilities.

Some key Christian leaders identified in our research have published articles and/or books. Professor Nestor Mamadou Nali of the CAR has published over a hundred medical reports. Mrs. Marie Paule Balezou of the CAR, a successful business woman, wrote a book that was widely circulated in the CAR, although subsequently it was withdrawn from circulation because of errors and needed corrections. Dr. Esther Mombo of Kenya has published many theological articles and a book focused on contemporary African realities. Simon Mbevi, founder and director of Transform Kenya, has published several books related to prayer, sexual purity, boys, and being a good father. Pastor Dinis Eurico published a book in Brazil and has several other completed manuscripts that have not yet been published. These, however, are the exceptions, not the rule.

Again and again key leaders expressed a desire for more writings by African Christian leaders, relevant for "daily use at home, school or church" (Mugambi 2013, 110). Several of the organizations we studied have formally stated the importance of improving the quantity and quality of African Christian writing. FOCUS Kenya, a nationwide student ministry, reported having recently begun a department of research and publication, and indicated it would like to become "a publisher like InterVarsity Press." However, resources for this are not yet available.

Thus our research demonstrates a gap. Even though a high proportion of African Christians named a favorite author who was African, and a large proportion of African Christians named a favorite author who was Christian, in our survey only a small percentage of African Christians named a favorite author who was both African and Christian. This merits careful consideration. What are the factors contributing to this?

FACTORS CONTRIBUTING TO THESE PATTERNS

The first factor is the central role of the educational sector in book sales and book exposure. One influence on what Africans read, and thus on their selection of favorite authors, is quite naturally their national educational systems (Chakava 1996). In Kenya, for example, since 2004 the Kenya Institute of Education (now the Kenya Institute of Curriculum Development) has specified approved books for Kenyan schools to assign, and many favorite authors come from this list of approved books. The books *Gifted Hands* and *Think Big* by Ben Carson are on this approved list, doubtless influencing Carson's selection as the #1 favorite author in Kenya. Four books by Kenyan Ngugi Wa Thiong'o (#3) are approved, one of which is in Swahili. Five of Nigerian Chinua Achebe's (# 4) books are on the approved list; seven by Wallah Bin Wallah (#14), in Swahili; eleven by Ken Walibora (#17), ten of them in Swahili; one by William Shakespeare (#19), fourteen by Said Ahmed Mohammed (#20), all in Swahili; one by Francis Imbuga (#30); one by Elechi Amadi (#45); three by Kithaka Wa Mberia (#48); one by Ali Mazrui (#58), one by Shellomith Nderitu (#58), and four by Marjorie Oludhe Macgoye (#70). A majority of assigned authors are African. Clearly, the fact that Kenyan schools are assigning these authors contributes to their economic success as authors and also exposes their work to a broad readership, thus influencing the likelihood of people selecting them as favorite authors. Younger respondents were significantly more likely to choose one of these education-endorsed authors than older respondents.[10] Similarly, books assigned in Angolan government schools are authored by favorite authors António Agostinho Neto (#1), Pepetela (#2), Oscar Ribas (#8), and Wanhenga Xitu (#14). And books assigned in government schools of the CAR are authored by favorite authors Pierre Sammy Mackfoy (#1), Étienne Goyémidé (#2), Ahmadou Kourouma (#5), Camara Laye (#8), Amadou Hampâté Bâ (#8), Ousmane Sembène (#8), Léopold Sédar Senghor (#12), Aimé Fernand David Césaire (#13), Albert Camus (#14), Victor Hugo (#14), and Jean Jacques Rousseau (#19).

Christian educational institutions do not function under a comparable list of approved authors. However, they do signal which authors are deemed important in other ways, such as by which books are stocked in theological libraries. So we examined the library holdings of five key Christian universities or theological institutions in Kenya (Africa International University, Daystar University, International Leadership University, Pan African University, and St. Paul's University) as a way of exploring the extent to which they stocked books by authors from our list. The following fifteen authors, in order, were the authors from our list with the largest presence in these libraries. All fifteen are Christian:[11]

Table 10–3. Top Fifteen Favorite Authors Ranked by Library Presence

1.	John Stott
2.	Andrew Murray*
3.	Billy Graham
4.	James Dobson
5.	C. S. Lewis
6.	Charles Spurgeon
7.	Tim LaHaye
8.	John Piper
9.	Watchman Nee
10.	Philip Yancey
11.	John Mbiti
12.	Max Lucado
13.	John C. Maxwell
14.	Bill Hybels
15.	Derek Prince

* While Andrew Murray was South African, we treat him in his era (1828–1917) for purposes of this chapter as part of a European world.

---

[10] $T(3706) = 7.79, p < .001.$

[11] We took the number of separate titles from each author in each library and added them together for a final number per author across the five libraries.

Mainstream evangelical European and American authors are featured centrally here. The only African Christian to make this top-fifteen list was John Mbiti (#11). Other favorite African Christian writers either were completely absent from these libraries (such as Joe Kayo, Chris Oyakhilome, David Oyedepo), or had a single book in one library (Dag Heward-Mills) or in two (Simon Mbevi). According to Phiri and Warner (2013, xxix), it is common across Africa for the libraries of theological institutions to be "full of donated books from the global north that address contextual theological questions from other contexts which the African church itself is not asking." Since the libraries of theological schools and Christian universities in Kenya, as elsewhere, are expensive to stock, and thus rely heavily on donations from non-African individuals and organizations (such as the Theological Book Network), it should not be surprising that the values of donors influence the acquisitions process with, in many cases, foreign authors themselves contributing their own books to the libraries. John Stott's Langham Trust contributes heavily to the libraries of theological institutions in Africa. Not surprisingly, his books show up in these libraries more frequently than any other authors from our list. Moreover, if donor values influence acquisitions, then it makes sense that library holdings would affect the authors who theological students and university-educated African Christians know.[12] When African pastors who have studied in such schools draw from and make reference to books they've read, it is to be expected that these are often books by Christian authors from outside Africa.

The primary way in which our respondents were exposed to African authors was through the national educational systems of Angola, the CAR, and Kenya, which had curricula that required and prioritized the reading of these authors. This requirement meant that books by these authors sold widely. It also gave people a chance to learn to appreciate them. One reason that respondents were less likely to choose favorite Christian authors who were African is because the curriculum and libraries of Christian educational institutions provide less prioritized support for African authors and less exposure to African authors than do national schools.

Because we were also interested in books being sold in Nairobi, we examined six Christian bookstores (two Keswick stores, one New Day, one Scripture Union, and two Wakestar stores), three nonreligious commercial book sellers (Nakumat, Uchumi Hyper, and Textbook Central Ltd[13]), and

---

[12] At Africa International University (AIU) the campus bookstore had books by the following authors on our list: Charles Spurgeon—15 titles; John Piper—7 titles; John Stott—5 titles; Bill Hybels—2 titles; John C. Maxwell—2 titles; and Max Lucado and Andrew Murray—1 title each. It would be interesting to examine the syllabi of such schools to see which authors from our list show up as assigned readings.

[13] Nakumat and Uchumi are major department store chains (with thirty-four and twenty-eight branches, respectively) in Kenya, and each has a large book section.

a large number of street vendors in order to determine the fifteen authors whose books are most present in each of these three categories of sales arenas (see Table 10–4).

Table 10–4 is interesting as much for what is absent as for what is featured. In positive terms, all three categories were dominated by the presence of Joyce Meyer, T. D. Jakes, Myles Munroe, and Joel Osteen—megachurch pastors and/or television personalities, all charismatic and/or Pentecostal, and all non-African. None of these four appeared in the top-fifteen list of library holdings. It is also worth noting that John Stott, the #1 author present in theological libraries, did not make any of the top-fifteen lists for booksellers. We did not find any of Stott's books for sale from street vendors.

In the Christian Bookstore list, Ghanaian megachurch pastor Dag Heward-Mills (#6) was the only African author in the top fifteen; Simon Mbevi was #30. No other African Christian authors from our list were present in any of the Christian bookstores. Among the commercial booksellers no African Christian author made the top fifteen, and Heward-Mills was the only African Christian author from our list that had even one book in one store. When it came to street vendors, while none of our African Christian authors showed up in the top fifteen, several did have publications being sold there (Heward-Mills, Kayo, Oyakhilome, Oyedepo).

In addition to placement in libraries and bookstores, visibility and publicity on radio and television also shape outcomes in terms of book exposure and reading. Consider the role of Christian television in Kenya. A perusal of the television channel Family TV shows that much of the programming is Christian. However, on examining the schedule for the week of May 19, 2014, we find that American religious personalities are central. Joel Osteen (#2) was featured Sunday at both 9 a.m. and 7 p.m., as well as Saturday at 1:30 p.m., and in the early morning on Monday and Friday. Joyce Meyer (#6) was featured at 10:30 a.m. and 10:30 p.m. Monday through Friday, and Sunday afternoon at 4 p.m. T. D. Jakes (#8) appeared at 12 noon on Saturday, at 2:30 p.m. on Thursday, and early mornings the other weekdays. Billy Graham (#25) was featured at 5 a.m. and 10:30 a.m. on Sunday mornings. Benny Hinn (#32) was featured Monday through Friday at 3:30 p.m. Max Lucado (#32) appeared at 12:30 p.m. on Wednesday. John Hagee (#58) appeared at 7 p.m. Monday through Friday and at 11:30 a.m. on Sunday. Robert Schuller (#70) appeared on Sunday at 4 a.m. Not a single Kenyan religious personality appeared with a regular program, and only one other African personality, Nigerian megachurch pastor Chris Oyakhilome (#32), appeared on the schedule, on Monday at 7:30 p.m. and Wednesday at 2 p.m.

Alternatively, one might consider radio, where some of the same authors have a pervasive presence. One radio station in Nairobi (Hope FM) features a book review program, where books by the following authors on our list

Table 10–4. Top Fifteen Favorite Authors Ranked by Bookstore Presence

Christian Bookstores	Other Commercial Book Sellers	Street Vendors
1. Joyce Meyer	1. Joyce Meyer	1. Joyce Meyer
2. T. D. Jakes	2. T. D. Jakes	1. T. D. Jakes
3. John C. Maxwell	3. Myles Munroe	1. Myles Munroe
4. Myles Munroe	4. Joel Osteen	4. C. S. Lewis
5. Karen Kingsbury	5. Robert H. Schuller	5. Tim LaHaye
6. Dag Heward-Mills	6. Stormie Omartian	6. Robert H. Schuller
7. Francine Rivers	7. John C. Maxwell	6. James Dobson
8. James Dobson	8. Ben Carson	8. Benny Hinn
8. Joel Osteen	9. James Dobson	8. Karen Kingsbury
10. Derek Prince	10. Rebecca Brown	8. John C. Maxwell
10. Kenneth Hagin	10. Steve Farrar	8. Joel Osteen
12. John Mason	10. Billy Graham	12. Stormie Omartian
13. Max Lucado	10. Karen Kingsbury	12. Ben Carson
13. Andrew Murray	10. John Mason	14. Billy Graham
13. Stormie Omartian	10. Francine Rivers	15. Francine Rivers

from outside Africa have been reviewed: Reinhard Bonnke, Juanita Bynum, Ben Carson, Morris Cerrulo, Stephen Covey, James Dobson, Billy Graham, John Hagee, Bill Hybels, T. D. Jakes, C. S. Lewis, Max Lucado, John Maxwell, Joyce Meyer, Myles Munroe, Stormie Omartian, Joel Osteen, Derek Prince, John Stott, Rick Warren, and Philip Yancey. Accrording to a staff member of Hope FM, African authors Simon Mbevi and David Oyedepo from our list were also reviewed. However, the charges to the author or publisher for a one-hour book review are expensive.[14] Such a cost is prohibitive for the ordinary African author.

If, then, we are to identify some of the key factors contributing to a situation where African writers have provided an extensive body of African literature that is not explicitly Christian, but that an otherwise vibrant African Christianity has not produced the literature that African

---

[14] If the author is present in the studio to talk about the book, it costs US$330; if the book is discussed without the author present, it costs US$200 (Kirimi Barine).

Christians seemingly desire and need, the following would be core dynamics to keep in mind.

1. Publishing and marketing are expensive and require adequate economic underpinnings. Most African Christians live within socioeconomic settings that are quite different from those faced by Christians in North America, Europe, and parts of Asia. The current global financial market patterns related to Christian publishing work against the flourishing of African Christian authors. Intentional correctives are needed.

2. While a billion people live in Africa, a large potential market, these people are spread across an enormous geographical area and are divided by numerous political and language boundaries—with a significant proportion being functionally illiterate. Would-be authors from the CAR work within a geographically vast country with poor transportation infrastructure and with a small population of 4.5 million, many of whom are illiterate or speak different languages. Unlike American would-be authors with an open market of more than 300 million fellow Americans speaking a single language, authors in the CAR encounter linguistic, geographic, and political barriers, as well as demographic realities, that work against broad dissemination of their work. Angolan Christian would-be authors, with a market of 21 million fellow Angolans, are isolated by political boundaries and language from all near neighbors and exist in a country where publishing historically has been "largely under the control of state-controlled monopolies" (Zell 1995, 4). The Angolan Christian author has limited options: self-publish or publish in Brazil with an established publisher that has a limited presence in Angola. There are no Christian publishers in Angola. Even in Kenya there are few publishers, and they have limited distribution outside of Kenya. A high proportion of the African Christian authors in our lists have self-published, and they market in rather ad hoc and limited ways—few with wide distribution. Some write for publishers in the USA or Europe, but such books are commonly far too expensive for African individuals or institutions to afford, sometimes costing the equivalent of US$100 or more. The system again works against an African Christian presence in print.

3. Publishing is a competitive arena, where those with a greater presence on television and radio are better positioned with major publishers (that provide high-quality editing and printing along with reasonable prices and good market placement). They also have a stronger financial base, which is a distinct advantage. While it is not true that each book sold by an American author precludes a book being sold by an African author, it is true that if a Nairobi television station fills its airtime with American authors, those slots of time are necessarily not available for African authors. Moreover, most African authors are not in a position to compete on a financially level playing field. It is worth considering possible ways in which the very success of Joyce Meyer, Joel Osteen, T. D. Jakes, and Myles Munroe—all of whom build off impressive platforms—compete

with and inhibit the flourishing of African Christian authors. Like these others, John Stott has achieved significant global success. However, unlike them, through Langham Partnerships he has leveraged his success into strong support for African Christian writers.

4. Christian missionaries historically distributed publications that were subsidized or free. The functionality of the publications was sometimes more important than their quality. Similarly, international Christian publishers often shipped their unsold books to African venues to be given away or sold at reduced rates. Given such patterns, authors were understood to be making a gratuitous spiritual contribution through writing. They were not expected to make an actual living by writing excellent books that would sell in a competitive market. One result is that African Christian expectations about Christian publishing sometimes work at cross purposes to the cultural habits, competencies, and values needed for writing success in the modern world. For example, older patterns—where Christian books were subsidized or free—have created cultural expectations that make it hard to ask buyers to pay full value for a Christian book. Moreover, publishers report that many African Christian leaders are reluctant to market and sell their books actively, feeling that this is not spiritual.

5. Book distribution in Africa is a problem (Chakava 1996, 2007). Most books by African authors are published locally, seldom marketed across their own country, much less beyond, and rarely see a second printing. Of the twenty-three Anglophone countries in Africa, only four have fairly adequate wholesale book distributors—Kenya, Nigeria, Ghana, and South Africa. In those countries bookshop owners can acquire their stock locally. Since most English-language titles come from other countries, in the other nineteen countries local booksellers need to import most of the books they sell—a daunting task. To complicate matters further, it is often difficult if not impossible to import books from neighboring African countries (because of border tensions, weak or nonexistent infrastructure, import duties, and bribes being extorted at customs). Thus, it is often far easier to acquire books from the United States or Great Britain.[15]

IMPLICATIONS AND WHAT IS NEEDED

Jesse Mugambi, a long-time publisher and theologian writes:

How can Africa's elite chart the future of this continent when its education is based on policies and ideas intended for other cultures? How can Africa's youth develop new insights to solve problems in the context of its own culture, while it is exposed only to literature

---

[15] Most of the information in this paragraph can be attributed to Edward Elliott of Oasis International.

coming from other cultures? The time has come for Africa's elite to contribute toward shaping the future of this continent through publication of the knowledge and experience accumulated at home and abroad. (Mugambi 2013, 1102)

The problem Mugambi points to is particularly true for the African Christian church. African writers have produced a significant body of high-quality literature that other Africans are familiar with and appreciate, but for the most part this literature is not Christian. On the other hand, African Christians have not produced a sizeable parallel body of high-quality explicitly Christian literature. The result is that African Christians read favorite African authors, and they read favorite Christian authors, but the number who name a favorite author who is both African and Christian is very small. And yet, as our analysis above suggests, change will happen only if the broader structural factors are understood, and if a wide variety of Christian stakeholders, both inside Africa and around the world, come to the following recognitions and commitments:

1. Writing and reading, and not merely orality, are important in the contemporary world for the strength of the African church.

2. A reading culture must be supported and fostered. This requires publication of context-appropriate children's books that foster pleasure in reading. It requires efforts to promote reading in homes, schools, and churches, with libraries encouraged for each (Chakava 1996). Book clubs and other initiatives intended to foster reading and its enjoyment as well as to encourage wider reading as a part of spirituality should be promoted (Chakava 1996; Hedstrom 2013).

3. The flourishing of African Christian writers is essential to the long-term strength of the African church in addressing the realities that African Christians need help with. Deep commitments on the part of diverse stakeholders are necessary to help bring about such an outcome.

4. Christian publishing and book distribution in Africa must be strengthened and prioritized, as is being attempted by Oasis International or by Hippo Books, in partnership with Langham Trust. There are lessons to be learned from the successes of secular publishers in Africa such as Longmans (Davis 2015) or Heinemann, as exemplified in Bejjit's (2015) fascinating exposition of the way in which Heinemann contributed to the writing success of Ngugi Wa Thiong'o. Again, Henry Chakava's (1996) outstanding book *Publishing in Africa* is filled with practical, real-world experience from a successful Kenyan editor and publisher (see also Chakava 2007; Mlambo 2007; Zell 2013). There is a need "to circulate books from one African region to other regions" (Phiri and Werner 2013, xxix). Electronic publishing and print on demand should be put to use.

5. A culture of writing must be fostered. This should include writing contests; public celebrations of writing success by African Christians; and writing courses in seminaries, universities, and Bible schools. One of the

reasons for the proliferation of Francophone African writers was a long-term "history of prize culture for [French-language] African literature," that created "significant structures of recognition and reception in the literary field" (Bush and Cucournau 2015). Similarly, in Kenya, the "Jomo Kenyatta Prize for Literature established in 1972 contributed to a burst of creativity" (Chakava 1996, 36), although the prize later died for lack of funding. Successful African Christian writers should be celebrated. Their books should be read and discussed by reading groups, assigned in course syllabi, purchased for libraries, and marketed across the continent as well as worldwide (Phiri and Werner 2013, xxix).

6. The identification, coaching, and training of Christian writers in Africa must be strengthened and expanded. This is already being done to a certain extent, for example, by Kirimi Barine of Publishing Institute of Africa through Media Associates International, and by David Waweru of Word Alive Publishers. However, much more is needed.

7. A wide variety of support for writers (royalties or royalty advances, sabbaticals, coaching, editing support, writing groups, writing partnerships) should be expanded from current levels. Among the leaders we studied, Esther Mombo exemplifies a pattern of high-quality and sustained writing. Moreover, The Circle of Concerned African Women Theologians is credited with having provided this support structure for her—support for engaging contextual realities theologically in high-quality writing (Phiri 2009).

8. Research about Christian reading and writing must be prioritized. Such research must examine the interests and needs of readers, and it must underpin strategic initiatives and planning related to writing and publishing.

9. Finally, it is important that we carefully examine the extent to which, and the ways in which, European and American Christians who attempt to engage Africa may contribute to neocolonial and unhealthy patterns that inadvertently work against the flourishing of African Christian literature.

The time has come to prioritize the value of African Christian leaders contributing to shaping the future of African Christianity through the publication of knowledge and experience accumulated at home and abroad. How to help this happen should be of interest to a broad range of concerned parties.

REFERENCES CITED

Barna Group. 2014. "The State of the Bible Report 2014." American Bible Society website. <http://www.americanbible.org.
Bejjit, Nourdin. 2015. "Heinemann's African Writers Series and the Rise of James Ngugi." In *The Book in Africa: Critical Debates,* ed. Caroline Davis and David Johnson, 223–44. New York: Palgrave Macmillan.

Bush, Ruth, and Claire Cucournau. 2015. "Francophone African Literary Prizes and the 'Empire of the French Language.'" In *The Book in Africa: Critical Debates,* ed. Caroline Davis and David Johnson, 201–22. New York: Palgrave Macmillan.

Chakava, Henry. 1996. *Publishing in Africa: One Man's Perspective.* Nairobi, Kenya: East African Educational Publishers, Ltd.

———. 2007. "Scholarly Publishing in Africa: The Perspective of an East African Commercial and Textbook Publisher." In *African Scholarly Publishing: Essays,* ed. Alois Mlambo, 66–75. Uppsala: Dag Hammarskjold.

Commeyras, Michelle, and Bontshetse Mosadimotho Mazile. 2011. "Exploring the Culture of Reading among Primary School Teachers in Botswana." *The Reading Teacher* 64/6:418–28.

Davis, Caroline. 2015. "Creating a Book Empire: Longmans in Africa." In *The Book in Africa: Critical Debates,* ed. Caroline Davis and David Johnson, 128–52. New York: Palgrave Macmillan.

Hedstrom, Matthew S. 2013. *The Rise of Liberal Religion: Book Culture and American Spirituality in the Twentieth Century.* Oxford: Oxford University Press.

Jewell, Dawn Herzog. 2009. "LittWorld Boosts Creation of Culturally Relevant Books and Articles." Lausanne World Pulse website. http://www.lausanneworldpulse.com.

Julien, Eileen. 2014. "Literature in Africa." In *Africa,* 4th ed., ed. Maria Grosz-Ngate, John H. Hanson, and Patrick O'Meara, 209–32. Bloomington: Indiana University Press.

Mlambo, Alois. 2007. "The Case for Publishing African Scholarship in Africa." In *African Scholarly Publishing Essays,* ed. Alois Mlambo, 11–24. Uppsala: Dag Hammarskjold.

Mugambi, Jesse N. K. 2013. "Challenges for Theological Publishing and Scholarly Books in Africa." In *Handbook of Theological Education in Africa,* ed. Isabel Apawo Phiri and Dietrich Werner, 1101–5. Oxford, UK: Regnum Books International.

Nsehe, Mfonobong. 2011. "The Five Richest Pastors in Nigeria." *Forbes Magazine* website. June 7. http://onforb.es/nkBSd4.

Otike, Fredrick Wawire. 2011. "Reading Culture, Cultivation, and Its Promotion among Pupils: A Kenyan Perspective." *International Research Journal of Library, Information, and Archival Studies* 1/1:1–5.

Pew. 2014. "A Snapshot of Reading in America in 2013." Pew Research Center website. http://www.pewinternet.org.

Phiri, Isabel Apawo. 2009. "The Circle of Concerned African Women Theologians." *The Ecumenical Review* 57:34–41.

Phiri, Isabel, and Dietrich Werner. 2013. "Editorial: Handbook of Theological Education in Africa." In *Handbook of Theological Education in Africa,* ed. Isabel Apawo Phiri and Dietrich Werner, xxvii–xxxiii. Oxford, UK: Regnum Books International.

Woodberry, Robert D. 2012. "The Missionary Roots of Liberal Democracy." *American Political Science Review* 106/2:244–74.

Zell, Hans M. 1995. "Publishing in Africa." In *International Book Publishing: An Encyclopedia*, ed. Philip G. Altbach and Edith S. Hoshhino, 366–73. New York: Garland Publishing.

Zell, Hans M. 2013. "How Many Books Are Published in Africa? The Need for More Reliable Statistics." *The African Book Publishing Record* 40/1:397–406.

Chapter 11

Developing Transformational Leaders— Curricula Implications from the Africa Leadership Study

John Jusu

Excellence in leadership development in Africa is often equated with quality of instruction in formal institutions of learning. The quality of instruction is often measured by the degree of central focus on institutional inputs (buildings, library, faculty), outputs (numbers of leaders formed), and outcomes (the competency of leaders produced). Consequently, training institutions with large libraries, high-profile faculty, and impressive campuses attract the most attention from stakeholders. But all too often curriculum development in these institutions is narrowly focused on meeting the requirements of accrediting agencies by replicating the curriculum of other educational institutions.

The true measure of excellence, however, in any institution intending to produce transformational leaders is whether those leaders end up having a significant impact in their communities. Answering this question requires research. The ALS has provided such research. By identifying Christian leaders that local believers identify as being effective and having impact, and by looking closely at the nature of their leadership, the ALS provides foundations for identifying relevant areas in leadership training curricula that need attention.

Curriculum in this chapter refers to all institutional processes involved in developing leaders in theological colleges, Christian liberal-arts universities, and church leadership-training institutions—leaders who will serve churches, Christian organizations, and society at large. The curriculum incorporates the entire experience that would-be leaders encounter under the guidance of formal Christian educational institutions.

This chapter explores the implications of research findings discussed in preceding chapters for the review, development, and administration of curricula within Christian higher education institutions that are intended to train transformational leaders. It discusses the ramifications of these findings for educators, curriculum developers, and administrators in pursuit of excellence in leadership development in Africa.

FAMILY IN THE CURRICULUM
OF FORMAL CHRISTIAN EDUCATIONAL INSTITUTIONS

The leaders we studied often began acquiring characteristics and competencies relevant to leadership success long before they pursued advanced formal education. The earliest formative influences came from family. Again and again, as explored in Chapters 2 and 3, we learn that parents, grandparents, and other caregivers played formative roles in the development of African Christian leaders. Psychologists such as Erik Erikson have long stressed the critical importance of parenting to ego or personality development of children. It is from parents and other family members that children learn to address conflicts and overcome challenges.

Educators must recognize the strategic role of "more knowledgeable others" (Vygotsky 1978) in the educational formation of children. Key people outside formal educational institutions, such as parents, also offer profound insights, understandings and skills acquired through experience and cultural transmission. And these "knowledgeable others" demonstrate and model ideas, values, and strategies that children internalize. It is important for educators to recognize and effectively interface with these knowledgeable others.

Given that the home is a critical factor in leadership development, it is important for formal educational institutions to move beyond school walls to engage parents and caregivers in curriculum enterprises. On the one hand, this involves recognizing that experienced and gifted African parents truly have knowledge that can benefit educational institutions. Inviting selected parents into seminars and classrooms to share enriches the curriculum by supplementing assigned readings (such as Chapters 2 and 3 herein) with the experiential knowledge of primary caregivers.

Alternatively, professors can require students to report on interviews they conduct with experienced and successful parents about family and parental dynamics and challenges in Africa today. Doctoral students or faculty can themselves conduct systematic research (using interviews, focus groups, or questionnaires) on parenting in Africa today and publish what they learn. That is, they can help generate an expanded literature on parenting that is responsive to the African context, builds on African wisdom, and can then be used in educational settings. Through such patterns of engagement, educators will be helped to conceptualize, develop, and implement a contextually appropriate curriculum for leadership training.

Formal educational institutions must not merely learn from parents and other caregivers. They must also take what they learn and implement formal educational programs designed to empower the knowledgeable others within the family to carry out their responsibilities successfully. Often families lack skills to meet the demands of parenting. It is, therefore, important that formal leadership-development institutions help them sharpen their parenting skills through community outreach programs, workshops, and other events. Institutions should design parent-leadership programs that provide opportunities for personal growth and that help develop the skills, knowledge, and dispositions to function as leaders with the voice and charisma to shape their sons and daughters. Institutions should strive to create meaningful partnerships with parents and to support them in creating an environment that will nurture their children's growth—one devoid of strife, conflict, drugs, or abuse.

In summary, institutions will enhance their leadership-development programs if they receive input from primary caregivers to inform their curriculum processes. At the same time, caregivers will continue to enhance their skills if educational institutions support them through parenting programs.

SECONDARY INSTITUTIONS IN THE CURRICULUM OF FORMAL CHRISTIAN EDUCATIONAL INSTITUTIONS

While the family is the most foundational socialization institution, children soon come into contact with other influences or secondary socialization units, including schools, churches, and parachurch organizations. The leaders we studied often reported having been influenced positively in childhood or young adulthood by a variety of institutions that were not schools, but that nonetheless contributed to their formation as leaders. Indeed, leaders were less likely to name formal educational institutions as crucial to their formation than these secondary institutions. Secondary institutions include Angolan organizations such as Mocidade para Cristo and Formação Feminina, Kenyan organizations such as FOCUS Kenya, Transform Kenya, Scripture Union, Magena Youth Group, St. Martin's Catholic Social Apostolate, and Kenya Students Christian Fellowship; and organizations from the CAR such as Campus pour Christ and Perspective Reformées.

Schools do, of course, foster thinking habits and patterns that allow people to succeed in life. They provide knowledge for future use. But frequently, when such knowledge or competencies come into use, the original educational influence is hardly acknowledged. The leaders we interviewed were more likely to acknowledge and articulate what they learned in relational, natural, real-life settings, such as those provided by these informal secondary socialization units, than to highlight what they learned in formal schools removed from context.

These complementary institutions design curricula of various types to help their target groups develop leadership potential. While using non-formal modes of socialization, these secondary units provide an environment in which people of all ages learn to interact with their peers, to compete, and to cooperate as they build life skills. They play a significant role in career development and cultural content learning. They also provide avenues for placement, volunteering, and internships for students in formal education.

To have an impact, institutions of higher education wishing to form African leaders should expand their stakeholder base for curriculum development. Key leaders in these secondary socialization units should be heard, and, as appropriate, their views should be incorporated into the curriculum. Schools should encourage the inclusion of secondary socialization units in their educational activities to provide students with an informal space to build their cultural, social, and spiritual capital. Assigned readings should feature these institutions. For example, students could be asked to read and discuss the ten-page reports of the ALS study on thirty such organizations.[1] Graduate students and faculty should be encouraged to research and write about the strategic work of this kind of African institution, and then should make these a focus of classroom instruction.

QUALITIES AND ROLES OF INFLUENTIAL LEADERS IN THE CURRICULUM

Our research identified a profile of outstanding leaders that most institutions would be proud to have as alumni. Such leaders are committed to the church, connected to the community, and display vocational excellence and cultural flexibility within the framework of servant leadership. Having this profile in view, and using "backward design" (Wiggins and McTighe 2005), curriculum developers can now ask: What do we need to provide for leaders to develop and display these qualities? This approach of beginning curriculum development with the end in mind is completely different from other design models that start curriculum writing from course development rather than from the perspective of the desired outcomes. Thus, instead of curriculum design starting with a focus on what courses to teach, it should focus on desired outcomes and from there select appropriate courses and other learning activities. This approach might exclude some traditional content-driven courses, while including others that are new and issue based.

---

[1] Available at www.AfricaLeadershipStudy.org.

Desired characteristics cannot be cultivated within the walls of the classroom alone. Educational institutions need to connect with other agencies within the community. The curriculum, in design and implementation, should foster a commitment to the church. It should encourage cultural flexibility through intercultural internships and relevant courses. The bottom line is that the curriculum should lead students to engage with the church and community through contextually challenging transformative activities.

African Christian leaders are involved in a variety of arenas frequently related to social justice and rehabilitation. They address drug abuse, alcoholism, prostitution, education for children and youth, health, and business. Often there is not a close fit between the educational curriculum and professional training of a given leader, and what that leaders ends up doing. And yet the successful leaders we examined often had an entrepreneurial spirit and abilities that clearly were enhanced by advanced knowledge, cognitive competencies, and critical thinking skills acquired through advanced education. They were able to identify social, moral, and economic problems and respond to them in transformative ways, whether or not the precise situations they were responding to had been the focus of their formal, professional training.

Our research suggests that any adequate leadership curriculum must feature critical and creative thinking skills regarding both content (in particular courses) and processes (exemplified in all courses). The teacher role must be reframed, not with the professor as the primary source of knowledge but rather as a facilitator of learning—helping students acquire knowledge and critical-thinking skills. Classroom practices should avoid dependence on a teacher-controlled environment characterized by "content dumping," but rather should feature learning-oriented methodologies and should encourage independence and creativity in learning.

Educational institutions must also work to enhance subject-area integration. All too often academic programs and departments operate as "silos" with low levels of curricular integration. African realities and issues need to be engaged in the curriculum through multidimensional and cross-disciplinary strategies. For example, if the curriculum is to address issues related to poverty, the design must be such that theological, missiological, economic, social, political, and environmental topics that touch on poverty are integrated into a specific course. Graduates who come out of a course like this would be empowered to see poverty in a holistic and integrated manner, and hence have the competencies to respond in new and transformative ways.

The criticism levied against higher education is that there is often a disconnect with contextual realities, with the result that people with high cognitive abilities have little practical impact. The integration of faith, life, and learning should lessen this criticism, as leadership development encompasses much more than cognitive abilities.

SOCIAL CAPITAL IN THE CURRICULUM
OF FORMAL CHRISTIAN EDUCATIONAL INSTITUTIONS

The ALS research, as summarized in Chapter 4 by Steven Rasmussen, revealed that social relationships of reciprocity and trust are essential to all effective African Christian leadership. This finding poses a significant challenge for the way leaders are developed. The curricula of formal institutions often work against the acquisition of social capital. Students usually sit in rows facing and listening solely to the lecturer. They are normally required to work alone, even in competition with one another, and are assessed as isolates. With heavy workloads factored in, students often find it difficult to develop the personal relationships that are critical to leadership success. But if the acquisition of social capital is truly a desirable educational outcome, then adjustments are needed. This may be as simple as rearranging seats into circles so that students face one another as they interact in the learning space. More substantively, the adoption of a collaborative teaching and learning paradigm, where students spend significant time working on projects in groups, will clearly have a positive impact on social capital.

Rasmussen points out that Christians often already have strong "bonding social capital," strong social ties with those in their own church or ethnic group. By contrast, distrust, hostility, and conflict often characterize relationships across ethnic and religious boundaries—and the sort of social capital that bridges these divides ("bridging social capital") is much less common. And yet, as Rasmussen points out, the highly effective leaders we studied were often rich in bridging social capital. That is, they were often highly successful as leaders precisely because they had strong ties of reciprocity and trust with people in other denominations, other ethnic groups, and even other religions. Thus educational curricula must not merely encourage relationships with other people of the same denomination or ethnic group but must foster strong relationships across denominational, ethnic, and even religious lines.

Since institutions of Christian higher education often bring together people of different ethnicities and denominations, they are optimally positioned to contribute to bridging social capital, especially if they design the curriculum to foster this. A curriculum that promotes learning in community through projects, mission trips, exchange programs, internships, practicums, games, fellowship groups, and chapels not only has the potential to contribute to bonding social capital, but rightly structured, has the potential for contributing to bridging social capital as well. Course work and readings that feature culture, ethnicity, anthropology, Islam, and intercultural communication can foster sensitivity and understanding that enhance bridging social capital.

Finally, Rasmussen points to incredible hierarchies of wealth, status, and power that characterize the modern world, both within communities or nation-states, and globally. Significant relationships of trust and mutual obligation that link people vertically across such hierarchies of education, status, power, wealth, and influence ("linking social capital") are extremely rare and extremely important. His chapter points out that many of the most effective leaders studied had unusually strong linking social capital, extensive relationships of trust and shared commitment with other people across these vertical divides, upward and downward, locally and internationally. Often it was in the context of shared Christian commitments that these local and international relationships were forged. And Rasmussen shows that such linking social capital was pivotal to their leadership success.

The educational curriculum must recognize the importance (and challenges) of this kind of relationship and should create structures that help produce healthy forms of linking social capital. This could involve interfacing with groups like FOCUS Kenya, which brings thousands of young people into close mentorship relations under older, well-educated, and highly successful Christians practicing a wide variety of professions. It could involve fostering international relationships through exchange programs, study abroad, or mission trips. Course work should focus both on communities characterized by poverty and on the global or locally resourced partners with whom collaboration is envisioned. Internships and practicums that involve collaboration across hierarchies of education, status, power, wealth, and influence on behalf of kingdom purposes should be valued.

African doctoral students and faculty should study such collaborative projects as case studies and should provide written materials that can be used in course work to coach others in the challenges and benefits of linking social capital for kingdom purposes. Educational materials should also feature the acquisition of character traits, competencies, and skills related to developing and maintaining the trust relationships needed in such partnerships. Entrepreneurial action and vision casting within the framework of transcendent shared commitments are key. Leaders must develop relationships with Christians with cultural capital and material resources, whether located nearby or in distant places, and should help such Christians understand how their resources can truly serve kingdom purposes. They must help to foster a culture of philanthropy within African churches, rather than merely seeking partnerships from abroad. Furthermore, the ability to foster and maintain trust over time is critical. Resource partnerships flourish best where there is deep conviction that those who handle resources are trustworthy. Trustworthy stewardship requires character but also relevant acquired skills and habits. Where relationships and partnerships span not only economic divides but also divides of nationality and culture, the potential for failures of understanding which damage healthy relationships is present. All of this must be addressed in the curriculum of Christian leadership development in Africa today.

EQUIPPING LEADERS
FOR ORGANIZATIONS WITH IMPACT

Chapter 7 by Michael Bowen looks beyond the leaders to the organizations they manage. Both male and female leaders oversee Christian organizations that provide a wide range of services related to sustainable agriculture, community health, governance and democracy, gender equality, environmental and institutional development, water projects, microfinance, theological education, educational services, health, peace and reconciliation, and personnel training. He observes that these faith-based organizations (FBOs) have the potential to mobilize massive numbers of people and resources for specific causes using their networks. They have high levels of faith motivation and grassroots presence. They have local knowledge and local trust. And they often espouse Christian values that merit the attention of theological education.

A common criticism of formal theological education relates to its lack of connection with contextual realities. Theological education, and formal education in general, has locked itself into the prison of "school" to the extent that its presence is rarely felt outside the institution's walls. Some entities in Africa are striving to break that pattern through the establishment of special departments or institutes, such as Africa International University's Institute for the Study of African Realities.

FBOs provide a ready research constituency for theological institutions and universities interested in African realities because they deal directly with these issues. FBOs can also provide avenues for placement, internships, and practicum experiences for leaders-in-training through the development of relationships and networks with organizations that have demonstrated impact in communities.

The institutions featured in Chapter 7 are rarely among the organizations that students learn about in their study of organizations. They tend to learn about formal bureaucratic systems and well-resourced service organizations with defined structures and steep control hierarchies. FBOs are usually different, and hence need special management and leadership skills. Theological training programs for leaders need to review their organizational management curriculum to reflect FBO realities. For example, people in these organizations consider their work as a ministry and a service to humanity. They see their jobs as a personal responsibility to God and feel that they have a significant role in the organization. If, however, the human-resources personnel in these FBOs have a distinctively management theory focus, they may see the workers as mere employees with a limited stake in the organization and hence treat them as such. This naturally creates conflict. Our curriculum should train leaders to be competent enough to understand these organizations and how to lead them.

Theological institutions and universities can also help these FBOs by adding value to their processes, for example, by helping them produce training manuals and by training their facilitators. Thus, for example, the educational service provider More than a Mile Deep has helped provide the training manuals used by the Church Missionary Society to train thousands of people, with significant impact in places such as Kenya, Uganda, and South Sudan. Educational institutions should build such partnership bridges for the benefit of both parties.

MODELING, MENTORING, COACHING, AND DISCIPLING IN LEADERSHIP DEVELOPMENT

Chapter 9 by Jurgen Hendriks observes that effective leaders demonstrate certain traits, such as servant leadership, that may be difficult to teach through formal course content. Indeed, academic institutions may all too easily model the opposite, with teachers exercising blatant power in ways that do not empower, but rather foster status hierarchies. Hendriks identified qualities of servant leadership such as accessibility, mentorship, the ability to identify and provide others with opportunities, and the wisdom to guide them through difficult terrain. These are less about the explicit curriculum than the implicit curriculum. Servant leadership is about values, habits, and attitudes that teachers need to model for students to see and emulate. Their responsibility is not only to teach knowledge and skills but also to mold men and women to be effective leaders in the image of Christ. Mentoring programs, skills coaching, and lifestyle discipleship should be used to foster servant leadership. Students should be able to see how "powerful" teachers use their authority for the benefit of those they serve. Students need to see that their teachers have a genuine interest in them and are willing to help them grow. Educators should make themselves available to their students in non-formal and nonthreatening settings where leadership traits are "caught rather than taught." When faculty participate with students in a variety of nonacademic activities and working groups, this gives scope for modeling and mentorship. Faculty-guided independent studies might also provide flexibility to pursue special interests and contexts of students in ways that empower and mentor.

A curriculum that would enable leaders to learn to multiply themselves must have mentoring at its core. For example, it could make provision for senior students to mentor incoming junior students as both go through their programs of study. Subsequently, these junior students would mentor the next generation. The institution should coordinate such relationships with significant input from students regarding how those relationships are formed and operate. In this way the implicit curriculum becomes formational in leadership development.

READING IN THE CURRICULUM
OF CHRISTIAN EDUCATIONAL INSTITUTIONS

Kennedy Buhere (2016) has observed that "some of the most accomplished people in academia and the world of affairs—in business, politics, and government—nurtured their intellect and that which we admire in them through extensive reading." This observation is consistent with the findings of Priest, Kirimi, and Salombongo, that many African leaders read extensively for purposes of personal, spiritual, and professional development. Reading stimulates inquiry; it helps leaders generate ideas, motivates them to think beyond their ordinary scope of influence and specialty, and encourages open minded and flexible thinking. Reading increases vocabulary and language skills that enhance leadership communication. Leaders who read relevant materials in their areas are likely to know more about leadership responsibilities than those who do not (Coleman 2012).

Curriculum renewal efforts to improve the reading abilities and habits of leaders-in-training must start with faculty, because they control what students read. The selection of assigned readings is critical. Textbooks must provide relevant content for the specified course and should be selected for understandability and contextual relevance. And yet the practice of reading textbooks and highly academic assigned writings in preparation for exams may not contribute to a lifelong habit and love for reading. Thus, it is important also to assign or give credit for readings with a strong contemporary human interest side and books with personal narrative, practical relevance, and ease of reading. It is important that African contexts, and African authors, be a part of this mix. Students should be given readings that will foster a love for reading.

Our research indicated that African leaders, even those in professions such as engineering or business, do read their bibles. Faculty should encourage and capitalize on this by designing a curriculum that ensures that even Christians studying in other fields are provided with tools to understand and apply the Bible. This could be done through short courses or modules, or through interfacing with other organizations that train for this, such as Bible Study Fellowship.

Educational institutions must foster critical reading skill development, not only for engaging with the Bible but for all reading. The ability to evaluate and draw meaningful conclusions and judgments from what is read is a critical competency for leaders. Critical thinking will empower leaders with the capacity to make informed judgments about which ideas to incorporate into their leadership practices and which ones to avoid.

Non-classroom activities, often referred to as the implicit curriculum, are also important. Both in and out of the classroom, faculty should demonstrate a love of reading and joy in talking over with students what they might be reading. Faculty can encourage students to organize a reading club in which they read materials with practical applications for the issues that they engage with in the classroom. These might relate to student lifestyle, career success, balanced and holistic living, global issues that affect careers, poverty, power and money, and/or "how to" materials. According to Priest, Kirimi, and Salombongo (Chapter 10 herein) these sorts of materials seldom appear in the libraries of institutions that train leaders but are widely read and valued by African readers more broadly.

WRITING IN THE CURRICULUM
OF CHRISTIAN EDUCATIONAL INSTITUTIONS

Closely related to reading is writing. Indeed, one of the challenges identified by Priest, Kirimi, and Salombongo is that African Christian readers encounter a scarcity of writings by African Christian authors, and thus mainly read Christian authors who are not African. This poses significant challenges that institutions of Christian higher learning need to address. It is critical that African Christian writers acquire and share contextually appropriate wisdom and understanding through writing and publication. Educational institutions must contribute to this.

Faculty should demonstrate the habit of writing not only academic books and articles but ones that broader audiences will find accessible, interesting, and helpful. This needs to be part of the faculty's sense of calling. Faculty should assign student writing and give careful support and feedback on the writing craft. Assigned writing could include reading reports, academic papers, informal journaling, reporting on news items, and even publishing magazine entries.

The schools should encourage writing groups, academic conference presentations, and student publications, and should sponsor magazines or online blogs that students can work on and contribute to. Schools should use new print-on-demand technology to expand their role in publishing. Excellence in writing should be recognized, rewarded, and honored. To develop leaders with a lifelong capacity and commitment to writing, faculty members should explicitly prioritize training for writing in the curriculum. The exceptional importance of African Christian writing must be affirmed and supported in a wide variety of ways.

GENDER ISSUES IN THE CURRICULUM
OF FORMAL CHRISTIAN EDUCATIONAL INSTITUTIONS

Our ALS research revealed that many African Christian women are exercising effective leadership in a wide variety of venues. And yet these women often encounter major hindrances and challenges to their leadership, as examined by Kwaka-Sumba and le Roux (Chapter 8 herein). Both cultural traditions and ecclesiastical systems can contribute to barriers and stigmas for women, making the leadership journeys of these women difficult and labyrinthine.

Kwaka-Sumba and le Roux show that enrollment of girls and women in formal educational institutions is increasing, with the percentage of female primary students in Kenya a full 50 percent. Nevertheless, at other educational levels and in Angola and the CAR, the proportion of female students is still much lower than for males. At advanced educational levels, and especially with theological education, there is usually less support for female than male students. And the attrition rate for young women is higher due to early marriages, financial difficulties, and pregnancies.

How then should the curriculum of educational institutions engage gender? Coursework must include a focus on the lives and experiences of women as well as men. This should include a focus on realities in the everyday lives of ordinary women, such as pastoral issues raised by experiences of female infertility in cultures that define female identity largely in terms of motherhood. But it should also include a focus on the stories of female leaders. For example, in church history and missions many women have made significant contributions to the development of the church, but they are rarely mentioned in our lessons. Male and female students need to read about these women—their struggles, challenges, and victories—to be able to change and enlarge their perspectives about women. Teachers and lecturers should deliberately use illustrations that are relevant to women. The higher education classroom should include women as professors, thus providing models of female leaders.

The curriculum must not merely include a focus on women, their lives, and their flourishing, but must also consider the unequal opportunities, prejudice, discrimination, and oppression they often encounter—even in contexts of Christian higher education. Course lectures and assigned readings and discussions should include this as a focus. The whole curriculum should be reviewed to consider and address ways it might unintentionally foster negative outcomes for women. The importance of mentorship for women, and of creating "safe spaces" to consider the issues, are crucial. Pedagogies featuring inquiry, dialogue, multiple perspectives, and critical consciousness are needed. Theorists (such as Paulo Freire) who articulate methods for bringing critical consciousness into the pedagogical process should be positively engaged. Both males and females should be invited into a discussion of how best to support the flourishing of girls and women in the modern world (as well as the flourishing of boys and men). Strong advocacy for women in educational and ministry settings should be championed by all. Male faculty and administrators must be advocates for female students as well as male.

Those women who have experienced leadership success should be given extra support to mentor younger women in navigating the leadership labyrinth. They should be encouraged to document their struggles so that other women can learn from their experiences as they signpost alternative leadership routes. Graduate students and faculty should research and write about leadership realities and dynamics related to gender in general, and women in particular. Such writings should be featured in class readings and discussions.

LEADERSHIP IN CONFLICT SITUATIONS

Wars and other conflicts pose challenges and opportunities for leadership ministries across Africa. In Chapter 5, Elisabet le Roux and Yolande Sandoua examined violence and conflict in the CAR. They show that Christian leaders played a key restorative role as they preached a message of reconciliation, extended hospitality to warring parties and their victims, and participated in interfaith activities intended to foster peace.

These findings regarding conflict situations present important considerations for the design of leadership curriculum in most educational institutions. Such curricula often assume predictable circumstances and are designed to empower leaders to act in situations of relative peace and safety. But in much of Africa, stability, predictability, safety, and peace cannot simply be assumed or taken for granted. When we consider the recent violence in the CAR, the ongoing interreligious violence in the coastal and eastern regions of Kenya, the 2007–8 Kenyan post-election violence, or the long civil war in Angola (1975–2002), it is clear that peace and stability must never be assumed or taken for granted in curricula for leadership development.

Those designing curricula for leaders should be mindful of such conflicts and of the dynamics involved, and they should ensure adequate engagement. Course content should focus on common sources of conflict in contemporary Africa. Readings should include case study material, such as one finds in Chapter 5 or in the ALS reports of pastors and organizations near Mombasa. The analysis of inequities, injustices, and old grievances should be considered. The role of Christian churches and pastors in contributing to prejudices and conflicts or in contributing to reconciliation and peace should be discussed. The possible roles of Christians in government, business, media, and civil society should also be analyzed. Students should be encouraged or required to visit conflict regions and refugee camps; they could be part of a food-aid program, or be volunteers in peacebuilding and disaster-intervention groups. In the classroom students should engage in problem-solving activities using real conflict situations.

In short, the careful analysis of war and conflict situations in contemporary Africa should inform curriculum design for leadership. The analysis of FATEB's role in peacebuilding through education should underpin curriculum development that would contribute to conflict resolution, peacebuilding, and community resilience. The curriculum should not merely respond to conflict, but should be active in avoiding conflict and promoting peace.

DEVELOPING LEADERS IN AN AGE OF CONSTANT CHANGE

In a world of constant change, it is important that godly Christian leaders be prepared to engage this complex reality not only through church ministries, but in politics and governance, business, economics, development, health, gender, communications, and education. While in an earlier era Christian higher education in Africa often focused primarily on theological education intended for church leadership, theological schools all across the continent are broadening their focus and becoming universities. They usually retain a focus on theological and pastoral training, but also are committed to engaging the academic disciplines more broadly and work to prepare graduates to serve in a wide diversity of professions in society at large. This broadened educational focus coincides, as Nupanga Weanzana points out in Chapter 6, with a shift on the part of African Christians away from an exclusive focus on word and gospel toward a widespread holistic emphasis on word and deed accompanying each other. Nearly all of the major Christian ministries in Africa today combine social concerns with biblical and gospel concerns.

What this means is that Christian higher education is undergoing rapid expansion, preparing graduates for church-based ministries as well as for vocations in society at large. Thus leadership curricula must address the knowledge needed for leadership impact in a wide variety of professions such as architecture, engineering, journalism, and law. But it also requires that our educational institutions cultivate theological judgment in architecture, engineering, journalism, and law—not merely in pastoral work. In short, universities must cultivate "the heart, hands and mind of Christ in all things" (Wood 1985, 86–87).

Many of the leaders studied in the ALS were walking in two worlds: the church and the community. The training that leaders receive should prepare them for both worlds. Theology must continuously shed the light of biblical truth on contextual realities, whether economics, gender, or politics.

If lawyers, architects, environmentalists, and soldiers are providing Christian leadership in the community, as attested to by the ALS, then it becomes the business of Christian higher education to ensure that their leadership principles rest firmly on theological and biblical foundations. If leaders are taking Christ into society through their passion for justice, then they should carry the authentic message of Christ. We cannot expect the secular universities to provide such Christian foundations. Given the supremacy of Christ in all things (Col 1:15ff.) and, by extension, in all knowledge domains, theologically informed education should open up to include other disciplines. When this is done, we will start to have Christian professionals, not just professionals who "happen to be" Christian.

CONCLUSION

The ALS identified and studied key Christian leaders, male, and female, clergy and non-clergy. This chapter has drawn from the ALS findings to make suggestions related to the role of Christian higher education in leadership development. The book itself is intended to serve as an important leadership-development resource to be used in African educational institutions as a class text, not merely as a library resource.

We hope that faculty and administrators in African Christian institutions of higher education, as well as accrediting bodies, will recognize the value of this chapter, this book, and the accompanying website for the conceptualization, design, development, and implementation of curricula for transformational leadership formation to serve the church and society in Africa. We also hope that, outside Africa, missiology faculty and those who teach about African Christianity will find these resources to be of value in their own curricula and that students will develop up-to-date understandings of Christianity in contemporary Africa and cultivate the understanding needed for wise partnerships with African Christian leaders and the institutions they serve.

WORKS CITED

Buhere, Kennedy. 2016. "Voluntary Reading of Books by Students Has Immense Benefits." https://tuko.co.ke.

Coleman, John. 2012. "For Those Who Want to Lead, Read." *Harvard Business Review.* August 15.

Vygotsky, Lev. 1978. *Mind in Society: The Development of Higher Psychological Processes.* Cambridge, MA: MIT.

Wiggins, Grant, and Jay McTighe. 2005. *Understanding by Design.* Alexandria, VA: Association for Supervision and Curriculum Development.

Wood, Charles. 1985. *Vision and Discernment: An Orientation in Theological Study.* Atlanta, GA: Scholars Press.

Chapter 12

Engaging Africa—
The Tyndale House Foundation's Story

Mary Kleine Yehling

ONCE UPON A TIME . . .

Storytelling is an essential part of life and held in high regard throughout much of Africa. In listening to the events of a story, our minds and hearts experience truth and insight. We participate, we engage, and we may be changed. Similarly, much of Christianity has come to us through the art of storytelling. The roots of this art, nurtured in African soil by the early church fathers of North Africa and the Mediterranean, have dramatically shaped our faith history (Oden 2010). Threads of truth hidden in the parables Jesus told are interwoven into our understandings of the kingdom of God. Consider Jesus's parable of the sower:

> "Listen! A farmer went out to plant some seed. As he scattered it across his field, some seed fell on a footpath, and the birds came and ate it. Other seed fell on shallow soil with underlying rock. The plant sprang up quickly, but it soon wilted beneath the hot sun and died because the roots had no nourishment in the shallow soil. Other seed fell among thorns that shot up and choked out the tender blades so that it produced no grain. Still other seed fell on fertile soil and produced a crop that was thirty, sixty, and even a hundred times as much as had been planted." Then he said, "Anyone who is willing to hear should listen and understand." (Mark 4:3–9, New Living Translation)

As in this parable, the fruit of the Africa Leadership Study (ALS) was the result of seeds that were planted earlier by various of the story's characters. This chapter tells the story from the vantage point of the Tyndale House Foundation (THF) and its engagement with Africa and the ALS. The foundation was only one character among many in the larger story.

215

This story begins in 1955 with Dr. Kenneth Taylor, a publishing executive in Chicago, who read the Bible to his ten children each day. The children had difficulty, however, in understanding the Authorized Version (KJV) from which he read. When he questioned his children about the day's reading, they often could not answer. So each day as he traveled by train from his home in Wheaton to his work at Moody Press in Chicago, he laid an open bible on one knee and a notepad on the other. Working paragraph by paragraph through the letters of St. Paul, he paraphrased a portion of the Bible to read to his children the next day. Soon, when he asked questions, they understood and could answer.

Over a seven-year period Dr. Taylor worked to paraphrase the epistles, and in 1962 he published *Living Letters*, establishing Tyndale House Publishers. The following year, using the royalties, Dr. Taylor and his wife, Margaret, founded the Tyndale House Foundation. His work paraphrasing the scriptures continued until 1971, when *The Living Bible* was published. This was a step of faith into the unknown territory of modern Bible translations that is now familiar to us all. This easy-to-understand paraphrase of the Bible generated high sales, and the Tyndale House Foundation received all the royalties. When the New Living Translation, translated by teams of scholars from the original ancient biblical texts in the style of *The Living Bible,* replaced it in 1996, those royalties were also assigned to the

Figure 12–1. Ken and Margaret Taylor with their ten children (1957)

foundation. In 2001, not many years before his death, Dr. and Mrs. Taylor donated Tyndale House Publishers to the Tyndale House Foundation.

Kenneth and Margaret Taylor could have been wealthy. Instead, they gave the majority of their net worth "to minister to the spiritual needs of people, primarily through literature consistent with biblical principles." They invested their wealth in the kingdom, and God has richly multiplied these seeds—thirty, sixty, and even a hundredfold.

Since its inception the foundation has encouraged ministries around the world, primarily through grant making. In his autobiography Dr. Taylor describes his "introduction to mission" during his seminary days in the early 1940s and expresses the conviction that missionaries should "work themselves out of their jobs and move on to new territory, leaving behind a self-directed, self-supporting church" (Taylor 1991, 119). Dr. and Mrs. Taylor were deeply committed to worldwide Christian missions, a commitment exemplified when they invited missionary statesman Dr. Edwin (Jack) Frizen, Jr., to join the newly formed Tyndale House Foundation board. The Taylors, together with Jack and his wife, Grace, were deeply involved in visioning, working with, and supporting a wide range of organizations.

Even before he published *Living Letters*, Dr. Taylor dreamed of setting up a foundation to invest in Christian organizations around the world (Taylor 1991, 284). His work with Moody Literature Mission and his interest in the spread of the gospel had taken him on many travels. In the 1962 Taylor family Christmas letter he describes traveling earlier that year through "Europe, Africa, Malagasy, the Mideast, Hungary, and Yugoslavia." But Africa, with its newly independent nations, received special attention. He wrote in that letter, "I visited 14 of the 28 new nations of Africa that have been formed" (Taylor 2000, 295–96). Such travels evidenced his deep interest in and commitment to Africa. One suspects he would have greatly valued the Africa Leadership Study and would have encouraged us, as was his way, to take "all to God in prayer."

ENGAGING AFRICA

An African grantee once said, "Your support provides a base for us to work together to make a space for God to act." What an elegant description of the interaction among vision, hard work, and provision. It highlights the dynamic impact that unity in relationships, the hallmark of Christian community, can have. When everyone involved works together in unity, this makes space for the Holy Spirit.

Involvement in the ALS represented a new chapter in the story of the Tyndale House Foundation's work in Africa. Ideally, one should hear this story over hot tea with milk and a biscuit, sitting comfortably in the shade, rather than reading it. Instead, readers will have to use their imagination to see the characters and events.

Figure 12–2. Dr. Kenneth Taylor (with Margaret Taylor) presents Kenyan
President Daniel Arap Moi with an English Living Bible and a Swahili New
Testament (1984), as Dr. George Kinoti observes

From its founding in 1963, the THF invested in Africa. Over the years
we have watched organizations develop to meet the needs of a continent
facing many challenges. We watched the demise of colonial rule and the
emergence of independent nations. The foundation has been privileged
to work with many of the organizations vital to these changes and to the
growth of Christian leaders.

Consider three of the educational organizations that received THF
support from their beginnings. Daystar University was founded in the
mid-1960s with a vision for training Christians in a variety of professions. Today, with over four thousand students, this Kenyan institution is
a leading Christian university, with unusual strengths in communication
sciences. Similarly, in the late 1970s to early 1980s, the Association of
Evangelicals in Africa (AEA) was instrumental, through its networks, in
founding both the Faculté De Théologie Evangélique de Bangui and the
Nairobi Evangelical Graduate School of Theology (now part of Africa
International University). Both schools are achieving the AEA dream of
equipping African Christian leaders. In all three cases, the THF provided
early funding. Now the graduates of these institutions serve across the
continent and beyond. THF has reaped an unanticipated benefit from
this early investment: faculty and students from these schools played vital
roles in the ALS.

THE CASE FOR ENGAGING IN THE ALS

The foundation's experience over the years affirmed that our investments in Africa were wisely managed by the recipients and were strategically important. The world, however, was swiftly changing. We recognized weaknesses in our understandings of contemporary Africa. We wanted to learn about initiatives and opportunities that might better suit current circumstances. Most of the organizations with which we had worked had Western rather than African roots. Many were in Anglophone countries, fewer in Francophone nations, and fewer still in Lusophone ones. We wondered what was happening in the Francophone and Lusophone church. More important, we suspected that ministries with African roots could better understand cultural context, define programs, and address priority needs in Africa.

Over a previous five-year period we had participated with other Christian foundations in a study in India—the India Leadership Study (ILS).[1] Initially, the THF board envisioned a study in Africa along similar lines. Edward Elliott, a board member who has devoted much of his professional life to publishing in Africa, agreed to explore this possibility. After many conversations and meetings with principals from various foundations, it became apparent that there were significant challenges to embarking on such a joint initiative with multiple foundations. We came from varying circumstances, had different mission statements, and envisaged different priorities for the study. The ILS was ongoing, and for some of those involved, additional work in Africa was not possible. Recognition of this reality was a pivotal point in our story because it pushed us into considering a new approach altogether.

In 2008, a second pivotal development occurred. Ed Elliott invited Dr. Robert Priest of Trinity Evangelical Divinity School in Deerfield, Illinois, in the United States, and Dr. David Ngaruiya of the International Leadership University in Nairobi, Kenya, to research and identify the key issues that such a study should consider. They spent three weeks in Nairobi interviewing a wide array of Africans and others involved in service and leadership training across the continent. Their report outlined what

---

[1] It was out of a desire by foundation officers to make good leadership development grants in India that various foundations (at the initiative of First Fruit) collaborated in supporting the India Leadership Study, carried out by Dr. David Bennett and designed "first, to draw a map, as it were, of leadership development in India today; second, to define principles for strategic, catalytic, capacity-building grants; third, to discover the trailblazers, that is, the key people and organizations in whom God is strongly at work; and fourth, to develop collaboration, especially between Indian leaders who had complementary visions and objectives" (David Bennett, "Insights from the India Leadership Study," presented at The Gathering, September 14, 2002). Christian foundations found the results of this India Leadership Study to be enormously helpful to their own grant making.

they learned regarding contemporary realities in Africa. It informed our understanding of the need for an Africa leadership study and provided a base for the study's organization and implementation.[2]

The involvement of Robert Priest and David Ngaruiya in this initial work drew them into the story. In time, Robert Priest moved into a leadership role overseeing the process of designing and implementing the research. Dr. Michael Bowen of Daystar University joined David Ngaruiya in jointly overseeing the project in Kenya and provided training and supervision for the student research teams.

Robert (Bob) Reekie, from South Africa, had recently retired from the THF board. Bob was co-founder and first president of Media Associates International and had trained publishers and writers throughout the world. Convinced that Bob Reekie's experience and maturity would strengthen the study, Ed Elliott asked him to join the initial planning group. By this time it had become clear that the leadership study in Africa would definitely not be the joint effort of a group of foundations. Bob Reekie took a strong leadership stance in encouraging us to take action: "We need to do this on our own. It's too important to let it die." If any of us had doubts about continuing, Bob's words overcame them. The THF board proved itself willing to make a significant investment in the project, and we were up and running.

STEP BY STEP

If you were hearing rather than reading this story, you would observe me leaning forward in my chair, speaking with quiet intensity, underscored by the hand gestures I use when I get excited. You would see that I consider this portion of the story of key importance. It laid the basis for all the work to come.

The decision to move forward without other foundations gave us greater space to work with African partners and to ensure that their interests, concerns, and insights were paramount. This new focus informed the design and implementation of the research. The India Leadership Study, which had involved over three dozen distinct foundations, had been organized, designed, and carried out by foundation personnel. It had identified strategic projects for funding and developed a structure for foundations to work closely with Indian partner organizations. In short, foundation interests had been the central and driving force behind the study.

By contrast, in the space created by having only one foundation involved, the ALS was able to proceed in ways that placed the African partners at the center of the research project. While the ALS would retain a focus on matters of interest to the foundation, it would broaden its focus to include

---

[2] See http://www.africaleadershipstudy.org/about/#background.

leadership issues and dynamics that African Christian scholars and other leaders identified as priorities. With African Christian scholars playing central roles in designing, implementing, and carrying out the research and analysis, the hope was that the results might challenge, shape, and inform our understandings of investing in Africa. Through its participation as one of many characters in this process the foundation itself was shaped and changed.

Once the decision was made to push forward, we immediately faced the task of clarifying our purpose and seeking appropriate partners. The initial planning group, with valuable guidance from Mark Taylor, the foundation president, drafted an initial ALS purpose statement delineating what we hoped would be accomplished from the foundation's perspective.

And so began a process of interaction and communication, of seeking to discern what the next step should be. As we stepped out in faith we trusted our path would become clearer. This was time consuming and required a high level of commitment on the part of the THF planning team, who met regularly over the life of the study. At certain steps along the way we seemed continually to circle the same issues. The positive tension of patiently waiting together for clarity was a humbling and empowering experience. We were learning to walk by faith in community. The ongoing support of the foundation board provided us with space for such a walk.

As we moved forward, it became apparent that our small circle needed to grow. We needed expertise, insight, and context to make well-informed plans. So we turned to those with whom we had worked in Africa over the years. We began with an online survey, which yielded helpful information, not least that online surveys achieve uneven results in Africa. Bob Reekie continually reminded us that in Africa, it is important to listen to the elders and invite their support. Association with individuals and institutions that are known and respected is essential. We were getting our first lessons in the high value of social capital in African culture.

These early experiences made clear our next step: we needed to gather a wider group of both African and Western stakeholders for several days so we could listen to one another and design the study jointly. We sought a balance of men and women, English and French speakers,[3] academics and practitioners. We invited those who worked in research, training and teaching, youth and leadership development, development of higher education and graduate programs, women's ministry, and writing and publishing. We drew from African universities that offered training in research and from ministries with which the THF had worked over the years. We invited some of Robert Priest's colleagues and former research partners to join in. This group became the crucible for the design and implementation of the project.

---

[3] Only later did we come to realize the importance of Portuguese. By our second meeting, we had two Angolan theological leaders present and playing a continuous and core role in our research.

Our first task as a wider group was to come to a common mind on the purpose and guiding parameters for the study. The participants from the THF outlined the foundation's intentions and what we hoped the study would accomplish. Significant time was then spent in group discussion to define goals that other participants hoped to achieve. This was a critical step, which if not given the priority it merited, could have doomed the project from the start.

We all wished to discover people and organizations with a high level of influence as judged by informed local African Christians. But we needed to dialogue frankly. Why did we want to discover them? We clarified that the THF goal was not simply to compose a list of potential grant recipients. Rather, it was to identify key leaders and organizations in order to understand what formed them. It was to shed light on priority areas of ministry needs that, if addressed, had the potential to effect significant positive change. With that information in hand, the THF could create a template to use in evaluating any project in Africa.

Conversely, participants from Africa wanted to use what was learned to inform and shape their planning, their ministry, their curriculum, their daily lives and work. They would be designing and implementing programs, projects, and practices that would effect change. Thus, they hoped for documentation of areas of highest impact and highest need. They wanted context and tools for designing effective strategies to address those needs.

The clarity provided by this open conversation enabled us to craft a purpose statement that reflected both perspectives (see Appendix A). We concluded that each of our purposes could be satisfied by the same research data if we took care to design the study keeping all purposes in mind.

This process became a framework for ongoing dialogue within the group. With a foundation of trust, where the input of each was truly valued, each participant expressed willingness to commit fully to the project. This personal, self-motivated commitment was reliable because all participants were achieving their own personal goals as well as the goals of the group. This proved to be one of our major strengths.

The collaborative nature of this project required patience, sustained conversation, and much time. We talked, prayed, emailed, and Skyped. We met regularly to plan, solve problems, work, and worship. We sensed the Holy Spirit at work, quietly and persistently drawing us together into a community. As we gathered to evaluate and discuss data from questionnaires and interviews, we became a team. We worked together across miles, languages, and cultures. Africans and Westerners alike experienced firsthand the day-to-day challenges facing leaders in other countries: Kenya, the CAR, Angola, South Africa, and the United States.

Problems that first appeared simple could quickly turn into major hurdles that drained time and energy. Circumstances in each country presented unique challenges, but one common thread was clear: Africa holds great treasure, the men and women who love the Lord, desire to serve his purposes, and are effectively leading and preparing others for leadership.

Prominent on the ALS website[4] is its seedbed logo: seeds flourishing in the open hand of an African. It embodies the ALS team's united prayer for leadership development in Africa. Ours is a story of celebration and joy.

IMPORTANT DECISIONS

With this groundwork laid, we began to define and refine the elements of the study under a process guided by Robert Priest. We agreed on specific information we wished to gather. We built our group collaboration skills as we designed the initial questionnaire and the protocol for its implementation. We discussed the basics that have to be addressed in any project: budget, timeframe, and areas of responsibility. Important decisions were made based on our collective wisdom.

We defined the geographic parameters of the research based on practical factors. The three major languages of education on the continent are English, French, and Portuguese. We had people on the ground in Kenya (English) and the CAR (French), and with access to Angola (Portuguese), so it seemed wise to gather our information from these three nations. In this way we would sample similarities and differences, discovering common factors related to leadership development.

The foundation committed to supporting additional training in research methods and practical skills for students administering the questionnaires. The process, we hoped, would support leadership development at the same time that we were researching it. Students became an integral part of the success of the study as they administered over eight thousand questionnaires (see Chapter 1). In the process we developed tools that others can use either in research or courses on research methods. These tools are available under "Resources" on the ALS website.

It was agreed that our research would be implemented under the auspices of the educational institutions where our research professors taught and the students studied. These institutions were generous with the time and talent of their staff and students. Each partnering institution is featured on our website. The commitment of leaders from these organizations provided the essential endorsement of respected elders. This approach served a key function as we asked potential respondents to give their time and provide thoughtful input. With respected local organizations sponsoring the research, the research process remained separate from any interest in the THF as a funding source. Indeed, the foundation's name was not featured at all in the research process itself.

---

[4] Africa Leadership Study: A Seedbed Resource. Http://www.africaleadershipstudy.org.

THE RESEARCH AND THE DATA

An overview of the ALS research process is presented in Chapter 1 of this book. It would be difficult to exaggerate how much better prepared the THF would now be to consider additional research. We hope that transparently sharing our ALS story will benefit other organizations. It was a unique and formative experience to be a part of such a diverse group functioning with singleness of purpose, generosity of spirit, humility toward one another, and significant success. The complete data and the research instruments and protocols are available on the ALS website for download in Portuguese, French, and English for use by others.

THE FINDINGS

Data review and analysis took place over a period of many months. Conferences were held with the full team to share information and insights, for prayerful discussion and evaluation, and to plan next steps. Guests from outside the ALS team with expertise in various fields were invited to attend and contribute. A private ALS website with a discussion Forum was established to facilitate ongoing conversations and serve as a place for all members of the team to easily access data, reports, and working documents. We became proficient in using online meeting tools, although we experienced the limitations and frustrations faced daily in much of Africa with limited and unreliable Internet access.

The research team developed a findings document[5] that distilled and organized key concepts into an overview. This served as a tool for the THF board in its oversight role as a source of important critique and funding. It also served the members of the ALS team as they chose findings of particular interest to them and began the collaborative development of the chapters of this book. Conferences provided space to read and critique one other's work and to maintain cohesion. This process is treated in depth in Chapter 1.

An oft-repeated theme emerged during our discussions. Participants often commented that certain findings fit with what they already sensed was true, but they had had no research or data to support their belief. They were excited to discover that the data supported their perceptions. In other cases the data brought unexpected information to light, surprising us with the results. It was a joyful journey of discovery that we were privileged to take together.

The ALS is the fruit of seeds planted many years ago; it hopes to be the seedbed for much fruit to come. To that end we have developed the ALS

---

[5] Tyndale House Foundation "17 Insights into Leadership in Africa" (2016), http://www.africaleadershipstudy.org/findings.

website. With many photos and graphics it tells the ALS story in great richness and depth. It supplements and supports the insights of this book and makes the full research data available for download in Portuguese, French, and English so others who wish can benefit from and build upon it.

PLANTING SEEDS TOGETHER

An important component of the website is its Resource Page. Organized around interest topics, it is a place where the ongoing growth and development of the seeds that have been planted can be made available, and the fruits can be celebrated and shared. The THF envisions the users of the site involved in an ongoing process of gathering, presenting, and adding materials that will be important to those engaged in leadership development, education, training, writing, and publishing. Some of the topics have been treated in depth in the chapters of this book. Some of the resources listed under the topic headings are based on the ALS findings. We hope others will join us in continuing to learn from and build on the data gathered in the ALS. There has been much work done by many others in the field of leadership development. Links to those organizations and their materials are also included by topic on the Resource Page. It will be enriched and expanded as the users of the site participate. We anticipate materials will be added in French, Portuguese, and English.

Included with the Resource Page is an ALS discussion Forum. It provides a space for users to post additional information. Conversations will provide an opportunity for users to get to know each other. It is a place for those with common interests to learn what each is doing and perhaps discover ways to work together. The Forum can be used to suggest the addition of Interest Topics and resource links to both the Resource Page and the Forum. In particular, Africans who use the site will have a knowledge of resources unknown to the foundation. As new and emerging resources are developed, they can be added to the various Interest Topics.

The initial Interest Topics that have been identified grew out of suggestions from the full ALS team. It is inherent in the process that the list will grow and links and resources will be added to each topic as others participate.[6]

HOW THE TYNDALE HOUSE FOUNDATION WAS HELPED

When the THF committed to the ALS, we hoped to improve our discernment as we invested funds in Africa. We wanted to support the development

---

[6] For a full list, see Appendix C in this book or visit the website, http://www. africaleadershipstudy.org/als-forum/, and join the conversation.

of strong, godly leaders in all areas of society. As the project moves forward, we continue to monitor the effects of our involvement in Africa and what we as an organization are learning along the way. A research project of such scope and depth was uncharted territory for the foundation board, and its flexibility—evidenced in its openness to an alternative review process and willingness to offer consistent funding for ALS's ongoing research—yielded important results. The THF continues carefully to balance the investment review process and strategic collaborations, all while keeping in mind the larger long-term goals of the project. Furthermore, our involvement in the ALS has had an impact on board considerations and decisions, with THF patterns of giving in Africa influenced by what we have learned through the ALS.

Consider two examples of recent THF initiatives. First is our involvement in Engagement de l'Afrique, a collaborative effort involving three theological schools in Francophone Africa, three international ministries with expertise in theological education, and three foundations committed to understanding the critical needs and issues of Francophone Africa. These nine organizations have committed to working together over the long term to equip leaders to train the next generation of leaders and to address the issues faced by the church in Francophone Africa. A component of the collaboration has been a process similar to the one the ALS team took in defining and planning together. This is a model radically different from the traditionally understood pattern of interaction between foundations and their funding applicants. We would not have understood the urgency and depth of the opportunities in Francophone Africa, and we would have been less open to this kind of collaborative effort, had we not participated in the ALS.

The second instance centers on issues outlined in Chapter 10. Although it will be a long-term effort, we are pursuing ways to address the need for more African publishers and authors. Because of our long history of funding literature projects, we entered the ALS with some knowledge and assumptions regarding writing, publishing, and distribution in Africa. ALS research tested our assumptions, verified some, and disproved others. Now, with data and findings in hand, we have a clearer picture that can help us with the strategic components that have the potential for greatest impact.

The training, development, and empowerment of African writers addressing African issues are crucial for the training of leaders. Publishing is a critically important way to give the church a voice. At the same time, publishing and distribution is a huge challenge throughout the continent. We are asking questions: Who is best able to train writers and publishers? Who is experienced in African publishing? Will print-on-demand systems or eBooks solve the problems of distribution? Experience gained from the ALS has sharpened our attention. We are seeking organizations that work in each of these fields to share information and expertise, collaborating in ways that will empower all involved to fulfill their mission.

These are two examples of how the ALS has fulfilled the original purpose. Not only have the data and findings given the THF a base of knowledge when evaluating potential grants in Africa, but the process has also changed us and opened us to a wider understanding of how a collaborative effort can be of inestimable benefit. While it is a difficult lesson to live out, we must remain open to being changed as we work with others and as we are shaped into a community focused by agreed-upon goals. This is a hallmark of the church—that others can see our love for one another worked out in community. If it can be interwoven in our working relationships, it will transcend denominational, cultural, and ethnic divides. It "makes a space for God to act."

RELEVANCE TO THE WIDER FUNDING COMMUNITY

THF is a part of a wider community of foundations, churches, and individuals interested in supporting kingdom work around the world (Wuthnow 2009). The members of this community range from foundations with large staff and multimillion-dollar endowments to megachurches to high-net-worth individuals to those with more limited means seeking to exercise stewardship of the resources with which they've been entrusted. As in any community a wide spectrum of purposes and the means to put them into practice exist. Some operate with traditional models that have served them well over the years. Many are re-examining and exploring how to adapt to the fast pace of change in our world.

There is an increasing recognition that research should inform giving. For instance, the mission statement of the Foundation Center is "to strengthen the social sector by advancing knowledge about philanthropy in the U.S. and around the world."[7] One example of such research may be found in Robert Wuthnow's *Boundless Faith: The Global Outreach of American Churches,* in which he examines the strategic ways in which American churches have utilized their material resources in service of Christian purposes around the world (Wuthnow 2009). The ALS thus provides both research that others may take advantage of in their giving, and it provides a model for others to imitate in their work. This model involves support for and collaboration with scholars and researchers in acquiring relevant knowledge.

There is a growing understanding in this funding community that we can be more effective if we work together rather than independently. Funders with interest in specific goals or geographic areas can share information and experiences with one another and with a wide variety of stakeholders, even if they do not have a formal framework for working together. Conversations need to take place between scholars and field practitioners,

---

[7] http://foundationcenter.org/.

as well as among scholars in various disciplines including missiology, education, the social sciences, and business. Greater awareness by each of the whole, and of the parts that various actors play in that whole, increases the chance of effecting change.

Today, as life is experienced more and more in the virtual world of Internet information and social networks, the funding community continues to recognize the vital importance of in-person relationships to kingdom work. The experience of the THF in the ALS has provided strong verification and documentation of this. We hope our experience can contribute positively to the ongoing funding community conversation.

THE STORY CONTINUES

The story of the ALS includes many characters. You have met some of the main ones in this book. You have gotten to know them as their carefully crafted chapters gave you a glimpse into the gifts, insight, and wisdom they have brought to their task. When you visit the companion ALS website, you can meet the larger ALS team and learn of its members' roles in this narrative, as well as their vision for it. While this chapter tells the THF's story, we were only one of many complementary participants in the ALS. Each person was drawn to this project for different reasons. But all brought an attitude of respect and humility accompanied by the strengths of their training, wisdom, and life experiences.

I suspect that all of us who seek to participate in the story of the kingdom of God, whatever our roles may be, have moments when we could use a word of encouragement. The principles at work in God's kingdom are radically different from those at work in the world around us. In my years of service with the foundation (since 1975), it has been a privilege and a personal challenge to observe the many examples of those who humbly live by faith, sometimes at great cost. This reflection has served as that encouragement for me. I pray it may do so for you also.

REFERENCES CITED

Oden, Thomas C. 2010. *How Africa Shaped the Christian Mind*. Downers Grove, IL: InterVarsity Press.

Taylor, Ken. 1991. *My Life: A Guided Tour*. Wheaton, IL: Tyndale House Publishers.

Taylor, Margaret. 2000. *The Way I Remember It! (The Memoirs of Margaret West Taylor)*. Wheaton, IL: Taylor Press.

Tiegreen, Chris. 2003. *365 Pocket Devotions: Inspiration and Renewal for Each New Day*. Walk Thru the Bible/Tyndale House Publishers.

Wuthnow, Robert. 2009. *Boundless Faith: The Global Outreach of American Churches*. Berkeley and Los Angeles: University of California Press.

A Reflection on Faithfulness—
When I Wonder If My Service Has Any Impact

We serve in a Kingdom of wheat kernels, mustard seeds and hidden pearls—small things with huge impact. The world cannot see their value. In our more discouraging moments, neither can we. . . .

[But] do not be discouraged if your faithful service to God has imperceptible results. They are imperceptible only to the naked eye. They are highly valued in the eternal Kingdom, where those who give away their lives find them again.

I tell you the truth, unless a kernel of wheat is planted in the soil and dies, it remains alone. But its death will produce many new kernels—a plentiful harvest of new lives. JOHN 12:24

(Tiegreen 2003, Day 154)

Conclusion

Lessons Learned through the Africa Leadership Study

Kirimi Barine, Michael Bowen, Edward Elliott,
H. Jurgens Hendriks, John Jusu, Elisabet le Roux,
David K. Ngaruiya, Robert J. Priest,
Steven D. H. Rasmussen, Wanjiru M. Gitau,
Nupanga Weanzana, and Mary Kleine Yehling

African Christian leaders and organizations are creatively and energetically working to address a wide variety of local problems and opportunities within the framework of Christian understandings, communities, and resources. In our final gathering at Brackenhurst in Kenya, the full ALS team met to discuss what we had learned through our research. Team members had prepared ahead of time by reading all of the survey results, interviews, and reports.[1] The following is a brief summary of what our full ALS team believes our research reveals.

1. *Pastors are very influential.* When asked to "name a Christian, outside your immediate family, who has influenced you the most," more than half of the respondents in Kenya and the CAR, and over one-third in Angola, named a pastor. This suggests that where there are important issues to be addressed in African societies (such as the challenge of ethnic political violence or the widespread problems with HIV/AIDS), it makes good sense for initiatives to partner with pastors in influencing people for good. Particularly influential pastors from Kenya that we interviewed and reported on include John Bosco, Joseph Maisha, and Oscar Muriu; from

---

[1] Space constraints do not allow us to include the full reports we prepared on the influential Christian leaders that our surveys explored or the full reports on highly effective African-led Christian organizations. Each of these reports and a variety of other resources are available in English, French, and Portuguese at http://www.africaleadershipstudy.org.

the CAR, David Koudougueret and René Malépou; and from Angola, Adelaide Catanha and Dinis Eurico.

2. *Non-clergy leaders also play strategic roles in a wide variety of arenas.* Outstanding non-clergy leaders that we interviewed included an architect (Edouard Nvouni), a medical doctor (Nestor Mamadou Nali), an environmentalist (Patrick Nyachogo), a retired military general (General Kianga), professors (Eunice Chiquete, Esther Mombo), the founder of a large and successful NGO (Alice Kirambi), an agricultural trainer (Joseph Kimeli), a teacher of sex education in schools (Isaac Mutua), and the founding director of two organizations that work with drug addicts (Cosmas Maina). Not only did these individuals accomplish a wide variety of strategic goals through their vocational work, but their professional positions and reputations positioned them to serve and influence more broadly than would be the norm for clergy. Furthermore, in contexts where the growth of the church has outstripped the presence of trained pastoral leaders, lay Christian leaders often fill the gap by serving as ministry leaders in and through their churches. For example, Angolan Manuel Missa is a highly respected primary school administrator and teacher but also serves in his church as singer, choir director, Bible study teacher, and deacon. Such influential non-clergy leaders are often less visible than clergy leaders, sometimes receiving little encouragement and support from churches, but they are extremely important to the strength of the church and its witness in Africa.

3. *On a continent where 60–70 percent of the church is female, women are strategic to the strength of the church but are often under-acknowledged and under-supported.* Countries varied in the extent to which respondents indicated that their churches provided opportunities for women in leadership; only half of CAR respondents and three-quarters of respondents in Kenya affirmed this. A majority of the organizations identified as having a maximum impact were led by men, with primarily male boards. It was not uncommon for leaders being interviewed to express regret over the lack of female presence on the board—but without any stated plan for changing this. The spouses of male leaders often played a strong partnering role (such as with Word of Life or Redeemed Academy). The same was true of leading pastors' wives, who were sometimes named in their own right as top leaders. Several women's guilds that we reported on, such as Mothers' Union, were identified as having maximum impact. Women identified as key leaders (such as Esther Mombo and Alice Kirambi) provided compelling evidence of the strategic influence and role of women in contemporary Africa, but also of the challenges women face. Clearly, this is an important area for further consideration and better support. *Churches play a variety of strategic roles in the lives of African Christians and communities.* When asked to name a Christian who had influenced them the most, 59 percent of Angolans, 70 percent of Kenyans, and 76 percent of respondents in the CAR listed a church leader of one kind or other (including, but not limited

to pastors). Not only are churches a base for mentorship and leadership training, but also for strategic influence on youth, poverty-alleviation efforts, care for widows, education about financial matters, education about HIV/AIDS, education about issues of ethnic violence and political process, and dissemination of Christian books.

4. *African-led parachurch Christian organizations are central to evangelism, discipleship, and social engagement on a wide variety of fronts.* Not belonging to a single church, such ministries foster interdenominational unity and are often led by entrepreneurial personalities—frequently laypeople—who identify needs, devise programs to meet those needs, formulate strategies to solicit support, and carry out programs with high impact. Such faith-based organizations face a variety of challenges, but many are facing these challenges with success. The interdenominational culture that is fostered is in itself a great strength for the wider church and merits consideration as a strong criterion for support.

5. *The Bible as the word of God is important in the lives of African Christians.* Not only is the Bible central in preaching, but over 60 percent of our respondents, nearly all of whom were literate,[2] indicated that they read their bibles daily (with Pentecostal Christians reading at highest levels and Catholics at lowest levels). Our research highlighted the central role of the Bible as God's word in some of the Kenyan youth-focused ministries that we examined in-depth, such as FOCUS Kenya, Kenya Students Christian Fellowship (KSCF) and Scripture Union, but also the role of vernacular Bible translations in the CAR (see the report on the Central African Association for Bible Translation and Literacy).

6. *Many Africans read books, especially books that are motivational, practical, and oriented toward helping readers achieve success.* One-third of respondents reported having read at least six books in the prior year, with roughly 60 percent of pastors having read six or more books in that time period. Pastors also report buying books at significantly higher rates than others; they are less likely to read fiction than others. The books of megachurch pastors from the United States (Joel Osteen, T. D. Jakes, Rick Warren) and elsewhere (Myles Munroe, David Oyedepo, Dag Heward-Mills, Chris Oyakhilome) were widely mentioned as favorites by Kenyan respondents, and many of these books have an emphasis on how to achieve success. Books by Ben Carson and John Maxwell were also favorites. Books that were practically oriented toward helping readers achieve success were central. Many of the leaders we interviewed indicated that they read extensively, although it is clear that only a few do serious academic reading.

7. *There is a strong need for local Christian authors.* While most Kenyan respondents who listed a favorite author listed an author who was explicitly Christian (67.4 percent), fully 61.5 percent of these authors

---

[2] We intentionally prioritized surveying those who were literate, a subset of the larger populations.

were from the United States. Fewer than 2 percent of Kenyan respondents who listed a favorite author listed a Kenyan Christian author. In the CAR, 38 percent listed a favorite author who was explicitly Christian, but fewer than 1 percent (0.6 percent) listed a favorite author from within the CAR who was explicitly Christian. To summarize this in other terms, while 41.6 percent of African Christian respondents named a favorite author who was African, and 58.2 percent named a favorite author who was Christian, the degree of overlap between the two was relatively small, with only 9.5 percent naming a favorite author who was both African and Christian (see Figure 10–1).

Our sense from the interviews is that many African Christian leaders have interesting and compelling stories, but they are not in print. Interestingly, most of the leaders that we interviewed stated that they would like to write a book or books about their life or ministry, which they believe would be of interest to others, but many indicated that they do not have the time or skill. Given the fact that these leaders understand their local context well, and given the apparent lack of Christian books by local authors, there is a strategic need for supporting initiatives aimed at helping local Christian leaders write and publish quality books.

8. *African Christian leaders and organizations achieve success through relational networks.* A surprising percentage of leaders with the greatest impact have lived and/or studied abroad (Brazil, Canada, France, India, Italy, Portugal, UK, the United States) and draw on global relational ties on behalf of local strategic ends. Successful leaders and organizations also build on extensive relationships of reciprocity and trust within their countries. The ability to forge cross-denominational relationships was pivotal to the success of most leaders and organizations we examined (with notable examples being NCCK and Mombasa Church Forum). Even the ability to forge trust relationships with Muslim leaders turns out to be a key dimension of leader and organizational success within Muslim-dominant regions (Bishop Bosco, Mombasa Church Forum, Redeemed Academy, Word of Life). Sociologists point out that in our modern world leadership is exercised less through top-down control within bureaucratic structures than through the ability to activate relational networks on behalf of strategic ends. Our ALS research would confirm that African Christian leadership is exercised through such a networked body of Christ. It would also seem to follow that if partners from abroad wish to be involved in a strategic way, they need to understand these networks, supporting and adapting to them in a culturally contextual way in addition to any financial support being provided.

9. *African Christian leaders minister within ethnic and inter-ethnic settings where intercultural skills, competencies, and commitments are crucial to success.* Our survey confirmed that Christian leaders come from all major ethnic groups. When our respondents were asked to name a pastor or non-clergy leader with the most impact, a majority in Kenya and

Angola named someone from their own ethnic group, while a majority of respondents in the CAR named someone from an ethnic group different from their own.[3] Thus the evidence suggests that shared ethnic/cultural identity remains an important dynamic in Africa, even while inter-ethnic relations are also central. Our interviews suggested that the success of many leaders is due in significant measure to their intercultural experiences, competencies, and commitments. That is, the fact that so many have lived abroad or in regions away from home appears to have contributed not only to their networks but to comfort and skill in relating with people across diverse cultural lines. Bishop Bosco, for example, moved away from his roots in Nairobi to Mombasa, where he learned to minister in Swahili and to make other cultural adjustments that won him respect among the Muslim Digo. Many who were interviewed called attention to the ethnic diversity of their staff or board, and clearly some felt it was important that Christian leaders provide modeling and guidance for healthy inter-ethnic relations.

10. *African Christian leaders are increasingly part of a connected world, although with marked constraints.* Over eight out of ten respondents in the CAR and over nine out of ten in Angola and Kenya had cell phones. Pastors in all countries had even higher rates of cell-phone ownership.

Roughly one-third of our Angolan and Kenyan respondents indicated they owned computers, although fewer than one-sixth did so in the CAR—and pastors in all three countries owned computers at lower rates than other respondents. One-third of CAR respondents (32.7 percent), less than half of Angolan respondents (48.8 percent), and nearly two-thirds of Kenyan respondents (63.3 percent) indicated that they had access to the Internet. Of those with access, CAR respondents were most likely to gain access through an Internet café, while Kenyans and Angolans most frequently accessed the Internet through their cell phones, followed by computers at home or work. Kenyans reported the highest frequency of Internet usage, with Angola a close second and the CAR a distant third. While pastors report less access to the Internet than others do, pastors who do have access report higher rates of Internet usage than others. The high-impact Christian leaders we interviewed report extensive use of various forms of communication, often downloading information from the Internet and having a Facebook web page. Most of the high-impact organizations we examined use email, Facebook, and other forms of social

---

[3] In Angola, 77 percent of respondents named a pastor from their own ethnic group and 80 percent named a non-clergy leader from their own ethnic group as having most impact. In Kenya, 65 percent named a pastor from their own ethnic group, with 66 percent naming a non-clergy leader from their own ethnic group. In the CAR, 37 percent named a pastor from their own ethnic group, and 48 percent named a non-clergy leader from their own group.

media as a means for communicating with and educating those they serve. Those organizations that have not yet done so (such as Mothers' Union), classify this as a weakness of their organization. The fact that organizations request assistance from donors in setting up the infrastructure to enable digital communication is thus valid and is a need that should be addressed.

11. *Initiatives that focus on youth are strategic.* In a continent where anyone under the age of thirty is considered a youth, 74 percent of the population in Angola, 69 percent in the CAR, and 72 percent in Kenya is less than thirty years old. Fifty-nine percent of respondents in Angola, 58 percent in the CAR, and 82 percent in Kenya indicated that their congregation focused either "a good bit" or "very much" on youth leadership development. Especially in Kenya, it was clear that a majority of the leaders and organizations with maximum impact were focused on youth. Larger congregations increasingly have youth pastors on staff. There is a widespread perception that youth face specific challenges and vulnerabilities but are also uniquely open to being influenced. Christian leaders and organizations can generally count on support from a variety of Christian, governmental, and civil society agencies when they focus on working with youth. Furthermore, many of the leaders we examined had themselves been shaped in their youth by ministries such as KSCF, Scripture Union, or FOCUS Kenya. Strengthening such ministries and expanding them within the CAR and Angola would appear to be a high priority.

12. *Mentoring is central to leadership development in Africa.* The majority of leaders we interviewed made reference to having been mentored by others and also to the mentoring in which they were involved (such as Bishop Maisha, Professor Mombo, Oscar Muriu), sometimes using internship programs along with mentoring. In our survey we asked if key leaders and organizations played a strong role in developing others as leaders, and if so, what means were used. More than half of our survey respondents who named a key leader as being particularly good at leadership development answered that the person used mentoring as a tool. Organizations that were identified as being unusually strong at developing leaders (such as FOCUS Kenya, KSCF, Scripture Union, Campus pour Christ) were also identified as strong in using mentors—with some of the student groups utilizing alumni to help with internships and mentoring, creating a self-sustaining loop.

13. *Formal education is clearly a central part of leadership development.* Our surveys, administered among groups of Christians and Christian leaders, indicated an unusually high level of formal education. The high-impact leaders we examined, even when they sometimes wished to stress the benefits of their own informal leadership development programs, had unusually high levels of formal education themselves. Unfortunately, our questionnaire failed to ask explicitly about the role of universities and seminaries, and thus we are somewhat limited in what can be said. In the CAR, FATEB was selected by the highest number of respondents as being

the organization with the most impact—which is somewhat surprising since the wording of our questionnaire emphasized other sorts of organizations rather than educational institutions. From the interview results it appears that most leaders have been shaped by some combination of high-quality formal education along with other forms of informal and mentoring relationships—with the combination being more important than any single one of these alone.

14. *Many African Christian leaders are ambivalent about politics but recognize that much is at stake and thus often engage the political arena on behalf of the common good.* Most leaders we interviewed associated politics with corruption and conflict. One natural response is avoidance. In both Angola and the CAR, more than 50 percent of respondents checked "not at all" when asked if their churches provided education related to political realities; another 25 percent checked "very little." This was especially true of Pentecostal churches. And yet some key Christian leaders were deeply appreciated for the strategic roles they had played in government (such as Nestor Mamadou Nali in the CAR). Some organizations (such as the NCCK and Mombasa Church Forum) were appreciated for providing Christian input into vetting political candidates and laws, and not simply conceding the political arena to Muslims or secularists. In Kenya, only 19 percent of respondents indicated that their church provided no education on political realities, with almost half saying their churches provided either "a good bit" or "very much." The recent peaceful election in Kenya almost certainly owes a great deal to the work of Kenyan churches in coaching their members on the importance of a political process not characterized by ethnic or religious violence. African Christians in other countries might benefit by learning through the experience of Kenyan churches.

15. *While most Christian churches, organizations, and leaders have minimal focus on relating to Muslims, a minority are doing an impressive job in this strategic area.* While Islam has a significant presence in the CAR and Kenya, most respondents indicated that their churches did little or nothing to focus on Islam. But 11 percent in the CAR and 18 percent in Kenya indicated their churches did "very much" in the area of Muslim outreach. Our Phase 2 research, especially on leaders and organizations on the coast of Kenya where Al Shabaab has been active and where tension and conflict with Islam is high, revealed a variety of ways in which Christians were engaging Muslims on behalf of peace and positive relationships, as well as on behalf of Christian witness. Bishop John Bosco received the highest number of nominations as the pastor with the greatest impact, and his ministry has been in a largely Muslim community with a central focus on serving that community and establishing positive relations. Cosmas Maina, who received the second-highest number of votes for a non-clergy leader, similarly has partnered with Muslims in working with drug addicts. The NCCK and Mombasa Church Forum have worked to cultivate Muslim leaders as conversation partners, providing support for Muslim political

candidates who exemplify positive approaches to interreligious relations, partnering with community policing against interreligious violence, and so forth. At the time of our research Bishop Bosco's Redeemed Gospel Academy, which operates in a primarily Muslim region and initially came under attack, had 350 students attending, more than half of whom came from Muslim families. The patterns of engagement being forged by these Christians need to be shared with African Christians across the continent.

16. *Better support structures for Christian institutions and leaders exist in Kenya than in Angola or the CAR, and it is much more difficult to acquire knowledge about leadership realities in Francophone and Lusophone Africa than in Anglophone Africa.* Everything from the availability of Christian books in the national language, to ease and safety of travel, to the availability of high-quality Internet access, differed significantly between Kenya and the other countries. The fact that Kenyan Christians speak the same language as American Christians makes communication and partnership much easier. And this affects not only ministry partnerships but the level of difficulty encountered in partnering for effective research on leadership dynamics. There are more demanding hurdles to be faced in the CAR and Angola than in Kenya in order to gain high-quality understanding of leadership realities. The implications are significant. If the global body of Christ is to partner wisely in the non-English speaking parts of Africa, we will need to work much harder to find information related to the challenges and opportunities affecting African Christian leaders.

After reviewing the data and identifying what we had learned, ALS team members reported that they were gratified that our research provided strong confirmation and evidence for what we had already sensed was true: African Christians are exercising great energy, initiative, and vision in responding to African realities and perceived needs. Through our research we learned a great deal about the specific ways in which African Christian leaders and organizations are creatively and energetically working to address a wide variety of local problems and engage opportunities within the framework of Christian understandings, communities, and resources. Participants expressed the hope that our research results would go far in counteracting the widespread perception that Africans are doing little to change the prevailing culture of poverty, conflict, violence, and foreign dependency.

Appendix A

ALS *Purpose Statements*

AS ORIGINALLY ARTICULATED BY THE TYNDALE HOUSE FOUNDATION LEADERSHIP TASK FORCE

The purpose of the Africa Leadership Study is to identify strategic opportunities for supporting the development of Christian leaders in Francophone, Anglophone and Lusophone[1] Africa. In conjunction with African Christian leaders, this will be accomplished through these strategic steps:

Assessing what is already being done in terms of leadership development.

Identifying opportunities where Western donors can and should be investing their resources for optimal effect.

Identifying challenges that will work against effective deployment of resources.

Creating a means of following up to assess the effectiveness of resources invested in leadership development.

AS FORMULATED BY AFRICAN SCHOLARS INVOLVED IN THE ALS PROJECT

The benefits and outcomes of the study will also inform the African Partners of the ALS Project and can serve as a resource for Africans in understanding current patterns, practices and programs of leadership to be used in their visioning and planning for the future. In that context these are the strategic steps:

Providing African churches and market-place leadership with details of effective initiatives as resources they can learn or draw from and in some cases replicate appropriately.

Providing case studies for institutions of higher learning.

Generating data that Governments can use for leadership development and intervention.

Generating literature on leadership.

---

[1] The original statement did not include Lusophone, which was added at the 2011 Nairobi conference.

Appendix B: ALS Survey Results

From Angola (N=1783), Central African Republic (N=2294), and Kenya (N=3964)

Unless otherwise noted, any percent listed is valid percent.

Q I: Name one Christian man or woman, outside your family, who has influenced you the most?

Sample of results for this question, with frequency of mention. Most names given appeared only once or twice in the list.

Angola		CAR		Kenya	
Ananias Alberto	14	Jean Balezou	13	John Bosco	38
Adelaide Catanha	10	Ferdinand Bassala	17	Gideon Karanja	12
Abias Cauto	6	David Bendima	13	Julius Kilonzo	21
Bernardo Chimoiya	5	Paul Change	26	Wilfred Lai	21
Alberto Daniel	11	George Offong Edet	14	Steve Macharia	13
Diamantino Doba	7	Daniel Halola	22	Joseph Maisha	21
Eduardo Domingos	5	Theodore Kapau	40	Simon Mbevi	16
Dinis Eurico	15	David Koudougueret	17	Edward Munene	12
Marcello Malukissa	7	Paul Mbunga-Mpindi	13	Mathews Mururu	13
José Manuel	7	Jean-Pierre Mobia	25	Timothy Musonye	19
Luiza Mateus	4	Corneille Nguepelego	14	Isaac Mutua	11
Daniel Pinto	4	Gaston Oumonguene	18	Sammy Ngewa	11
Nelson Samaria	6	Jean Lefort Pougaza	31	Furaha Semo	13
Faustino Sikila	5	Geris Appolinaire		Philip Shitsukane	14
Mario Velho	4	Sengueteli	20	John Waweru	1
		Valentin Yakoma	15		

Q 2: This person is or was:

	Angola	CAR	Kenya
A pastor	35.4%	50.4%	56.2%
Another church leader	23.2%	25.3%	13.7%
A teacher	8.5%	8.1%	10.1%
An employer	1.6%	2.0%	2.4%
A friend	21.5%	9.5%	15.4%
Other	9.8%	4.6%	2.2%

Q 3: In what one area has this person impacted you the most?

	Angola	CAR	Kenya
In your relationships with others	8.3%	5.9%	10.0%
Spiritually, in your relationship with God	73.3%	68.8%	67.0%
Vocationally, in your work and career decisions	5.9%	5.2%	9.0%
Ethically	2.0%	5.0%	4.1%
Financially	1.3%	3.4%	1.9%
Educationally (skills)	6.8%	10.4%	7.2%
Other	2.5%	1.3%	0.8%

Q4: What is the average number of people that attend your church on a given weekend?

	Angola	CAR	Kenya
Less than 40	6.7%	5.8%	8.5%
41-100	12.2%	26.0%	24.6%
101-250	20.2%	27.3%	22.9%
251-500	21.8%	15.4%	19.7%
501-1000	21.8%	9.0%	12.4%
More than 1000	17.2%	16.5%	11.9%

Q 5: What is the name of your local church?

[Results not provided here]

Q 6: What is the name of this church's head pastor?

[Results not provided here]

Q 7: What is the name of your church's denomination?

Angola	Frequency	Percent
Asamblea de Deus Pentecostal	88	5.1%
Convenção Baptista de Angola	6	0.3%
Igreja Adventista do Sétimo Dia	27	1.6%
Igreja Apostólica Africana em Angola	2	0.1%
Igreja Católica	62	3.6%
Igreja Cristã Evangélica	4	0.2%
Igreja Evangélica Batista de Angola	298	17.2%
Igreja Evangélica Congregacional de Angola	605	34.9%
Igreja Evangélica dos Irmãos de Angola (Plymouth Br)	50	2.9%
Igreja Evangélica Reformada de Angola	118	6.8%
Igreja Evangélica Sinodal de Angola	209	12.1%
Igreja Luterana	30	1.7%
Igreja Metodista Unida de Angola	19	1.1%
Igreja Nova Apostólica	8	0.5%
Igreja Presbiteriana de Angola	6	0.3%
Igreja Visão Cristã	19	1.1%
Missão Evangélica Pentecostal em Angola	10	0.6%
Uniao de Igrejas Evangelicas de Angola	82	4.7%

CAR	Frequency	Percent
Assemblée de Dieu	15	0.7%
Centre Evangélique Béthanie	15	0.7%
Communauté des Eglises Apostoliques en Centrafrique	470	21.4%
Eglise Adventiste du Septième jour	10	0.5%
Eglise Catholique	168	7.7%
Eglise Coopération Evangélique en Centrafrique	147	6.7%
Eglise de la Fraternité Apostolique	13	0.6%
Eglise de Plein Évangile	8	0.4%
Eglise Evangélique de Réveil	14	0.6%
Eglise Luthérienne	34	1.6%
Eglise Méthodiste en Centrafrique	11	0.5%
Eglise Protestante du Christ Roi	13	0.6%
Eglises Baptistes*	830	37.9%
F.E.E.P.A.C	24	1.1%
Fédération des Eglises Evangélique des Frères	138	6.3%
Independent/Nondenominational	50	2.3%
Mission des Eglises Evangéliques en Centrafrique	16	0.7%
Mission Internationale d'Evangelisation Vie Abondante	10	0.5%
Union des Eglises Evangélique de Elim	52	2.4%
Union des Eglises Evangélique des Frères	114	5.2%
Union des Eglises Evangéliques de la Fraternité Apostolique	15	0.7%

*The category Eglises Baptistes (Baptist Churches) encompasses at least five different large Baptist denominations: UFEB, UEB, ANEB, CEBI, CEBEC.

Kenya	Frequency	Percent	WCD*
Africa Inland Church	374	9.7%	5.4%
African Brotherhood Church	28	0.7%	0.6%
African Gospel Church	96	2.5%	0.5%
African Independent Pentecostal Church of Africa	35	0.9%	3.0%

African Orthodox Church of Kenya	9	0.2%	1.4%
Anglican Church	336	8.7%	10.9%
Baptist Church	160	4.1%	3.0%
Christ is the Answer Ministries (CITAM)	87	2.3%	--
Church of Christ in Africa	18	0.5%	0.7%
Church of God in East Africa	7	0.2%	0.4%
Church of Restoration	29	0.8%	--
Deliverance Church	57	1.5%	0.2%
East Africa Pentecostal Churches	19	0.5%	0.3%
Evangelical Lutheran Church in Kenya	20	0.5%	0.3%
Free Pentecostal Fellowship	48	1.2%	0.2%
Friends Church (Quakers)	36	0.9%	--
Full Gospel Churches of Kenya	71	1.8%	0.8%
Glory Outreach Assembly	17	0.4%	--
Gospel Outreach	36	0.9%	--
Gracious Restoration Christian Church	14	0.4%	--
Independent or Nondenominational	129	3.3%	--
International Gospel Ministries Migori	18	0.5%	--
Jesus Celebration Center	23	0.6%	--
Kenya Assemblies of God	160	4.1%	2.8%
Methodist Church in Kenya	14	0.4%	0.6%
Nairobi Chapel	54	1.4%	--
Pentecostal Assemblies of God	98	2.5%	1.8%
Pentecostal Evangelistic Fellowship of Africa	74	1.9%	1.0%
Presbyterian Church of East Africa	120	3.1%	4.3%
Redeemed Gospel Church	178	4.6%	--

Roman Catholic Church	424	11.0%	19.9%
Salvation Army	78	2.0%	1.0%
Seventh-Day Adventist Church	389	10.1%	2.2%
Voice of Salvation and Healing Church	15	0.4%	0.3%
Winners' Chapel	42	1.1%	--
Worldwide Gospel Church	22	0.6%	--

*World Christian Database statistics on denominational breakdown as percent of Kenyan population.

Q 8: To what extent does your church provide care for elderly widows?

	Angola	CAR	Kenya
Not at all	13.6%	26.9%	8.9%
A little	46.8%	42.4%	29.4%
A good bit	27.4%	18.3%	33.5%
Very much	12.1%	12.4%	28.2%

Q 9: To what extent does your church provide job training?

	Angola	CAR	Kenya
Not at all	16.7%	50.7%	20.4%
A little	29.5%	22.1%	30.0%
A good bit	29.7%	13.4%	27.8%
Very much	24.1%	13.9%	21.8%

Q 10: To what extent does your church provide financial training?

	Angola	CAR	Kenya
Not at all	44.3%	21.1%	16.3%
A little	29.5%	22.7%	29.4%
A good bit	15.9%	27.6%	30.8%
Very much	10.3%	28.6%	23.5%

Q 11: To what extent does your church provide youth leadership development?

	Angola	CAR	Kenya
Not at all	13.6%	9.8%	3.2%
A little	27.7%	32.0%	15.0%
A good bit	30.7%	31.2%	32.9%
Very much	27.9%	27.0%	48.9%

Q 12: To what extent does your church provide education about HIV/AIDS?

	Angola	CAR	Kenya
Not at all	21.0%	20.6%	12.1%
A little	36.0%	36.3%	24.5%
A good bit	25.5%	19.6%	29.2%
Very much	17.5%	23.5%	34.3%

Q 13: To what extent does your church provide education about political realities?

	Angola	CAR	Kenya
Not at all	56.1%	54.8%	19.0%
A little	25.3%	25.7%	31.7%
A good bit	12.5%	11.4%	27.7%
Very much	6.1%	8.0%	21.5%

Q 14: To what extent does your church provide adult leadership development?

	Angola	CAR	Kenya
Not at all	16.7%	15.3%	6.3%
A little	31.6%	32.1%	20.3%
A good bit	28.5%	31.0%	34.1%
Very much	23.2%	21.5%	39.3%

Q 15: To what extent does your church provide opportunities for women in leadership?

	Angola	CAR	Kenya
Not at all	10.3%	13.8%	5.9%
A little	26.5%	31.7%	18.7%
A good bit	32.8%	29.1%	34.2%
Very much	30.5%	25.4%	41.2%

Q 16: To what extent does your church provide ethical teaching for all of life?

	Angola	CAR	Kenya
Not at all	9.5%	7.9%	4.5%
A little	24.6%	21.7%	14.5%
A good bit	29.7%	34.3%	29.6%
Very much	36.2%	36.0%	51.4%

Q 17: To what extent does your church provide models of servant leadership?

	Angola	CAR	Kenya
Not at all	17.7%	7.2%	4.4%
A little	32.5%	23.7%	14.9%
A good bit	28.8%	33.8%	32.9%
Very much	21.0%	35.3%	47.8%

Q 18: To what extent does your church provide outreach ministry to Muslims?

	Angola	CAR	Kenya
Not at all	85.8%	59.8%	41.5%
A little	7.5%	20.0%	23.2%
A good bit	3.1%	9.5%	17.1%
Very much	3.6%	10.7%	18.2%

Q 19: To what extent does your church provide access to Bibles and Christian books?

	Angola	CAR	Kenya
Not at all	6.0%	6.1%	6.2%
A little	15.6%	14.6%	18.0%
A good bit	25.2%	23.2%	24.0%
Very much	53.1%	56.2%	51.8%

Q 20-22: Please list three pastors that you believe are making an important difference in your local area?

[Results not listed here]

Q 23: Who of the above three pastors would you say is making the most significant impact?

The most frequently named pastors with impact are listed below, with frequency of mention:

Angola

Ananias Alberto	22	Luisa Mateus	11	Josue Binoua	54
Marcos Andre	13	Alberto Miguel	13	Raymond Gobo	30
Adelaide Catanha	20	Elioth Moraine	14	Theodore Kapau	111
Fernando Catanha	21	Matias Sambango	15	Pierre Keafei-Moussa	22
Lucia Chitula	23	Filipe Tchissingui	24	David Koudougueret	111
Martinho Diogo	21	Bernardo Vongula	14	Vincent Kpare	18
Afonso Dumbo	13			René Malépou	17
Dinis Eurico	49	**CAR**		Jean-Pierre Mobia	55
Manuel Felix	13	Daniel Alola	47	Thierry Moinamse	18
Manuel Aurelio Kapamu	21	Isaac Baletogbo	25	Corneille Nguepelego	44
Antonio Eurico Lucamba	28	Jean Balezou	20	Gaston Ouamonguene	32
Marcelo Malukisa	37	Ferdinand Bassala	34	Jean le Fort Pougaza	29
Adelaide Tomás Manuel	17	Marc Belikassa	20	Mathias Tofio	25
José Manuel	17	David Bendima	30	Isaac Zokoue	42

Kenya

Tom Arati	15	Walter Kimutai	11	Paul Mutua	14
Olutande Stephen Bakare	19	Wilfred Lai	27	Sammy Ngewa	11
		Steve Macharia	25	Kenneth Odhiambo	13
John Bosco	46	Simon Mbevi	15	David Oginde	11
Benson Kago	16	Edward Munene	14	Gregory Otenga	20
Gideon Karanja	11	Martin Munyao	18	Cephas Wango	15
Julius Kilonzo	32	Mathews Mururu	19	Muriithi Wanjau	13

Please tell us about this pastor.

Q 24: What is his or her gender/sex?

	Angola	CAR	Kenya
Male	90.2%	99.5%	92.2%
Female	9.8%	0.5%	7.8%

Q 25: How old would you guess that he or she is?

	Angola	CAR	Kenya
Less than 35	7.9%	3.5%	7.9%
Between 35 and 44	26.7%	22.0%	41.4%
Between 45 and 54	38.4%	41.9%	34.0%
Between 55 and 64	22.3%	25.9%	13.4%
More than 64 years old	4.6%	6.7%	3.3%

Q 26: What is his or her marital status?

	Angola	CAR	Kenya
Married	92.0%	90.0%	89.7%
Single	5.8%	9.4%	9.6%
Other	2.2%	0.5%	0.7%

Q 27: What is his or her ethnic group?

Ethnicity of named pastors compared with the population of this ethnic group in the country as a whole.

Angola	Pastor	Pop
Bakongo	30.3%	13%
Bangala	0.4%	
Chokwe/Cokwe	1.5%	5%?
Ganguela	3.4%	9%?
Kimbundu	5.7%	25%
Kwanyama	0.6%	4%?
Nyaneka-Humbe	0.8%	3%?
Ovimbundu	53.8%	37%

CAR	Pastor	Pop
Banda	17.2%	27%
Gbaya	18.3%	33%
Mandja	18.1%	13%
Mboum	1.1%	7%
Ngbaka	13.8%	4%
Ngbandi	12.0%	11%
Sara	3.0%	10%
Zande-Nzakara	2.0%	2%

Kenya	Pastor	Pop
Embu	0.9%	2%
Kalenjin	8.4%	12%
Kamba	17.2%	11%
Kikuyu	26.6%	17%
Kisii	14.3%	6%
Luhya	12.3%	14%
Luo	10.0%	11%
Maasai	1.4%	2%
Meru	1.9%	6%

Q 28: How broad would you say this pastor's influence is?

	Angola	CAR	Kenya
Mainly in one local area	33.0%	13.6%	24.9%
In one region of the country	23.3%	32.8%	29.5%
National	33.8%	31.7%	27.7%
International	9.9%	21.9%	17.8%

Q 29: To what extent is this person helping develop or train others as leaders.

	Angola	CAR	Kenya
Not at all	0.9%	1.7%	0.6%
Somewhat	9.3%	10.4%	6.3%
Quite a bit	30.9%	28.5%	26.1%
Very much	58.9%	59.5%	67.0%

Q 30: Which of the following best describes how this pastor is developing leaders?

	Angola	CAR	Kenya
Mentoring (setting good example, parenting, discipling)	61.5%	61.6%	61.3%
Formally (education in school, teaching, administration)	12.9%	18.6%	12.8%
Informally (internships, seminars, workshops)	23.7%	15.6%	18.0%
Financial Sponsorship/Support	0.8%	3.4%	3.0%
Other	1.2%	0.8%	4.8%

Q 31-33: Please list three confessing Christians that you know of (not a pastor) that you believe are making a difference in your local community in relation to some important area other than pastoral ministry.

[Results not listed here]

Q 34: Who of the above three would you say is making the greatest or most strategic impact?

Frequently named non-clergy leaders with impact are listed with frequency of mention:

Angola		CAR		Kenya	
Cris Avelino	4	Mme Brigitte Andarra	20	Jeremiah Kianga	14
Fred Barros	6	Mme Marie Paule		Joseph Kimeli	8
Simão Catombela	4	Balezou	11	Alice Kirambi	10
Albino Chicale	9	Mme Chantal Bobo	10	Judge Onesmus Makau	8
Eunice Chiquete	5	Jean Degoto	11	Kenneth Marende	9
Emidio Daniel	5	Joel Diboy	11	Timina Minyikha	9
Ernesto Daniel	4	Evariste Dignito	11	Elijah Munovi	6
Diamantino Doba	17	Louise Dindo	8	Councilor Mumo Mutua	6
Mariano Kusumua	4	Appolinaire		Isaac Mutua	28
Manuel Missas	8	Koyambenguia	9	Jackson Ngovi	7
Mata Mourisca	5	René Maleyombo	14	Patrick Nyachogo	6
Daniel Pinto	5	Prof. Mamadou Nestor		Chief Nyakinyi	6
Sofia Simão	11	Nali	14	John Oino	6
Januário Victor	4	Edouard Ngaisona	9	John Dache Pesa	11
Vasco Zage	4	Edouard Nvouni	8	Margret Simiyu	6
		Honora Yagossa	12	Councilor Irene Wacuka	10
		Mme Marie Louise			
		Yakemba	6		
		Mme Cecile Yakoma	8		

Please tell us about this person:

Q 35: What is his or her gender/sex?

	Angola	CAR	Kenya
Male	74.9%	65.3%	56.5%
Female	25.1%	34.7%	43.5%

Q 36: How old would you guess he or she is?

	Angola	CAR	Kenya
Less than 35	30%	11.7%	18.1%
Between 35 and 44	27.3%	33.5%	35.1%
Between 45 and 54	26.3%	35.8%	29.9%
Between 55 and 64	13.4%	16.8%	13.3%
More than 64 years old	3.0%	2.1%	3.6%

Q 37: What is his or her marital status?

	Angola	CAR	Kenya
Married	66.4%	65.5%	82.4%
Single	30.7%	31.8%	16.5%
Other	2.9%	2.7%	1.1%

Q 38: What is his or her ethnic group?

Ethnicity of named non-clergy leaders (Ldrs) compared with the population (Pop) of this ethnic group in the country as a whole.

Angola	Ldrs	Pop
Bakongo	32.3%	13%
Bangala	0.2%	
Chokwe/Cokwe	1.8%	5%
Ganguela	1.4%	9%
Kimbundu	4.8%	25%

Kwanyama	0.6%	4%
Nyaneka-Humbe	1.6%	3%
Ovimbundo	54.4%	37%

CAR	Ldrs	Pop
Banda	11.5%	27%
Gbaya	15.4%	33%
Mandja	13.2%	13%
Mboum	1.0%	7%
Ngbaka	5.6%	4%
Ngbandi	13.3%	11%
Sara	3.1%	10%
Zande-Nzakara	2.1%	2%

Kenya	Ldrs	Pop
Embu	1.0%	2%
Kalenjin	10.1%	12%
Kamba	16.9%	11%
Kikuyu	25.2%	17%
Kisii	14.5%	6%
Luhya	13.3%	14%
Luo	10.2%	11%
Maasai	1.5%	2%
Meru	2.0%	6%

Q 39: Which group does this person MOST influence?

	Angola	CAR	Kenya
Children	6.0%	3.9%	7.6%
Youth	29.2%	18.0%	28.0%
Women	8.5%	13.3%	12.2%
Men	5.6%	4.0%	2.7%
The Elderly	1.1%	3.4%	2.4%

The whole community	45.1%	47.0%	40.6%
The whole nation	2.8%	9.4%	5.6%
Other	1.7%	1.0%	0.8%

Q 40: Which of the following best describes the area of this person's influence? [Select the ONE best answer]

	Angola	CAR	Kenya
Business	3.8%	6.4%	6.7%
Church leadership develop-ment	27.1%	24.1%	23.4%
Communication/media	1.4%	2.7%	1.7%
Conflict Resolution	2.8%	3.8%	5.5%
Education	13.2%	12.1%	14.6%
Evangelism	33.7%	21.9%	12.0%
Farming/environment	1.2%	3.0%	4.1%
Government/Civil Service	3.3%	5.1%	5.5%
Health Care	6.4%	3.6%	4.7%
Homes and Families	2.0%	5.8%	9.4%
Music/entertainment	2.0%	2.7%	1.6%
Poverty alleviation	1.0%	6.7%	8.0%
Other	2.2%	2.1%	2.8%

Q 41: How broad would you say this person's influence is?

	Angola	CAR	Kenya
Mainly in one local area	62.1%	31.6%	39.5%
In one region of the country	19.0%	30.7%	30.1%
National	17.2%	31.0%	23.5%
International	1.8%	6.8%	6.8%

Q 42:To what extent is this person helping develop or train others as leaders.

	Angola	CAR	Kenya
Not at all	0.7%	3.4%	1.2%
Somewhat	14.9%	20.3%	9.0%
Quite a bit	46.4%	38.6%	33.9%
Very much	38.1%	37.7%	55.9%

Q 43:Which of the following best describes how this person is developing leaders?

	Angola	CAR	Kenya
Mentoring (setting good example, parenting, discipling)	56.8%	47.1%	50.8%
Formally (education in school, teaching, administration)	17.4%	25.9%	17.1%
Informally (internships, seminars, workshops)	20.3%	14.0%	18.1%
Financial Sponsorship/Support	3.0%	12.3%	7.9%
Other	2.5%	0.8%	6.1%

How would you rate this person in:

Q 44: Skill at their work.

	Angola	CAR	Kenya
Not High	2.5%	2.1%	2.3%
Somewhat High	16.4%	20.1%	13.8%
High	48.0%	43.6%	51.0%
Very High	33.1%	34.2%	32.9%

Q 45: Wisdom and knowledge of the local context.

	Angola	CAR	Kenya
Not High	2.1%	2.2%	1.7%
Somewhat High	22.5%	24.4%	13.3%
High	47.0%	47.8%	47.7%
Very High	28.4%	25.6%	37.2%

Q 46: Ethical integrity.

	Angola	CAR	Kenya
Not High	3.8%	5.6%	2.7%
Somewhat High	20.4%	28.3%	13.7%
High	45.3%	40.8%	44.7%
Very High	30.5%	25.4%	38.9%

Q 47: Love and service of others.

	Angola	CAR	Kenya
Not High	2.1%	1.5%	1.0%
Somewhat High	12.8%	15.5%	7.5%
High	41.3%	41.6%	39.8%
Very High	43.8%	41.4%	51.7%

Q 48: Positive reputation in the community.

	Angola	CAR	Kenya
Not High	2.2%	1.7%	1.6%
Somewhat High	14.2%	16.9%	9.0%
High	45.4%	42.4%	44.4%
Very High	38.1%	39.0%	45.1%

Q 49: Inspires teamwork/mobilizes community.

	Angola	CAR	Kenya
Not High	3.3%	2.4%	2.6%
Somewhat High	21.0%	23.1%	11.6%
High	41.6%	42.1%	42.4%
Very High	34.2%	32.4%	43.5%

Q 50: Uses resources efficiently.

	Angola	CAR	Kenya
Not High	8.0%	4.6%	2.8%
Somewhat High	30.9%	26.2%	13.5%
High	36.9%	42.4%	41.5%
Very High	24.3%	26.8%	42.2%

Q 51: With what agency or organization, if any, does this person work?

[Results not listed here]

Q 52: Please describe what this person does that is having an impact.

[Results not listed here]

Q 53-55: Please list the names of three Christian organizations, programs, or initiatives that you believe are having an important positive impact in your local area or region.

[Results not listed here]

Q 56:Which of these three would you say is having the most important positive impact in your local area, region, or country?

The most frequently named organizations with impact are listed with frequency of mention.

Angola	Organization	N
	Associação dos Escuteiros de Angola	34
	Centro de Formação Profissional da I.E.C.A	11
	Conselho de Igrejas Cristãs em Angola (CICA)*	25
	Departamento de Assistência Social Estudos e Projectos (DASEP)*	35
	EL SHADAI	12
	Formação Feminina (FOFE)*	28
	Grupo Biblico de Estudantes Cristaos en Angola (GBECA)	10
	Hora da Reflexão (Hour of Reflection)	11
	Instituto Superior de Teologia Evangélica no Lubango (ISTEL)*	11
	Jovens Com Uma Missao (JOCUM) = YWAM	11
	Mocidade para Cristo (Youth for Christ)*	57
	Mulher da Igreja Evangélica Reformada de Angola (MIERA)*	9
	Projecto Ester	27
	Projecto Uhayele	12
	Promaica	13
	Sinta-se	11
	Sociedade Média da Igreja Evangélica Congregacional em Angola (IECA)	12
	União Cristã Femenina (UCF)	15

CAR	Organization	N
	Action Chrétienne pour le Développement (ACDL)	10
	Adonai Mission International*	110
	Ambassade Chrétienne (Radio Evangile Néhémie)*	148
	Association Centrafricaine pour la Traduction de la Bible et l'Alphabétisation (ACATBA)*	22

Campus pour Christ *	161
Caritas	185
Ecole Theologique Évangélique des Freres	13
Emmaus	21
Faculté de Théologie Évangélique de Bangui (FATEB)*	186
Groupement Chrétien des Oeuvres Sociales	17
Jeunesse Chrétienne Conquerante (JCC)	14
Jeunesse Évangélique Africaine (JEA)	40
Mission pour l' Evangelisation et le Salut du Monde (MESM)*	32
Perspectives Reformées*	62
Radio Songo	12
Seminaire Évangélique	25
Union des Jeunes Chrétiens (U.J.C)	37

*Follow up interviews and reports were prepared on the starred organizations. These reports are available upon request.

KENYA Organization	N
Baobab Christian Home	23
Bomaregwa Welfare Association*	6
Cheptebo Rural Development Centre*	10
Christ is the Answer Ministries (CITAM)*	7
Christian Partners Development Agency (CPDA)*	6
Compassion International	55
Daraja La Tumaini*	15
Fariji Sacco	20
FOCUS (Fellowship of Christian Unions) Kenya*	21
Kenya Students' Christian Fellowship (KSCF)*	17
Kwiminia CBO*	13
Magena Youth Group*	16
Mombasa Church Forum*	10
Mothers' Union*	24
Narok Pillar of Development Organization*	11
Nation Council of Churches of Kenya (NCCK)*	10
Red Cross	44

Redeemed Academy*	29
Scripture Union*	32
St. Martin's*	21
Tenwek Community Health and Development (TCHD)*	13
Transform Kenya*	15
Word of Life*	18
World Vision	191

*Follow up interviews and reports were prepared on the starred organizations. These reports are available upon request.

Q 57: Which group is most helped by this organization or initiative?

	Angola	CAR	Kenya
Children	5.5%	3.7%	18.0%
Youth	24.7%	11.8%	20.8%
Women	8.9%	3.6%	8.6%
Men	1.9%	1.8%	0.9%
The elderly	1.8%	1.4%	1.6%
The whole community	42.5%	49.5%	40.0%
The whole nation	13.1%	25.8%	9.3%
Other	1.6%	2.5%	0.7%

Q 58: Which of the following best describes the area of this organization or initiative's influence?

	Angola	CAR	Kenya
Business	2.9%	1.7%	6.8%
Church leadership development	16.5%	20.7%	13.1%
Communication/media	1.7%	3.7%	1.7%

Conflict resolution	3.4%	0.9%	2.8%
Education	16.1%	12.6%	16.3%
Evangelism	29.1%	32.8%	9.4%
Farming/environment	1.5%	7.2%	7.1%
Government/civil service	5.1%	1.0%	2.9%
Health care	9.1%	4.1%	11.0%
Homes and families	6.3%	3.2%	11.1%
Music/entertainment	0.9%	0.6%	0.3%
Poverty alleviation	5.0%	9.0%	15.2%
Other	2.4%	2.6%	2.2%

Q 59: How broad would you say the impact of this initiative or organization is?

	Angola	CAR	Kenya
Mainly in one local area	35.0%	9.1%	26.0%
In one region of the country	17.5%	16.0%	24.3%
National	32.9%	47.9%	33.0%
International	14.6%	27.0%	16.7%

Q 60: To what extent is this organization or initiative helping develop or train people as leaders?

	Angola	CAR	Kenya
Not at all	2.1%	3.0%	2.5%
Somewhat	12.8%	8.6%	9.2%
Quite a bit	36.3%	28.5%	33.3%
Very much	48.7%	59.9%	55.0%

If the answer here is "very much," then please answer the following question.

Q 61: Which of the following best describes how this organization or initiative is developing leaders?

	Angola	CAR	Kenya
Mentoring (setting good example, parenting, disciplining)	37.4%	39.2%	30.1%
Formally (education in school, teaching, administration)	17.1%	32.1%	20.4%
Informally (internships, seminars, workshops)	34.7%	19.8%	23.9%
Financial sponsorship/support	4.0%	7.2%	20.0%
Other	6.7%	1.7%	5.5%

To what extent is the following true about this organization or initiative?

Q 62: It has a good reputation in the local community.

	Angola	CAR	Kenya
Not at all	1.2%	2.1%	0.9%
Somewhat	7.9%	13.7%	8.2%
Quite a bit	60.4%	36.4%	31.3%
Very much	30.5%	47.8%	59.6%

Q 63: Local churches provide it with strong support.

	Angola	CAR	Kenya
Not at all	7.1%	19.6%	7.2%
Somewhat	14.2%	34.0%	18.3%
Quite a bit	59.1%	26.2%	34.8%
Very much	19.6%	20.3%	39.7%

Q 64: Women participate in its leadership.

	Angola	CAR	Kenya
Not at all	3.9%	8.5%	3.6%
Somewhat	12.2%	28.8%	15.3%
Quite a bit	60.7%	35.0%	35.3%
Very much	23.2%	27.7%	45.7%

Q 65: It works wisely in the local context.

	Angola	CAR	Kenya
Not at all	1.3%	3.7%	1.4%
Somewhat	9.3%	14.8%	9.4%
Quite a bit	65.5%	33.5%	31.6%
Very much	24.0%	48.0%	57.7%

Q 66. Please describe what this organization or initiative does that is having an impact.

[Results not listed here]

Q 67. Please give us the name of someone who works in leadership with this organization or initiative?

[Results not listed here]

Q 68. Please give us contact information for this person (phone number and email) if you have it.

[Results not listed here]

Please tell us about yourself:

Q 69: What is your gender/sex?

	Angola	CAR	Kenya
Male	65.6%	65.8%	57.9%
Female	34.4%	34.2%	42.1%

Q 70: How old are you?

	Angola	CAR	Kenya
18 to 24 years old	39.7%	17.4%	23.6%
25 to 34 years old	23.4%	28.2%	33.4%
35 to 44 years old	17.5%	27.1%	26.4%
45 to 54 years old	11.8%	17.8%	12.1%
55 to 64 years old	6.2%	8.0%	3.7%
More than 64 years old	1.3%	1.4%	0.9%

Q 71: What is your marital status?*

	Angola	CAR	Kenya
Married	37.7%	35.3%	54.9%
Widowed	2.0%	4.2%	8.3%
Single	59.1%	57.2%	36.2%
Other	1.3%	3.3%	0.6%

Q 72: What is the highest level of education you have completed?

	Angola	CAR	Kenya
Less than primary	1.8%	4.2%	0.9%
Primary school	13.5%	7.2%	8.6%
Secondary school	61.3%	18.4%	29.2%

College/university (undergraduate, bachelors)	21.8%	52.2%	46.7%
Master's degree or doctoral degree at university or seminary	1.6%	18.1%	14.7%

Q 73: I am currently...

	Angola	CAR	Kenya
Employed	39.3%	29.2%	41.7%
Self-employed	13.1%	10.0%	22.1%
Out of work and looking for work	15.1%	18.3%	10.3%
Out of work but not currently looking for work	1.4%	3.9%	2.0%
Housewife/family caregiver	1.3%	10.7%	3.3%
Student	28.3%	24.8%	19.2%
Retired	1.5%	3.1%	1.5%

Q 74: If you are working, please describe your work.

	Angola	CAR	Kenya
Pastor or church employee	5.7%	7.5%	10.2%
Employee of a not-for-profit or charitable organization (NGO)	2.9%	6.4%	6.6%
Employee of a for-profit company or of an individual for wages	6.8%	8.6%	13.2%
Government employee	26.2%	13.1%	11.8%
Self-employed in own business, professional practice, or farm	13.2%	6.1%	16.6%
Working without pay in family business or farm	1.2%	6.8%	4.5%
Other or not answered	44.0%	51.6%	36.9%

Q 75: What is your monthly income, combined with your spouse's income if you are married?*

	Angola	CAR	Kenya
Less than $120	11.4%		23.3%
Less than $60		13.6%	
$60 to $120 a month		11.8%	
$121 to $480	14.4%	15.6%	27.8%
$481 to $1,200	17.0%	3.5%	11.2%
More than $1,200	8.6%	1.5%	3.1%
Not answered	48.5%	53.9%	34.6%

*Income was asked in local monetary units, but with amounts that were approximately equal to these amounts in U.S. Dollars.

Q 76: What is your ethnic group?

(Respondent ethnicity compared with country population.)

Angola	Resp	Pop
Bakongo	29.8%	13%
Bangala	0.1%	
Chokwe/Cokwe	2.6%	5%
Ganguela	1.4%	9%
Kimbundu	5.7%	25%
Kwanyama	0.9%	4%
Nyaneka-Humbe	2.6%	3%
Ovimbundo	54.4%	37%

Central African Republic	Resp	Pop
Banda	14.0%	27%
Gbaya	18.3%	33%
Mandja	14.9%	13%
Mboum	2.9%	7%

Ngbaka	6.5%	4%
Ngbandi	17.1%	11%
Sara	5.5%	10%
Zande-Nzakara	2.7%	2%

Kenya	Resp	Pop
Embu	1.3%	2%
Kalenjin	10.3%	12%
Kamba	15.5%	11%
Kikuyu	23.7%	17%
Kisii	15.3%	6%
Luhya	14.4%	14%
Luo	11.0%	11%
Maasai	1.0%	2%
Meru	2.3%	6%

Q 77: What is your relationship to your church?

	Angola	CAR	Kenya
I do not attend church regularly	7.1%	13.0%	8.2%
I am a church member and/or attend regularly	67.4%	53.9%	60.4%
I am a lay leader in my church	20.8%	20.4%	16.2%
I serve as a pastor in my church	4.2%	9.0%	13.2%
I am a denominational leader (such as a Bishop, Overseer, or Moderator)	0.4%	3.7%	2.1%

Q 78: Do you own a cell phone?

	Angola	CAR	Kenya
Yes	96.4%	82.1%	93.7%
No	3.6%	17.9%	6.3%

Q 79: Do you own a computer?

	Angola	CAR	Kenya
Yes	41.3%	15.3%	34.4%
No	58.7%	84.7%	65.6%

Q 80: Do you have Internet access?

	Angola	CAR	Kenya
Yes	48.8%	32.7%	63.3%
No	51.2%	67.3%	36.7%

If YES, then...

Q 81: How do you most often access the internet? (Percent of those with internet access)

	Angola	CAR	Kenya
Cell Phone	40.8%	16.0%	46.2%
Computer at Internet Cafe	12.7%	61.7%	22.0%
Computer at my home	37.6%	10.2%	14.6%
Computer at work or school	7.1%	12.1%	15.9%
Electronic tablet	1.8%	0.0%	1.3%

Q 82: Frequency of Internet Access? (Percent of those with internet access)

	Angola	CAR	Kenya
Several times a day	27.2%	15.9%	45.1%
Once a day	15.3%	20.8%	17.7%
Occasionally	43.7%	48.8%	27.6%
Rarely	12.6%	13.5%	7.5%
Never	1.2%	1.0%	2.3%

Q 83: Do you own an electronic tablet? (Such as a Kindle, iPAD, Android)

	Angola	CAR	Kenya
Yes	3.9%	1.0%	8.7%
No	34.8%	94.4%	74.8%
Not answered	61.3%	4.7%	16.5%

Q 84: How many books have you read in the last twelve months?

	Angola	CAR	Kenya
None	7.1%	18.6%	7.3%
1 or 2	34.3%	23.0%	26.9%
3 - 5	26.0%	23.3%	26.0%
6 - 10	14.8%	14.3%	16.8%
More than 10	17.8%	20.8%	23.0%

Q 85: Do you ever buy books at a Christian Bookshop?

	Angola	CAR	Kenya
No, there are none near me	29.0%	30.2%	13.1%
No, although there is at least one nearby	13.5%	13.0%	14.9%
Yes, but not often	47.8%	43.0%	56.9%
Yes, often	9.7%	13.8%	15.2%

How frequently do you read the following?

Q 86: Newspapers or magazines

	Angola	CAR	Kenya
Never	7.7%	31.8%	4.6%
Less than once a month	40.5%	30.3%	12.7%
At least monthly	16.3%	10.9%	11.1%
Weekly	22.3%	13.9%	32.5%
Daily	13.3%	13.2%	39.1%

Q 87: The Bible

	Angola	CAR	Kenya
Never	1.6%	5.8%	0.9%
Less than once a month	5.9%	8.7%	4.3%
At least monthly	5.1%	7.0%	4.9%
Weekly	27.4%	19.6%	25.8%
Daily	60.1%	58.9%	64.2%

Q 88: Fiction books (Novels)

	Angola	CAR	Kenya
Never	54.1%	56.3%	31.2%
Less than once a month	27.7%	22.2%	30.9%
At least monthly	6.1%	11.3%	19.8%
Weekly	6.7%	6.1%	11.9%
Daily	5.4%	4.1%	6.2%

Q 89: Other books (Non-fiction)

	Angola	CAR	Kenya
Never	17.6%	31.3%	23.7%
Less than once a month	33.1%	27.7%	31.6%

At least monthly	18.3%	16.1%	22.3%
Weekly	16.5%	14.5%	13.2%
Daily	14.5%	10.4%	9.3%

How frequently do you read news or magazine articles or books ...

Q 90: On a cell phone?

	Angola	CAR	Kenya
Never	31.2%	56.5%	40.9%
Less than once a month	18.2%	9.1%	13.3%
At least monthly	9.0%	4.0%	8.6%
Weekly	13.2%	5.8%	13.3%
Daily	28.4%	24.6%	23.9%

Q 91: On a computer?

	Angola	CAR	Kenya
Never	41.3%	72.5%	43.8%
Less than once a month	18.1%	9.3%	13.6%
At least monthly	10.5%	4.4%	10.2%
Weekly	14.7%	6.5%	15.7%
Daily	15.5%	7.3%	16.8%

Q 92: On an electronic tablet?

	Angola	CAR	Kenya
Never	42.2%	94.3%	77.8%
Less than once a month	15.3%	3.2%	8.1%
At least monthly	9.1%	0.9%	4.0%
Weekly	11.6%	1.1%	4.3%
Daily	21.9%	0.6%	5.9%

Q93: If you have a favorite author, what is his or her name?

(Listed three times or more)

Angola

Canguimbo Ananas	12
Bambila (Manuel Simão)	4
Rebecca Brown	20
Luis Camões	3
Cristiano Cardoso	3
Augusto Chipesse	5
Augusto Cury	9
Cristiano Cardoso	3
Billy Graham	9
Joaquim Hatewa	3
Benny Hinn	3
Jaime Kemp	4
Tim LaHaye	6
Fritz Laubach	4
Silas Malafaia	8
Antunes Manjolo	3
John Maxwell	24
Lor Mbongo	4
Joyce Meyer	4
Mike Murdock	4
António Agostinho Neto	45
Stormie Omartian	3
Pepetela	38
Oscar Ribas	9
Luís "Aires" Samakumbi	12
Penelas Santana	8
Irmã Sofia	16
John Stott	3
Rick Warren	5
Wanhenga Xitu	5

CAR

Silas Ali	15
Amadou Hampâté Bâ	17
Henri Blocher	5
Bill Bright	3
Rebecca Brown	5
Albert Camus	9
Dale Carnegie	3
Aimé Fernand David Césaire	13
David Yonggi Cho*	7
Bernard Binlin Dadié	4
Birago Diop	3
Emile Durkheim	5
Emmanuel Eni	3
Zacharias Tanee Fomum	26
Étienne Goyémidé	56
Billy Graham	23
Victor Hugo	9
Martin Luther King	9
Léon Kobangue	3
David Koudougueret	3
Ahmadou Kourouma	22
Alfred Kuen	20
Camara Laye	17
Martin Luther	3
Pierre Sammy Mackfoy	60
René Maran	3
Paul Mbunga Mpindi	20
Watchman Nee	4
Jules Marcel Nicole	5
Stormie Omartian	3
Tommy Lee Osborne	7
David Oyedepo	9
Ferdinand Oyono	4
René Pache	4
Derek Prince	5
Jean Jacques Rousseau	8
Jean Paul Sartre	3
Ousmane Sembène	17
Léopold Sédar Senghor	14
Socrates	3
Charles Spurgeon	3
John Stott	9
Voltaire	5
Emile Zola	4

*Formerly Paul Yonggi Cho.

Kenya

Chinua Achebe	98	Robert Kiyosaki	14	Joel Osteen	139
Elechi Amadi	6	Tim LaHaye	4	Chris Oyakhilome	10
Reinhard Bonnke	7	C. S. Lewis	9	David Oyedepo	31
William Booth	30	Max Lucado	10	James Patterson	7
Dan Brown	3	Robert Ludlum	4	Bill Perkins	3
Rebecca Brown	12	Wangari Muta Maathai	3	John Piper	4
Juanita Bynum	3	Marjorie Oludhe Macgoye	3	Derek Prince	6
Ben Carson	162	John Mason	12	Leonard Ravenhill	6
John Bairstow Carson	5	John C. Maxwell	72	Francine Rivers	10
Morris Cerrulo	4	Ali Mazrui	4	J. K. Rowlings	3
William Jefferson Clinton	5	Kithaka Wa Mberia	5	Robert H. Schuller	3
Paulo Coehlo	5	Simon Mbevi	5	William Shakespeare	17
Stephen Covey	11	John Mbiti	12	Robin Sharma	4
James Dobson	5	Joyce Meyer	52	Sidney Sheldon	24
Steve Farrar	3	Miguna Miguna	14	Charles Spurgeon	5
Mark Finley	4	Pepe Minambo	7	Danielle Steel	9
Marvin Gorman	3	Said Ahmed Mohammed	16	John Stott	20
Billy Graham	13	Mbugua Mumbi	4	Ngugi Wa Thiong'o	114
Robert Greene	3	Myles Munroe	41	Nancy Van Pelt	18
John Grisham	14	Andrew Murray	3	Ken Walibora	18
John Hagee	4	Prof. Makau Mutua	3	Wallah Bin Wallah	25
Kenneth Hagin	12	Shellomith Nderitu	4	Joyce Wamwea	3
Dag Heward-Mills	30	Watchman Nee	4	Rick Warren	52
Napoleon Hill	5	George Njau	3	Ellen G. White	50
Benny Hinn	10	Sabina Njeri	3	Philip Yancey	3
Bill Hybels	7	Clement Ogomo	5		
Francis Imbuga	11	Grace Ogot	5		
T. D. Jakes	50	Assa Okoth	10		
Joe Kayo	10	Stormie Omartian	3		
Martin Luther King	9	Erick Opingo	3		
Karen Kingsbury	4	Evans Orina	3		
John Kiriamiti	16				

Q 94: Research Assistants Who Collected Surveys:

Angola*	
Alberto, Agostinho	29
Amadeu, Lourenço	30
Arnaldo, Arão	29
Bapolo, Araújo	26
Bento, Helder	30
Calufele, Pedro	23
Cassoma, Edgar	30
Chissingue, Francisco	29
Chitumba, Moises	22
Cipriano, Enoque	21
Domingos, Elias	29
Fata, Mauricio	30
Gomes, Alberto	25
Gomes, Regunaldo	22
Isaac, Antonio	24
Mauricio, Clarice	24
Pedro, Martins	28

*In Angola 100 research assistants collected surveys. Here we list only those who collected 21 or more.

CAR	
Boydet, Belin	145
Codjia, Dzifa	105
Dongobada, Didacien	120
Kalemba, Mymy	73
Kongolona, Fatchou	91
Koyadibert, Max	264
Mataya, Viana Mathy	224
Mulume, Yves	139
Mushimiyimana, Jean-Claude	90
Muteba, Mayambe Elie	325
Mwambazambi, Kalemba	23
Nsamu, Mavutukidi Lopez	99
Nyongona, Franck	82
Rabariolina, Christopher	62
Razafimaharo, Frederic	60
Sakalaima, Paul	195
Sandoua, Yolande	28
Swebolo, Emmanuel	121
Tao, Elysee	73

Kenya	
Ananda, Zephaniah	96
Gitau, Wanjiru	165
Isolio, Godfrey	209
Karanja, Moses	106
Kariuki, Margaret	196
Kiragu, Ruth	201
Kisyula, Rachel	174
Maina, Ednah C	174
Malemba, Duncan	216
Momanyi, Job	174
Mutuku, Alex	174
Mutuku, Cyrus	198
Mwanza, Sebastian	304
Njuguna, David	188
Owilla, Hesbon	161
Owino, Ruth	195
Tinega, Philip	134
Weyama, Angela	213

Q 95a: Towns and cities in which survey administered:

Angola		CAR		Kenya*	
Andulo	18	Bangui	1426	Bomet	52
Bailundo	52	Bouar	288	Bungoma	56
Benguela	27	Damara	181	Eldoret	83
Caála	40	Mbaiki	259	Flyover	68
Cacungo	17	Yaloke	130	Githunguri	69
Caluquembe	110			Kagwe	36
Camacupa	13			Kericho	61
Catchiungo	74			Kiambu	56
Caxito	6			Kilifi	37
Chicala	19			Kisii	37
Chinguar	35			Kisumu	41
Chiugengo	30			Malindi	47
Ganda Embango	6			Migori	130
Huambo	79			Mogotio	50
Humpata	9			Mombasa	394
Kuito	198			Nairobi	475
Lobito	32			Nakuru	69
Longonjo	18			Narok	51
Luanda	546			Njoro	37
Lubango	335			Nyahururu	51
Namibe	30			Nyamira	133
Sede	18			Nyeri	99
Sumbe	30			Ukunda	125

* Partial list. We collected
surveys in over 65 cities,
towns, and villages of Kenya.

Q 95b: Provinces in which survey administered (all provinces listed):

Angola		CAR*		Kenya*	
Bengo	29	Bangui	1426	Central	524
Benguela	66	Bamingui-Bangoran	0	Coast	663
Bié	265	Basse-Kotto	0	Eastern	373
Cabinda	0	Haute-Kotto	0	Nairobi	475
Cuando Cubango	1	Haut-Mbomou	0	Northeastern	0
Cuanza Norte	0	Kémo	0	Nyanza	473
Cuanza Sul	30	Lobaye	259	Rift Valley	579
Cunene	0	Mambéré-Kadéi	0	Western	318
Huambo	348	Mbomou	0	Missing Province Data	559
Huíla	454	Nana-Mambéré	288		
Luanda	546	Ombella-M'Poko	311		
Lunda Norte	0	Ouaka	0		
Lunda Sul	0	Ouham	0		
Malanje	0	Ouham-Pendé	0		
Moxico	0	Vakaga	0		
Namibe	30				
Uíge	0				
Zaire	0				

We did not survey Northeastern Kenya for logistical and safety reasons. At the time of our survey, Kenya was divided into provinces, a governmental structure that in 2013 was abandoned and replaced with forty-seven counties.

* CAR is divided into sixteen Préfectures with Bangui a separate Commune, essentially a seventeeth Préfecture. In CAR, for logistical and safety reasons, we limited our focus to four Préfectures.

Appendix C

Africa Leadership Study: A Seedbed Resource

WEBSITE AND FORUM

Resource Page:
http://www.africaleadershipstudy.org/resources-als/

Forum:
http://www.africaleadershipstudy.org/als-forum/

The Resource Page is where the ongoing growth and development of the seeds gathered through the ALS research can be planted and the fruits can be celebrated and shared. The page is organized around interest topics suggested by ALS team members and friends. Each interest topic includes a list of resources. You may know of resources that can be added. Those of you living in Africa will have knowledge of resources we may not know about. You may want to suggest a topic.

Some of the topics have been treated in depth in the chapters of this book. Some of the resources listed under the topic headings are based on the ALS findings. We hope others will join us in continuing to learn from and build on the ALS data gathered.

There has been much work done by many others in the field of leadership development. Links to those organizations and their materials are also included by interest topic on the Resource Page. The page is not intended to focus on ALS materials exclusively.

We hope that you, the users, will be able to help us enrich and expand the resources found here. To that end, we have set up a Forum with discussions tied to the interest topics. You will be able to use the Forum to suggest additional topics, to carry on conversations about existing topics, and to suggest additional resources. We anticipate that the conversations will take place in French, Portuguese, and English. Resources can be suggested for each language, and they will be posted in that language. Tyndale House Foundation envisions and prays that the users of the site can be involved in an ongoing process of gathering, presenting, and adding materials important to those engaged in leadership development, education, training, writing, and publishing.

Please join the conversation and share information and resources. The following are featured interest topics:

Biblical Resources lists various Bible versions and study tools for those interested in studying and understanding scripture.

Prayers provides a space for us to encourage and support one another.

Developing Leaders features resources that are specifically focused on developing individuals.

Developing Organizations describes resources that are specifically focused on developing organizations.

Women in Leadership provides space to explore the critically strategic leadership role of African women in the church and the community, a role that is often unrecognized.

Christian Associations in Africa is a place to discover organizations, conferences, training events, and resources that have been developed to fit the African context.

Training in Writing and Publishing is especially for those interested in developing writing or editing skills or publishing materials.

Publishers and Publishing Associations provides a growing list of publishers currently working in Africa, including those that offer books by African authors.

Print on Demand is a forum to discover and discuss the role that the expanding number of print-on-demand systems in Africa play in the availability of reasonably priced Christian books and materials. This has strategic potential as a distribution channel for African writers.

Studies on Leadership and Education provides links to work being done in leadership development, research, best practices, and development of training resources.

Organizations Working in Leadership Development provides connections to groups with a high level of impact, some based in the West and many indigenous to Africa.

Educational Institutions lists schools and other educational opportunities for leadership development across Africa.

Microenterprise, Skills Training links to organizations that offer information on microenterprise development programs. Some may provide hands-on skills training in conjunction with preparation for Christian ministry.

Research Training—ALS Model is useful for those who want to study research methods and those who may want to use the ALS materials in their classrooms.

Building on the ALS Data—Further Research encourages and facilitates the use of the original survey data and includes ideas for further research. The results will be posted on the Resource Page.

Seedbed Fruit will gather and celebrate the projects and research that grow out of the ALS.

Thoughts for Funders is a place for individuals, churches, mission boards, and other funders to explore key concepts inherent in working in Africa in order to provide the greatest benefit and support to indigenous leaders and organizations.

Index